# GREAT CONTINENTAL RAILWAY JOURNEYS

INTRODUCTION BY MICHAEL PORTILLO

**SIMON &
SCHUSTER**

London · New York · Sydney · Toronto · New Delhi

A CBS COMPANY

## THE WORLD
### ON MERCATORS PROJECTION

# BRADSHAW'S
# RAILWAY MAP OF EUROPE
### BY J. BARTHOLOMEW, F.R.G.S.

Scale of English Miles

Scale of Kilométres

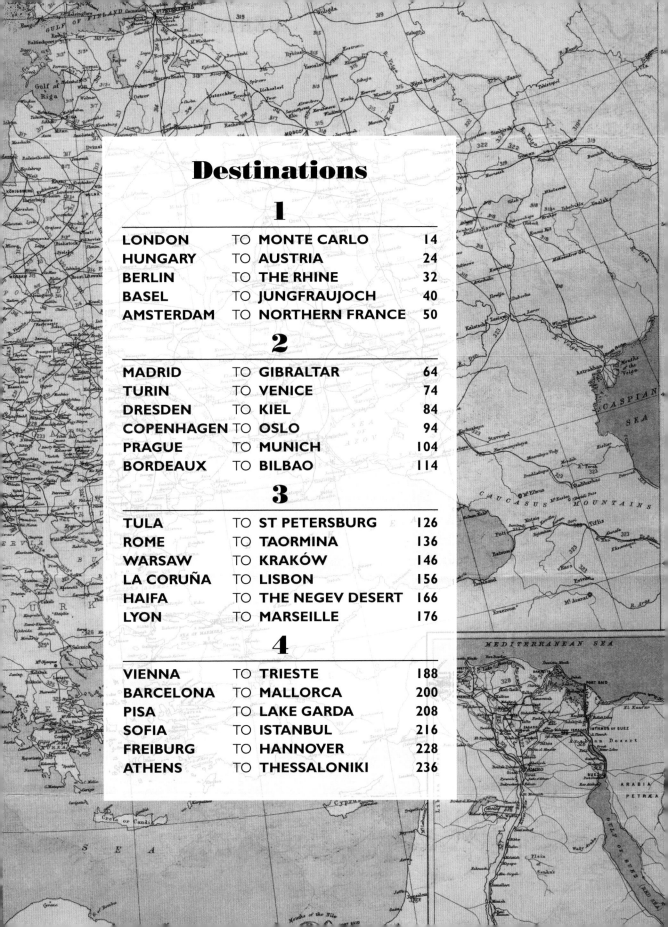

# **Destinations**

## **1**

| LONDON | TO | MONTE CARLO | 14 |
|---|---|---|---|
| HUNGARY | TO | AUSTRIA | 24 |
| BERLIN | TO | THE RHINE | 32 |
| BASEL | TO | JUNGFRAUJOCH | 40 |
| AMSTERDAM | TO | NORTHERN FRANCE | 50 |

## **2**

| MADRID | TO | GIBRALTAR | 64 |
|---|---|---|---|
| TURIN | TO | VENICE | 74 |
| DRESDEN | TO | KIEL | 84 |
| COPENHAGEN | TO | OSLO | 94 |
| PRAGUE | TO | MUNICH | 104 |
| BORDEAUX | TO | BILBAO | 114 |

## **3**

| TULA | TO | ST PETERSBURG | 126 |
|---|---|---|---|
| ROME | TO | TAORMINA | 136 |
| WARSAW | TO | KRAKÓW | 146 |
| LA CORUÑA | TO | LISBON | 156 |
| HAIFA | TO | THE NEGEV DESERT | 166 |
| LYON | TO | MARSEILLE | 176 |

## **4**

| VIENNA | TO | TRIESTE | 188 |
|---|---|---|---|
| BARCELONA | TO | MALLORCA | 200 |
| PISA | TO | LAKE GARDA | 208 |
| SOFIA | TO | ISTANBUL | 216 |
| FREIBURG | TO | HANNOVER | 228 |
| ATHENS | TO | THESSALONIKI | 236 |

# INTRODUCTION
## BY MICHAEL PORTILLO

*BRADSHAW'S* GUIDEBOOKS PROVIDE A DEEP INSIGHT into Britain's state of mind in the year of their publication.

The guide to the United Kingdom from the 1860s (which I use in the BBC television series *Great British Railway Journeys*) reveals a nation at the peak of self-confidence. The British empire is the largest that has ever existed and, at its heart, London is the world's first metropolis. The country leads the world in innovation, invention, science, engineering and manufacture.

But by 1913, the mood has changed markedly. The *Bradshaw's Continental Guide* of that year reveals a loss of self-assurance. Germany has taken the lead in engineering and scientific research. France dominates new industries like car manufacture and cinema. War approaches.

The guide doesn't say that explicitly, but it lists the sizes of Europe's armies and navies country by country. Germany's army is vast, Britain's tiny, but the Royal Navy is still as large as any two others put together. The book recounts the progress of the Balkan wars up to the moment of publication. It was to be in the Balkans where the fuse of the Great War was lit.

The Europe described in *Bradshaw's* has enjoyed decades of peace. The British have not been involved in a Continental war for nearly a century; and even Germany and France have been at peace for more than 40 years. It's the old Europe of empires: Tsarist, German, Austro-Hungarian and Ottoman. The coming war will sweep them all away. I have the impression that one of the causes of the First World War was that Europe undervalued peace, not realising how its institutions, prosperity and happiness depended on the absence of war.

The old order was threatened by other things too: by terrorists, for example. Among those assassinated were the Austro-Hungarian empress, the Russian tsar, and the Portuguese king and his heir. A bomber narrowly failed to murder the Spanish king and his British bride on their wedding day. British people have been led by the sentimental poems of Rupert Brooke to view their pre-war period through rose-tinted lenses. Perhaps there was honey for tea for some, but there was also intense industrial strife, violence against and by suffragettes, and an impending civil war in Ireland.

More subtly, artists like Picasso, Braque, Klimt and those of the Der Blaue Reiter movement undermined familiar certainties. Painting, literature and even architecture could be revolutionary, especially linked to nationalism, as in Ireland, or throughout the crumbling Austro-Hungarian empire; and in a different way, in an ever more self-assertive Germany.

Travelling by train with a century-old guidebook has been, for me at least, a wonderful way to learn about the political, cultural and social history of our continent. Just as broad advantage is now being taken of the centenary of the Great War to remember and to reassess, so I hope that the *Great Continental*

*Railway Journeys* programmes help us to understand what Europeans stood to lose.

But the programmes are full of joy too. We celebrate the eccentricities of nations as we build castells, 'people steeples', in Catalonia. I battled a huge mechanical dragon in Germany and 'impersonated' a ski jumper on a zip wire in Norway. I have been beaten with birch twigs in a Russian bathhouse, heated to melting point in a Swedish sauna, and I tumbled from a toboggan in Austria. I have 'danced' my way across the Continent: with a horse in Spain, with a man in Vienna, with a high school graduating class in Warsaw and in a Roman theatre in Bulgaria.

There have been some great railways to admire: the Schafbergbahn powered by a steam locomotive 'built on a slope', and the line that climbs through tunnels to Europe's highest station at the Jungfraujoch. I enjoyed the first trans-Alpine line through Austria's Semmering Pass and the tracks that hug the river banks between the steep vineyards of the Douro valley in Portugal.

You can read history in railways. In what was known in 1913 as the Holy Land, there was a railway for Christian pilgrims from Jaffa to Jerusalem, and one for Muslim pilgrims from Haifa towards Medina and Mecca. But the British feared that that line posed a military threat to India and Egypt, and during the First World War Lawrence of Arabia blew it up.

I like to give a potted history of Russia with three rail stories. Leo Tolstoy, the novelist, was also a social reformer and champion of the peasants at a time of mounting revolutionary sentiment. He died in a station in 1910. After the March revolution of 1917, Tsar Nicholas II signed his abdication in a railway carriage. Then Germany decided to allow Vladimir Lenin to cross its territory in a sealed train like a revolutionary virus, to foment the Bolshevik uprising that October, and so knock Russia out of the war. It must be the most significant train journey of all time.

I hope that the television programmes may be seen as a celebration of the diversity of nations. So many colourful customs have somehow survived the conforming pressures of globalisation. It's a celebration of peace as well. After Europe's terrible 20th century, most of our lives are untroubled by war. Even so, I filmed in Russia while Ukrainians were dying, and the tensions in Israel and the occupied territories are palpable. There are Mediterranean countries recommended in *Bradshaw's* that are presently off-limits because of war or terror.

I hope, too, that this book will help you to travel with me through beautiful scenery and impressive cities; to meet entertaining characters; to enjoy new foods; to marvel at extraordinary customs; and to laugh.

If it also stimulates your interest in and love of history I shall be very glad. We are what we are thanks to both geniuses and tyrants, because of both virtue and evil. Most of us are very lucky to live in our magnificent continent in the times that we do.

# FOREWORD

WHEN MICHAEL PORTILLO EMBARKED ON RAIL JOURNEYS around Europe, he took the doorstep-sized *Bradshaw's Guide*, published in 1913, as an immutable record of Europe as it was then.

This straight-talking guide is an antidote to the sentimental nostalgia that sometimes accompanies old-style railways, the flawed 19th-century icon that became etched on the ground and in the public consciousness.

The continent had been irreversibly changed by the ingenuity that put locomotives on the tracks some 80 years previously and by the industry drawn along in their wake. They were a triumph of technology, but there were still lessons to learn about safety, comfort and timetabling.

*Bradshaw's* was designed for the tourists who came later, to advise about the customs and practices of foreign lands. Michael walks in the footsteps of those visitors, experiencing Edwardian times from a European perspective and relishing the flavours of life in this bygone era.

Not every journey listed in *Bradshaw's* can be replicated today. Some lines have been diverted, many have closed. A few are new, as are the fast, sleek trains that generally run on them. In that sense, the railway guide is a better testament to the places visited by trains than the routes used to get to them.

Inspired by his schedule, this book aims to illuminate every nation's railway network expansion – or lack of it. But this is no dry engineering treatise. With the railway narrative comes another, darker chapter which progresses on a parallel track, that of how nations eschewed the economic prosperity that train services brought in order to wage war against one another.

These twin tales tell of intrigue, integrity, innovation, exploitation, old empires, new nations – with a smattering of royalty and anarchy, too. Featured are railway's great characters with extraordinary vision, those who strove but failed and the villains of the piece.

If the selection of journeys seems idiosyncratic it's because, diamond-like, the story of how trains shaped Europe has numerous different facets. Each one helps complete the picture, like a piece of a puzzle, making this beautifully illustrated book an ideal choice for rail enthusiasts, history buffs, all inveterate travellers – armchair or otherwise – or as a companion to the popular show.

# 1

**LONDON** TO **MONTE CARLO**
**HUNGARY** TO **AUSTRIA**
**BERLIN** TO **THE RHINE**
**BASEL** TO **JUNGFRAUJOCH**
**AMSTERDAM** TO **NORTHERN FRANCE**

IN THE WAKE OF THE FIRST WORLD WAR there were ruined villages, fresh cemeteries and a pockmarked vista that snaked for miles through Flanders and France. And the political landscape was irretrievably changed also, with the collapse of the Austro-Hungarian, Ottoman and Russian empires.

Yet a journey by train through Europe before the conflict revealed nothing of the cataclysm that lay ahead.

In truth, the golden age of railway travel, with its massive and swift expansion, was largely over. Europe was already crisscrossed with lines – *Bradshaw's* reflected this with its minute detail on numerous routes in existence all over Europe.

The challenge now was to make journeys quicker and more comfortable. Although many improvements were already in evidence by 1913 – such as a greater number of wheels per carriage, seat upholstery and the inclusion of heating, restaurant cars and even lavatories – trips by train were still far from smooth in the seat.

Beyond the view from the carriage window, France was riding high as an imperial power but was better known for being the architect of the 'belle époque', or beautiful era. As a consequence, Parisian living was filled with a level of expectation and innovation that glossed over problems created by increasing international tensions. In Germany – where trains were notoriously slow – manufacturing at least was going full pelt, but at a glance the country appeared to be concerned more with acquiring technology than territory. Switzerland was likewise revelling in its industry and a new-found tourist trade, while the Low Countries were shoring up their economies and culinary and commercial interests. As peace gave way to conflict, the incentive to improve trains for travellers vanished at a stroke and engines became the workhorses of war.

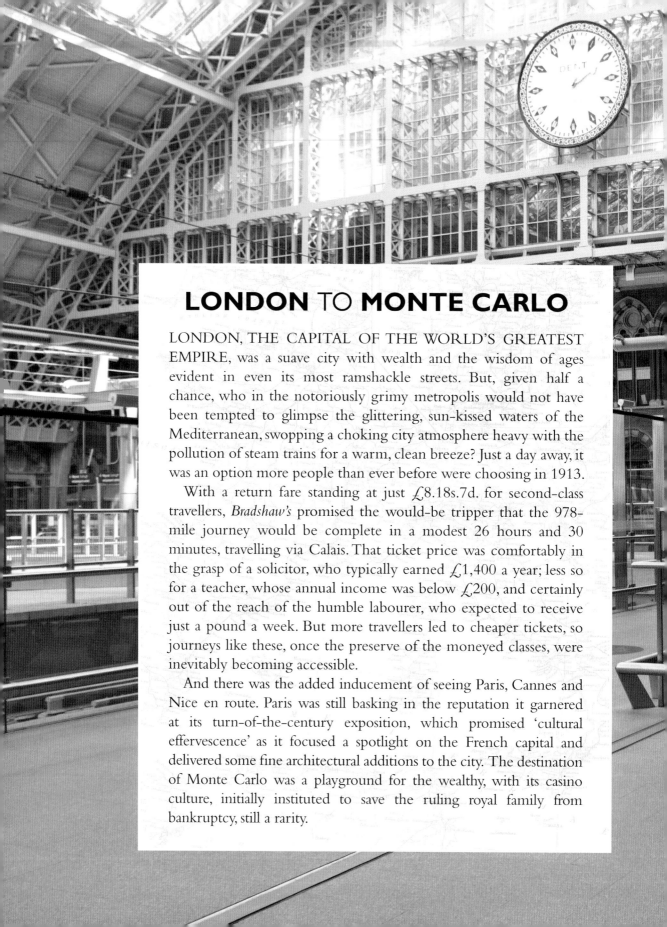

# LONDON TO MONTE CARLO

LONDON, THE CAPITAL OF THE WORLD'S GREATEST EMPIRE, was a suave city with wealth and the wisdom of ages evident in even its most ramshackle streets. But, given half a chance, who in the notoriously grimy metropolis would not have been tempted to glimpse the glittering, sun-kissed waters of the Mediterranean, swopping a choking city atmosphere heavy with the pollution of steam trains for a warm, clean breeze? Just a day away, it was an option more people than ever before were choosing in 1913.

With a return fare standing at just £8.18s.7d. for second-class travellers, *Bradshaw's* promised the would-be tripper that the 978-mile journey would be complete in a modest 26 hours and 30 minutes, travelling via Calais. That ticket price was comfortably in the grasp of a solicitor, who typically earned £1,400 a year; less so for a teacher, whose annual income was below £200, and certainly out of the reach of the humble labourer, who expected to receive just a pound a week. But more travellers led to cheaper tickets, so journeys like these, once the preserve of the moneyed classes, were inevitably becoming accessible.

And there was the added inducement of seeing Paris, Cannes and Nice en route. Paris was still basking in the reputation it garnered at its turn-of-the-century exposition, which promised 'cultural effervescence' as it focused a spotlight on the French capital and delivered some fine architectural additions to the city. The destination of Monte Carlo was a playground for the wealthy, with its casino culture, initially instituted to save the ruling royal family from bankruptcy, still a rarity.

# ST PANCRAS: A STORY OF SLUMP AND BOOM

ONCE IT WAS A GRAND GATEWAY to London for those who came to the capital by train from the north. Now the refurbished edifice of St Pancras is the exit point for those heading south to Europe by rail.

The fortunes of St Pancras, reflecting those of British railways, have also at times gone in two different directions.

It was built alongside King's Cross station in 1868 to accommodate the high number of new railway lines in London, on land that was once slum housing and a graveyard. No workaday design, its wrought-iron roof truss made it the era's largest space enclosed by a single span ever built – later mimicked across the world.

The iconic facade of St Pancras station, in central London. St Pancras International has been the home of Eurostar since November 2007

The first train to pull into the station arrived on 1 October at 4.20 a.m. carrying the overnight mail from Leeds. St Pancras became renowned as the delivery point for beer from Burton, stored in cool cellars beneath the station, and milk among other commodities.

With new wings of the Midland Grand hotel completed by 1876, the station was firmly established as a London landmark. But a bomb dropped in 1941, which wrecked the tram shed, together with a decline in the popularity of rail travel in subsequent decades put the station building under threat. By now, rail operations were nationalised and, hoping to wring new wealth from two railway relics, plans were made to replace both King's Cross and St Pancras with a single modern building.

Poet Sir John Betjeman, a champion of old England, was among opponents who campaigned vigorously against the idea and they were rewarded by the building's preservation. But still it languished in disrepair until plans for the Channel Tunnel were conceived. Today, with regular services departing to Europe, the palatial glassy and Gothic station, specially adapted for its new role, seems a fittingly grand stepping-off point for a technological triumph like the Channel Tunnel.

In 1913, long before engineers burrowed 75 metres (225 ft) below the English Channel, travellers departed from more southerly London stations like Victoria and Charing Cross, for ports that lay close to the French coast, including Dover, Folkestone and Newhaven.

The ships that awaited them were small steamers with a typically rolling gait which had been providing an often uncomfortable interlude between British and French railways for almost a century. Although Frenchman Louis Blériot had crossed the Channel by air in 1909, there was as yet no alternative for those prone to seasickness.

From the decks of just such a ship, German inventor Rudolf Diesel (1858–1913) threw himself into the Channel after being plagued by financial worries. Only after his death were the diesel locomotives that he helped pioneer brought into service.

## Old enemies, new friends

Opened in 1994, the 50 km (32 mile) link may have made European travel much easier but it also highlighted a difference in rail travel each side of the Channel. In Britain, the engines could manage only 86 miles per hour. In France, speeds of more than double that were achieved.

But the long-term lack of investment in the UK's railway infrastructure wasn't on most people's minds – rather it was the implied threat to Britain from rabies, which was commonly found in northern France. A huge anti-rabies vaccination programme kept the British countryside safe.

After snipping a ribbon, Queen Elizabeth labelled it the product of 'French élan and British pragmatism', while French newspaper *Le Figaro* hailed the end of British insularity.

Engineers thought differently and Lady Thatcher, who was prime minister when the project began in 1988, reflected their view. 'Every generation has to do something exciting that will affect the future.'

*With Paris as the country's railway hub, the city's stations soon had to be rebuilt to accommodate a growing number of lines*

# FRENCH RAILWAYS: A TROUBLESOME BIRTH

TWO YEARS BEFORE BRITISH ENGINEER George Stephenson unveiled his steam-powered *Rocket* in 1829, there was already a railway quietly hauling coal on a 21 km (13 mile) stretch near Lyon. Admittedly, it relied on a combination of gravity for the downhill stretches and horse power going up but, nonetheless, by the middle of 1830 it provided a passenger service for those content to squat in bumpy coal wagons.

Its lack of ambition was perhaps typical of French aspirations for railways at a time when the business of trains in Britain was exploding.

True, there were a few other attempts to get railway travel underway, but political instability following the Napoleonic Wars shackled progress and, between 1827 and 1842, only 569 km (354 miles) of line were built. Finally, a government bill was passed in 1842, designed to kick-start the industry.

The law decreed that the state would build the necessary infrastructure, including stations, and prepare rail beds. Meanwhile, private companies would lay rail and operate rolling stock.

On paper, it looked a fine ideal. In practice, the bureaucracy that plagued French governments of the era continued to hobble expansion despite monumental efforts by, among others, politician Alexis Legrand (1791–1848) to establish a national railway network. According to Legrand, the railways were 'the roads of power, enlightenment, civilisation'.

Within ten years the numerous private companies had combined to form just six major ones, wielding enough power to sidestep meddlesome government intervention on their projects. However, private firms weren't covered in glory either. Connections that would interlink the privately run lines remained inconveniently few, as companies focused on their own railway empires rather than the passengers' needs. Almost all radiated from Paris and passengers often had to make a detour via the capital to complete a journey to a city that was neighbouring their own.

As for the residents of the overcrowded medieval city, there was considerable upheaval with the construction of six major stations, all of which were duly expanded to accommodate an ever greater number of trains. The first platform to be constructed there was Gare Saint-Lazare in 1837. It was followed by bigger enterprises in the shape of Gare Montparnasse, Gare du Nord, Gare d'Austerlitz, Gare de l'Est, and the original Gare de Lyon. A decade later, the lives of the poor and displaced were disrupted once more when further swathes of the city were cleared for development in the grand plans drawn up by Baron Haussmann (1809–1891).

## Art Deco and diesel pull in the crowds

At the turn of the 20th century Paris hosted the Exposition Universelle. The French capital, which had so recently been transformed by the grand neoclassical designs of Baron Haussmann, was now lavishly decorated by its exhibits. The first World's Fair had been held in London half a century previously and there had already been four in Paris, including one in 1889 for which the Eiffel Tower was built. Events like these were now significant features in the international calendar. More than merely a commercial showcase, they were a celebration of innovation, and it was here in Paris that diesel engines were unveiled for the first time. An electric train toured the show site, which covered hundreds of hectares and attracted 50 million visitors during 212 days.

However, its greatest legacy was the promotion of Art Deco design, including the architecture of the Gare de Lyon. A station had existed on the site since 1852 and, despite four subsequent extensions, was too small for its task. The new Gare de Lyon had its 13 lines sheltered in a magnificent double-span iron and glass palace and was topped by a clock tower 64 metres (210 ft) high. Travellers remember it best for its ornate restaurant.

# TRAIN TRAVEL AND LA BELLE ÉPOQUE

IN A FEW SHORT DECADES after the arrival of the first trains Paris was transformed, and with its new edifices came a vibrancy that radiated around the world. The process to this golden age wasn't immediate but was inextricably linked to the effect of railways.

The population of Paris increased more during the 25 years that followed the opening of the first station than during the previous eight centuries.

People were fed by rural produce transported to the city on rails and each of the major stations on the outskirts became a hub for commerce. Wines from the south also made a commercial debut.

Meanwhile, the centre of the city benefited too, with the first modern department store, Le Bon Marché, opening in 1852.

Life in Paris was blighted by the Franco-Prussian war, which began in 1870 and amply illustrated the military value of railways. Well-supplied Prussian armies, as well as rail-borne artillery, were swiftly on the move towards the French capital, while France's army was partially paralysed by a poor railway network.

Afterwards, the French were determined to characterise the new Third Empire with confidence, prosperity and innovation. The country's industrial revolution, accompanied by further expansion in railways, stepped up a gear, fuelling a new age of conspicuous consumption, for the middle and upper classes at least. And the trains brought artists, writers, chefs, performers and designers to Paris, in a time that became known as the 'belle époque', or beautiful era, which would soon pervade most of western Europe.

German poet Heinrich Heine explained how the train made Paris feel like the centre of Europe. 'I feel as if the mountains and forests of all countries were advancing on Paris. Even now, I can smell the German linden trees; the North Sea's breakers are rolling against my door.'

But soon a new age was dawning – that of the motor car. Steam- and petrol-fuelled vehicles were pioneered in France, with Armand Peugeot

LA PREMIÈRE VOITURE AUTOMOBILE DANS PARIS
L'apparition de la première voiture automobile de Serpollet, qui portait le nom de "Voiture Miracle", dans les rues de Paris, en Avril 1891, fut la cause d'une émotion considérable dont se souviennent encore les vieux parisiens. (Voir l'article page 3).

The first car to arrive in Paris in 1891 created a stir among carriage drivers, whose livelihood would soon be under threat from the Métro

## Métro magic

Coach drivers had dreaded the coming of the train for fear of losing their jobs. After its arrival, those in Paris were in fact kept busy ferrying passengers from the major stations at the outer rim of the city to its heart.

However, their boom years were about to end as, alongside the motor car, came the Métro.

It was a project that had been discussed since the middle of the 19th century and at one stage even elevated sections were proposed to help cure congestion on the roads. When digging finally began in 1898, the project was nearly four decades behind its equivalent in London.

Opening in July 1900 to service the Olympic Games, held in Paris at the same time as the Exposition Universelle, the first line linked the Porte de Maillot to the Porte de Vincennes.

Cutting-edge technology was used to excavate further lines, with the ground beneath the River Seine being frozen with calcium chloride brine so that tunnelling could safely take place.

By 1913, when *Bradshaw's Continental Railway Guide* was published, there were ten lines and some 467 million passengers riding on them.

producing his first car in 1889, a year ahead of the Panhard et Levassor company and nine years prior to the first Renault being made. By 1903 France was the world's leading car producer.

There was a response from the railway companies, prompted not only by the arrival of the motor car but also by the increased size of coaches hauled by engines to house ever more passengers.

Thus, in 1907, the powerful Pacific 231 locomotive began service, with the figure denoting the number of axles it possessed. Later, Swiss composer Arthur Honegger, who confessed a passion for steam locomotives, wrote a symphony dedicated to that particular engine. 'To me they are living things and I love them,' he said.

# FEAR, LOATHING AND A LOST TRANQUILLITY

ASIDE FROM THE RAILWAYS, other technologies were advancing, including the art of movie-making.

In 1895, Auguste and Louis Lumière, whose father had made his fortune manufacturing plates for stills photography, had patented their Cinématographe, a combined camera, projector and film printer.

Based at the family home in La Ciotat, a resort in Provence, the brothers experimented by filming everyday subjects, including the arrival of a train hauling four freight wagons and at least 12 coaches at the station.

It was this 50-second unedited film taken from a static camera that they chose to premiere in Paris before a paying audience later that same year. A favourite story that's been a cornerstone of cinema history is that terrified audience members fled the venue, certain that the train would erupt from the screen.

**The sight of this locomotive on the big screen was said to have had customers fleeing the movie theatre**

Certainly, many in the audience might have had misgivings. Two months earlier, there was a derailment at Montparnasse, when an express crashed through the buffers at the terminus. The accident happened because the driver, running several minutes late, had been trying to make up for lost time.

Consequently, the locomotive careered into the station at speed, simultaneously suffering brake failure. It crossed the station concourse, crashed through the perimeter wall and fell on to the Place de Rennes below, where it landed on its nose. A woman in the street was killed by falling masonry. Later, the driver and a guard were fined. The train, left perched upright for several days, caused a sensation in Paris and was the subject of numerous photographs by both professionals and amateurs.

## The waterways fight back

Naturally blessed with a series of rivers, France had further enhanced the network of waterways from the mid-17th century after investing in canals. Now those with a vested interest hurled obstacles in the path of aspiring railway companies trying to establish a foothold in the early 19th century. That railways would be detrimental to agriculture and would threaten a traditional way of life were also given as reasons to curb their spread. In 1832, the chamber of commerce in Rouen turned down plans for a 136 km (84 mile) rail link with Paris, citing the damage that it could do to canal and riverside enterprises.

It wasn't the end for the railways in France but it certainly proved to be a hold-up. Inevitably, railways spread across the country and did indeed take freight off the waterways and on to the tracks. However, a short period of neglect was followed by further boom years on canals, as from 1860 it became apparent that a competitor to the railways would help cut prices. By 1893, there were more than 7,000 miles of navigable waterways in France carrying 25 million tons of freight. However, most traffic was on the River Seine, the canal that linked the Marne and the Rhône and other routes in the north.

But today there's some doubt about whether a panicked audience screamed at the film of the train. It may well be that a 3-D film by Louis Lumière on the same theme, screened 40 years later, was the one that spread alarm for, although the French may not have been used to moving pictures, they were by now accustomed to steam trains like the one filmed. By 1880, about 6,000 locomotives were fully operational, carrying more than 50,000 passengers a year.

However, it's true too that trains have always inspired fear. By 1840, French trains were driving at 40 mph and accidents like that at Versailles two years later, in which 55 people were killed, loomed large in the public consciousness. The fear of railways or train travel, properly called siderodromophobia, inspired one French railway company to employ a doctor to examine why people were scared. For some, though, their opposition was fuelled by hostility rather than fear, as a tranquil rural life vanished with the arrival of the trains.

# HUNGARY TO AUSTRIA

THE AUSTRO-HUNGARIAN EMPIRE was once a giant on the world stage. By the time Edwardian travellers were visiting the region the empire was fraying around the edges. But the authorities there were adept at papering over the cracks, not least thanks to a fine railway network. Before the First World War there were 20,760 km (12,900 miles) of railways in Hungary to serve a population of some 21 million, the vast majority of trains being operated by the state. In Austria, also largely state-owned, there was almost 12,875 km (8,000 miles) of track.

Budapest had an underground train system by 1896, the first in Continental Europe, and Vienna was just two years behind, operating steam trains beneath the streets of the imperial capital.

It was no coincidence that Emperor Franz Josef I – in power since failed revolutions in both Hungary and Vienna in 1848 – was a fan of railways. Not only did he personally support railway ventures across the territory, but he had his own sumptuously appointed royal train, known as the Imperial Express.

Ultimately, however, none of this could hold back the tide of nationalist feeling among the peoples of the dominion. Neighbouring Serbia was casting avaricious glances at the empire, hoping to carve off a slice for itself. When the emperor's heir presumptive, Archduke Franz Ferdinand, was assassinated in Sarajevo in the summer of 1914 by Serbian Gavrilo Princip, a challenge was thrown down. Franz Josef was in his imperial home at Bad Ischl when, on 28 July 1914, he signed the papers that signalled war with Serbia.

With that, Tsar Nicholas II of Russia mobilised troops to honour a Slavic alliance, which in turn provoked Germany to come to the aid of Austro-Hungary. When Germany declared war on Russia, France, being already paired with Russia through a diplomatic agreement, was then inevitably at war with Germany. Britain might have sat it out despite an existing three-way agreement with Russia and France. But when Germany invaded Belgium en route to France another treaty was contravened and Britain felt obliged to act. Thus, two rival camps lined up to do bloody battle.

# RAIL AS A STRATEGIC WEAPON

WHEN BRADSHAW'S 1913 GUIDE was published, the Austro-Hungarian empire was the largest political entity in Europe, covering 700,000 square kilometres (270,000 square miles).

Its history was complex, and the enforced union between peoples was frequently an unhappy one. Hungary, for example, won a long battle against Turkish rule in the 17th century, only to find itself under the dominion of the Habsburg empire centred in Austria.

The arrival of the railway in Hungary in 1846 became a symbol of a burgeoning rebellion against the status quo for radicals who dreamt of an independent state. One such patriot was poet Sándor Petőfi (1823–1849), who was among the passengers in the first rail service that ran between Pest and Vác. After noting that 'men can also fly today', he instantly appreciated the advent of railways and their potential for bringing about reform. He captured this optimistic mood in a poem:

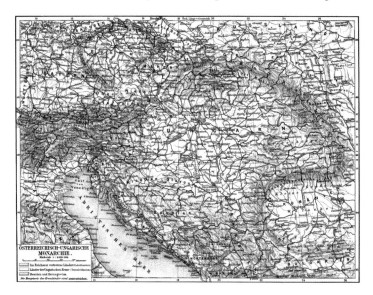

*The railways are the veins of earth*
*Culture and progress prosper where*
*They cause pulsations of the air*
*To nations' greatness they give birth.*

Two years later there was indeed a revolution in Hungary, with Petőfi dying in one of its last battles. It was one of a number in Europe in 1848 fired by liberalism – and doomed to failure. Without exception, each revolt was defeated and an even more oppressive regime than had previously existed was installed.

In Austria's case, Franz Josef I (1830–1916), deeply conservative and militarily minded after a spell in the army as a young man, became emperor of the Habsburgs.

Brooding resentment still festered in Hungary, where 14 generals had been executed by the Austrians in Transylvania in 1849.

The emperor, plagued by a series of wars, finally made two fundamental realisations: that he could not rule safely and successfully without co-operation from Hungary, and that railways were strategically important to the military wherewithal of the empire.

In 1867, Austria and Hungary agreed to a union which finally offered some status to Hungarians, granting them their own parliament and army.

A melting pot of peoples and cultures, the Austro-Hungarian empire was once a dominant force in Europe

Emperor Franz Josef was head of state for both – and encouraged major railway-building projects.

Unlike other imperial nations, Austria did not seek colonies overseas. But it was keen to keep its assets intact despite a rise in nationalism. Within its borders were not only Germans and Hungarians, but also Czechs, Poles, Italians and Serbs. Austria's major cities included Vienna, Prague, Trieste and Kraków, while Hungary counted Zagreb and Bratislava as well as a number of Romanian cities in its fold.

So railways that linked these far-flung outposts of empire could also be used to ferry in the army to quell any uprisings. Perhaps for that reason, both countries preferred a state-run system from 1879, although private companies played a small part in the railway story, too.

## Bridging the Danube

Not all Hungarians sought revolution. Statesman István Szechényi (1791–1860) was loyal to the Habsburgs and believed that economic prosperity would bring about change.

To that end, he employed William Tierney Clark (1783–1852) to link two sides of Hungary's main city, Buda and Pest. Clark, who was responsible for two bridges over the River Thames among others, designed and supervised the building of the Chain Bridge at a cost of £622,042, leaving Scotsman Adam Clark (no relation) (1811–1866) in charge of its day-to-day construction.

The bridge, 202 metres (600 ft) long, was finished in 1849, after which Adam Clark had to twice save it from being blown up, first by the Austrians then the Hungarians themselves. He did so by filling bridge compartments with water to mitigate the effects of explosives.

Afterwards, Tierney Clark praised the 'energy and perseverance' of Count Szechényi and reflected on the difficulties, including 'the magnitude of the river over which it is thrown, its depth, the nature of its bed, and the velocity of the current'.

# A TALE OF TWO CITIES

PARIS WAS NOT THE ONLY SUBJECT of an ambitious remodelling programme in the 19th century. Always anxious that his empire keep pace with the rest of Europe, Franz Josef I had grand plans for his capital, Vienna.

Perhaps the most significant contribution he made to change the face of this medieval city was to boldly tear down its fortifications – which the city had outgrown – and replace them with a broad and stylish boulevard. The elegant Ringstrasse, which was officially opened in 1865, set the tone for a city that began to fill its streets with magisterial buildings. Among them was a Greek-style parliament building, galleries, a grand opera house and a university. There was a park studded with statues and a world-famous walz in its honour.

Consequently, it was one of the most fashionable of European cities before the First World War, giving the semblance of being at the heart of a strong and resilient empire. *Bradshaw's* concurs with that view. '[Vienna]

The Ringstrasse. Vienna was ideally tailored to its well-heeled residents; but those living at the margins of society faced a hapless existence from which it was almost impossible to escape

is regarded as one of the brightest and healthiest of the large continental cities, with cheerful and courteous inhabitants.' According to the guidebook, the Ringstrasse, 'a fine broad thoroughfare', extends in a two-mile-long crescent around three sides of the inner town, with most of the city's principal buildings nearby.

On the flip side of its public face was a private agony unfolding in an underbelly where nothing of the glamour that enchanted overseas visitors rubbed off on inhabitants. Inadvertently, perhaps, *Bradshaw's* indicates what was at the core of the complacency in this divided city, which finally cost Austria its empire. Describing the exhibits of one of the main museums, the guidebook says the 'unrivalled accumulated treasures of many centuries' in the imperial collection 'is probably the richest and most valuable and historically interesting collection in existence of articles of gold and silver, gems, jewels, precious stones, crystals etc., historical curiosities and smaller works of art'.

But while these riches left Edwardian visitors awestruck, they were remote from the legions of poor people who inhabited this so-called 'city of dreams'.

## Royal railways

Austria's first railway opened in 1837, although it wasn't completed that year. Running northwards from Vienna, it would finally reach Kraków for a journey that by 1913 would take about seven hours. It was called Kaiser Ferdinand-Nordbahn, after the emperor, establishing a pattern for railway names that reflected the encompassing role of the royal family.

In the 1850s, Vienna was linked with Salzburg via the Kaiserin Elizabeth-Bahn, the railway named for the empress who would be assassinated by an Italian anarchist in 1898. By 1860 the Franz Josef line carried passengers between Vienna and Belgrade.

The first locomotives to run in Austria were made by Robert Stephenson's company in England and accompanied to Vienna by Scot John Haswell (1812–1897), who was persuaded to stay, becoming locomotive superintendent of the Austrian State Railways. He built the *Wien*, the first Austrian-made locomotive, in 1841 and helped establish the empire's first engine manufacturer.

In 1913, an estimated 1,500 Viennese people committed suicide, ostensibly to escape their piteous existences. Fewer than half the city's inhabitants were born there, so many were isolated not only by lack of money but also by language and custom.

The emperor, swaddled in luxury at the Hofburg Palace, was blind to the deepening chasm between the wealthy elite and the disconsolate masses. Although he had enjoyed popularity, fewer of his people than ever before now shared his imperial beliefs. Vienna-born historian Frederic Morton (1924–2015) summed up the contradictions by noting that imperial Austria was 'a byword for melodious decay'. 'In the Vienna of January 1913 illusion and reality embraced elegantly, seamlessly,' he wrote in his book *Thunder at Twilight*.

With the Western world teetering on the edge of a precipice, the city's veneer was poised to fracture.

A train speeds
through the high
mountain pass
between Salzburg
and Tyrol

# THOMAS COOK LAYS THE TOURIST TRAIL

WITH STUNNING SCENERY, a free-wheeling intellectual discourse and a robust pedigree in music history, Austria was an obvious choice for tourists in pre-war Europe.

As early as 1868, travel entrepreneur Thomas Cook had accompanied trippers to Vienna as part of a tour from Venice to Budapest. Five years later, he gave a further helping hand to Austria's fledgling tourist industry by publishing his first international timetable with details of trains, boats and horse-drawn carriage services.

But Emperor Franz Josef still believed more people could be enticed to Austria. Now railways would have a new role outside the military arena, as an initiative was launched by its state-run railway company.

On 23 July 1912 (in a report submitted by the Marconi Transatlantic Wireless Telegraph), the *New York Times* reported that observation cars from the Canadian Pacific line would soon be attached to express trains and used for local excursions. 'The Hungarian Minister of Commerce and Railways has entered into negotiations with the Canadian Pacific Company for the establishment of a similar train service of American cars on several lines of the

Hungarian railroad system, mainly to the Tatra Mountains and Transylvania,' the report said.

The Canadian Pacific had for years been using specially designed observation cars with larger-than-average windows and an open platform at the rear, so that passengers could enjoy the scenery of the Rocky Mountains as they travelled between Calgary and Vancouver.

Outside, the carriages – the longest in Europe – were made of varnished teak. Inside, there were 33 free-standing leather armchairs, as well as a library and a secretary and telegraph services.

As it turned out, the unprotected platforms proved too dangerous to be used in long Austrian railway tunnels, so glass was installed when the coaches were made in 1912 by a Prague company, to Canadian Pacific specifications.

According to *Bradshaw's*, in the summer of 1913 Austrian State Railways were once again due to include Canadian Pacific observation cars 'to the chief daylight express trains … traversing the most picturesque districts of Austrian Tyrol.' It's not known if this happened.

Previously warm relations between Canada and Austria dramatically cooled in the spring of that year. Ostensibly, the reason was a new steamer line launched in March 1913 that docked in Trieste, in direct competition to Austrian and German shipping lines, which had previously enjoyed a monopoly. In reality, it was the thousands of poor citizens of the empire who bought one-way tickets and emigrated, depriving the army of valuable conscripts, that grated. Observation car services were suspended following a bitter legal battle. If they resumed at all it was only for a short period, before the outbreak of war. The service didn't return to the timetables after the conflict had finished and dreams in Hungary of cashing in on a tourist bonanza were dashed.

## On the rack with the Schafbergbahn

Tourists who visited Austria were keen to appreciate the stunning vistas – but less enthusiastic about a long mountain hike.

Accordingly, the Schafbergbahn was built to take passengers to a dizzying 1,190 metres (3,904 ft) in carriages hauled by a steam cog railway. During its construction, 6,000 mules were used to take equipment up the mountain, which in places has gradients of 1:4. The line covers a distance of almost 6 km – around 3½ miles – on a track gauge measuring one metre (3 ft 3 in). Also known as rack railways, the engines grind upwards as teeth in its operating cogs mesh with corresponding gaps on the rails. The first locomotive arrived in bits, to be reassembled at the bottom of the mountain. Those workhorses that first went into service in the summer of 1893 are still doing sterling work today alongside more modern engines.

# BERLIN TO THE RHINE

AT THE START OF THE 20TH CENTURY, Germany had nearly 64,000 km (40,000 miles) of railway track, having increased its network by ten times in 50 years.

A juvenile state, established in 1871, Germany was nonetheless ambitious and the military advantages loomed large in the minds of Kaiser Wilhelm II and his army top brass.

One unintended consequence of the expanded rail capacity was a boom in the number of tourists that visited. For the many Britons who took advantage of the far-reaching railways in Germany, the start of the First World War seemed all the more baffling. To them, the German army's agenda wasn't immediately clear – although it had been in place for as long as the country had existed.

Strategically, the benefits of trains were clear. Prior to the railway there were horses, but these were used mostly for officers, while rank and file soldiers marched in columns to any designated war zone.

The speed at which Napoleon's troops travelled was often cited as a reason for his success. His men marched 15–50 km a day, without waiting for cumbersome baggage trains. When they got hungry, they lived off the land – which made them no friends among farmers.

However, now soldiers could travel 50 km (30 miles) in just two hours, or several hundred kilometres every day. And they arrived at their destination without undue exertion.

Trains in the industrial Ruhr would have even greater significance during the First World War, after weapons production increased to more than five times the pre-war level, to meet government orders.

Much later, it would be a different war that caused Japan to plan a railway that would link Tokyo and Berlin. The Japanese emperor's advisers proposed using German lines from Berlin as far as Baghdad, while the Japanese would make their way to Europe via Korea and across Mongolia and Afghanistan. As the Second World War took what was for them an unexpected course, the railway remained a pipe dream.

# TRAVELLING LIGHT IN GERMANY

BEFORE THE FIRST WORLD WAR, Germany was something of a 'must see' for British tourists. According to *Bradshaw's*: 'No country in the world can show so many nobly planned and well built towns or cities which have preserved so perfectly their ancient character.'

If they took to the railways during the trip, the trippers would find carriages 'clean and comfortable', the guide promised, with cheaper than average fares working out at less than a penny per mile in second class. Trains, unified on mid-European time (GMT +1) since 1890, had a reputation for being on time.

However, railway passengers in Germany faced additional costs that were not always levied elsewhere. No free allowance of luggage was made by German railway administrators, for example. *Bradshaw's* doesn't offer a guide price because there were 15 different luggage zones in Germany and the necessary information was held in a series of tables too large to publish in an already weighty tome.

GERMANY
IN THE BLACK FOREST
Information and handbooks from all tourist agencies and travel bureaus
German Tourist Information Office, 665 Fifth Avenue, New York City

But *Bradshaw's* wasn't the only source of information for travellers from the UK. Dresden, Berlin, Bremen, Cologne and Hamburg all had Thomas Cook offices by 1913, reflecting their popularity as tourist destinations. Prior to the 20th century, guidebooks produced by John Murray in England and by Karl Baedeker in Germany were also accurate and informative.

Without them, visitors to the German region might have struggled before 1871 because at the time Germany wasn't a single country but 40 loosely federated states. Before the Congress of Vienna in 1814–15, which better compartmentalised the regions, the outlook was even more confused.

Needless to say, this hotchpotch of powers did nothing to help speed the building of a railway network. One man is credited with helping to coalesce railway services after the country itself was unified in 1871, although his interests did not lie in tourism.

Helmuth von Moltke (1800–1891) was born in Prussia, always the most eminent of the German states. As he rose through the ranks of the army, he became a superb strategist and recognised the military potential of railways

## Berliners take to the tram

In 1881, the electric tram was built in Berlin, at the personal expense of its confident creator. Werner von Siemens (1816–1892) had trialled the world's first electric train – a pint-sized engine with a driver astride it, towing a line of back-to-back seating – two years earlier at the city's trade fair with some success.

In a letter to his brother Carl, he said: 'Our electric railway ... is quite a spectacle here. It is running even better than expected ... around a thousand people a day are being transported for a donation of 20 pfennigs to charity. The train carries 20 to 25 people and runs at roughly the pace of a horse-drawn tram. This is something we certainly can develop!'

And it was this train that evolved into a tram car 5 metres (16 ft) long, powered by direct current supplied through rails. Its maximum speed was 40 kph (25 mph) – heady stuff for the 20 passengers.

The tram replaced horse-drawn trams and steam buses and its technology led to electric underground trains. In 1929, there was more than 600 km (370 miles) of tram track in Berlin. Today, the figure is not quite 200 km (120 miles), most of it having been preserved behind the Berlin Wall in the Communist east.

almost immediately after their inception. Frustrated, he found himself unable to mobilise troops quickly enough to make a difference in the numerous wars that flared up on the Continent. His point was finally proved in 1870 when he masterminded the defeat of France, using armies that were transported by rail.

Afterwards, with Germany a single political entity, railway building increased apace, not least thanks to a series of improved technologies, and it was this programme that benefited tourists in the early 20th century.

Locomotive repairs being carried out at the Krupp works in Essen in the Ruhr valley, the industrial heart of Germany

# STEEL WHEELS AND A SAFETY DIVIDEND

MEN MADE AND LOST GREAT WEALTH on the railways throughout the 19th century. For Alfred Krupp (1812–1887), a happy collaboration with locomotive makers cemented a fortune that had already been established and turned his surname into a byword for steel.

When Krupp inherited his father's workshop in Essen in 1826 the future did not seem assured. But with the workshop and its seven employees came the secret of making high quality cast steel. Still a teenager, the able-minded Krupp got to grips with manufacturing steel rolls and went on to enjoy a healthy profit from producing cutlery and coins.

However, it was with the advent of large-scale railway engine manufacture that the possibilities for even greater riches began to unfold. Initially, his works – conveniently close to the Ruhr coalfields – made axles and springs from cast steel. But in 1852, after he made the first seamless steel railway tyre, money began pouring into his coffers.

Steel wheels made railway journeys much safer, as the ones they replaced were liable to fray. At a time when railway operators were frequently being sued after crashes and derailments, it was a particularly attractive option.

Its production made such an impact on the business that Krupp adopted the symbol of three rings, representing railway wheels, as a trademark.

But this highly profitable arena formed only part of the business. Krupp was an enthusiastic producer of armaments and, by the time of his death, had armed 46 nations.

He was the first to make anti-aircraft artillery with his modified one-pounder gun, installed on the back of a horse-drawn carriage. Known as the '*ballonkanone*', it was intended to down the hot-air balloons sent from besieged Paris during the Franco-Prussian war in 1870 and proved to be the humble beginnings of an entirely new facet of military hardware.

On his death, his son Friedrich (1854–1902) continued to cash in on what was now a European arms race, until his suicide. Between 1886 and 1910, steel production in Germany increased by 1,300 per cent.

## The Old Lady of Wuppertal

Wuppertal is now defined by the suspension railway that weaves around the roofline of the city.

First opened in 1901, the monorail still carries an estimated 25 million passengers a year, although locally it's been dubbed 'the old lady'.

Yet, astonishingly, there was nothing new about the idea, even back at the turn of the 20th century. It was in the 1820s that British civil engineer Henry Robinson Palmer (1795–1844) became convinced that suspended railways were the way forward.

In 1823, he wrote an illustrated book on the subject. It was called *Description of a Railway on a New Principle*, and in it he wrote: 'Having submitted my plan to such tests as were satisfactory to many of the most eminent engineers and men of science I am encouraged by their opinion and by my own conviction deduced from extensive observations on similar works.'

In his plans it was not steam engines towing the suspended carriages but horses. Perhaps bizarrely, he even set up a prototype in the Ruhr a few years later at the behest of a German entrepreneur who believed it would provide an ideal means of towing coal from the mines.

Unfortunately for Palmer, it would be another 75 years before his futuristic dream became a reality there. But that the 13 km (8 mile) line still runs at a height of 12 metres (39 ft) in Wuppertal, above traffic jams and road works, is surely the best tribute to his vision.

# FAIRYTALES IN THE RHINELANDS

ONE OF THE CELEBRATED RAILWAY TRIPS for travellers was alongside the Rhine between Cologne and Frankfurt, where the river banks are peppered with imposing castles, fairy-tale follies and grand statuary.

With Cologne a railway hub by the middle of the 19th century, the allure of the trip brought many overseas visitors. Other attractions included the chance to buy eau de Cologne, created in the 18th century by Italian immigrant Johann Maria Farina to disguise the smell of the city and its people. And after 1880 the fabulous *Dom*, or cathedral, was finished, standing tall over one of the railway lines leading into the city.

It was proposals for another extraordinary line that helped sow some of the seeds of war. There had been long-standing plans to link Berlin to Baghdad by rail, a project that had initially won British support when it was proposed by the Deutsche Bank in 1888.

*Railways carried tourists through a stunning river valley to Cologne where they could buy a celebrated scent. But Germany's railway ambitions elsewhere caused problems for the British government*

That support had evaporated by the turn of the century when it seemed the line would give Germany a quick route to the Middle East at a time when coal was giving way to oil as the fuel of choice.

A shorter line built by the Germans in Anatolia had won the favour of Abdul Hamid II, the sultan of the Ottoman empire. Consequently, the Germans won Turkish consent to build a 2,500-mile line between Constantinople, or Istanbul as it is now known, and Basra in Iraq.

In fact, it was a costly route, with numerous tunnels needed to breach the Taurus Mountains. In 1902, the Germans offered the French and English the chance to have a stake in the project. With concern about German naval aspirations occupying public thought in England, there was an outcry about the strategic threat the railway would pose and the offer was flatly rejected.

The line was eventually completed in 1940, a triumph in Germany's police state of 'Drang nach Osten', or 'push east'.

# Time travel on the Einstein Express

When Albert Einstein (1879–1955) published his paper 'Relativity: The Special and the General Theory' in 1916, he used the analogy of a train travelling at speed past an embankment. He was trying to explain one of the trickiest truths for non-mathematicians to grasp – that time passes differently depending on where you are and what you're doing.

Around this time, Einstein was working at the Swiss patent office in Bern, where the city's 12th-century clock tower was synchronised with clocks at the local railway station. Some patent applications wanted to synchronise the tower precisely with more distant timepieces using speed-of-light signals. Einstein saw a problem.

He asked readers to imagine standing on a railway embankment at the centre point of a forward-moving train. Suppose in that instant they observed a simultaneous lightning strike at either end of the train. To them it would indeed be simultaneous.

But a train passenger sitting at that same centre point would have been hastening towards the front strike and away from the rear one. This passenger (assuming he or she possessed superhuman senses capable of registering light-speed) would correctly say that the front strike occurred first.

In other words, the stationary observer and the moving passenger experienced the same event but at different times relative to each other. Einstein's train had helped overturn an assumption of physics by proving that time did not have 'absolute significance' but depended on motion.

# BASEL TO JUNGFRAUJOCH

FOR DECADES, SWITZERLAND has had a rail service that serves villages as well as towns and cities, even if those tiny centres of population are improbably perched on steep mountains.

This is no mean feat, especially as challenging landscape wasn't the only problem that the first railway companies faced. Three different languages are commonly spoken in land-locked Switzerland, with others also heard within its boundaries, and the country's network inevitably spills into that of its neighbours.

However, there's been stable government since 1815 which, together with its dearly held neutrality, enabled the railway to evolve for logical rather than military reasons.

The journey to network coverage – which was late in getting started – wasn't entirely smooth and, as a result of railway company bankruptcies, a series of rail strikes, a piecemeal approach by the regional cantons and resistance to foreign ownership, railways were nationalised in 1897.

Remarkably, given the circumstances, the web of main lines was completed as early as 1913. Typically, imposing and elegant bridges and viaducts with arched masonry feature strongly, all built with the pioneering use of reinforced concrete.

The First World War did have an impact on Swiss railways, although it wasn't a belligerent. Without natural resources to run locomotives at its disposal during the conflict, the nation struggled to secure fuel. A lesson was learned and afterwards all lines were electrified.

By the 20th century the value of the Swiss railway system, with its 671 tunnels and 6,000 bridges, was highlighted when research found that each of its residents travelled 1,751 km (1,088 miles) a year by rail, considerably more than fellow Europeans. A reputation for trains being clean, comfortable and timely undoubtedly plays its part. If nothing else, those impressive figures validate the aspirations and tribulations of a distant generation of engineers and investors.

## TRIUMPH AND TRAGEDY
## BENEATH THE GOTTHARD PASS

Working on the
Gotthard tunnel
was a risky
business. But
when labourers
went on strike for
better conditions
they were
confronted with
the Swiss army

DESPITE ITS DIFFICULT TERRAIN, Switzerland had to have a fully fledged railway system or it could not co-exist on parity with other European nations. That was the belief of far-sighted entrepreneur Alfred Escher (1819–1882), who is retrospectively remembered for bringing modern railways to Switzerland.

To help one railway company realise its plans, he founded a loans company that evolved into Credit Suisse. Yet perhaps his greatest achievement was to help steer to fruition ambitious plans for the north–south rail link beneath the rugged outcrops of the Gotthard Pass. To do so, he won support and finance from Italy and Germany. But this technological triumph was fraught with problems and, for a while, cost Escher his hard-won reputation.

The 15 km (9 mile) tunnel took ten years to dig and cost almost 200 lives, including that of chief engineer Louis Favre (1826–1879), who died aged 53 while inspecting it. Before his death, it was Favre who took centre stage in this story of misplaced pride, human degradation, national jealousy and, ultimately, extraordinary achievement.

Favre was a Swiss engineer with only limited experience in tunnel building. However, after promising to build the tunnel for 2,800 Swiss francs per linear metre, he won the contract with the newly created Gotthard Railway Company. So keen was he to secure the work that he agreed to a punitive 5,000 Swiss franc fine for every day the project was delayed, which doubled on the six-month mark.

If he had doubts about meeting deadlines, Favre comforted himself with the knowledge that technology was perpetually improving. Indeed, Alfred Nobel had patented dynamite in 1867. Favre even believed he would complete the tunnel in just six years.

A tunnel had already linked France and Italy, with the Mont Cenis – also known as Fréjus – tunnel. That 14-year project, under the supervision of French engineer Germain Sommeiller (1815–1871), not only had the latest pneumatic equipment on site that made some 15 feet of progress every day, but there were organised camps for workers which included schools, hospitals and a recreation room.

## Pastries galore on the Baden run

Switzerland's first train, linking Zürich and the spa town of Baden in 1947, has always been known as 'the Spanish bread train'. (It wasn't the first train on Swiss soil. That came in the form of a railway which linked the outskirts of Basel and Strasbourg, built by a French textile magnate and held in some suspicion by the Swiss.)

However, the 23 km (14 mile) entirely Swiss enterprise which terminated at Baden was used not only by the wealthy residents of Zürich seeking a soothing water treatment, but by servants who came daily to buy the popular pastries for the tables of their employers.

This proved something of a turning point in Swiss fortunes. Until then, there had been a succession of poor harvests, widespread poverty and a feeling of hopelessness manifested by a growing desire among the economically disadvantaged to seek a better life elsewhere.

Now the servants who were tasked with shopping felt the benefit of a technological breakthrough, catching a train into town – albeit in poorly appointed third class – rather than walking. At last there was optimism that the future would be better if they stayed in Switzerland to enjoy the fruits of a belated industrial revolution.

The Italians hoped Sommeiller would take on the Gotthard tunnel too, but he refused to compromise on costs.

To cut expenditure, Favre economised on safety measures for his labourers, who worked in menacingly dreadful conditions. (When this tunnel was being replaced by a longer, deeper one in 2010, temperatures of 45 degrees centigrade were recorded.) Men were injured by or perished in flood water; there were accidents with machinery and even a hookworm epidemic. A strike by workers in 1875 was crushed by the Swiss army, with a further four men dying.

All the while, Favre's personal debt was mounting as progress went far slower than predicted.

# THE PERILS OF NATIONAL PRIDE

IF FAVRE THOUGHT HIS PROBLEMS couldn't get any worse, he was woefully mistaken. His next monumental difficulty came in the form of Franz Rziha (1831–1897), a Bohemian reputed to be the father of scientific tunnelling.

When Rziha visited the tunnel site in 1874, he was chief engineer of the Austro-Hungarian department of trade. What he saw appalled him. It was not the plight of the Italian labourers working under duress in extreme heat and polluted air that troubled him, but the boring method chosen by Favre.

Both men favoured honeycombing the rock face with holes using the newly developed pneumatic drill, and inserting dynamite to generate controlled explosions. But Favre had opted for the Belgian construction technique, which involved starting work at the top of the tunnel and following through with tunnel supports.

In Rziha's opinion, Favre should have followed Austrian techniques, which involved working from the ground upwards – as outlined in a book Rziha himself had previously published.

*Opened in 1906, the Simplon tunnel was for years the longest tunnel in the world*

After the Austrian made public his criticisms, a row enveloped Europe's engineering community which rumbled on for years. Favre had his supporters and Rziha, detractors, mostly for making it an issue of nationality rather than science. But the truth of which tunnelling method – top or bottom – was superior simply wasn't clear.

The ensuing backlash, combined with lengthy delays, led to investor Escher's resignation from the Gotthard Railway Company board in 1878, a year before Favre died from a stroke. According to colleagues, Favre had aged visibly as a result of the stress and condemnation he endured.

So neither Escher nor Favre was in the spotlight to receive the plaudits when the railway began running. On its opening, the tunnel was compared as an engineering feat to the recently completed Suez Canal and even on a par with the pyramids of ancient Egypt. Much later, the reputation of both men was restored.

Soon it was followed by other major tunnels out of Switzerland. The westerly Simplon tunnel, designed by German engineer Alfred Brandt (1846–1899), was opened in 1906. At nearly 20 km (12½ miles) long, it was for years the longest tunnel in the world and provided a route from London to Istanbul for the Simplon Orient Express.

This time 67 workers perished out of the 2,000 employed daily during its eight-year construction, which was marked by workers' strikes. Nonetheless, progress was made at a steady 18 feet per day until temperatures reached 138 degrees Fahrenheit and the rock was too hot to handle after being hewn from the tunnel walls.

The Swiss side was sealed with an iron door until the Italian labourers completed their approach through the Alps.

Construction on a second tunnel parallel to the first began in 1912 and was completed nine years later. The building of the Lötschberg tunnel, designed for electric trains from the outset, also took its toll on the workforce, with 13 dying in an avalanche and 25 killed when the tunnel collapsed after a deluge of water. This single-bore tunnel was opened in 1913, with engineers solemnly recognising that lives would be saved with better geological investigation.

## An electrifying change

Aware that passengers could be harmed by inhaling carbon monoxide if a steam train broke down in the tunnel, a decision was made before the completion of the Simplon tunnel to use electric trains instead. The Zürich-based Brown, Boveri & Cie established electrification and sourced suitable locomotives.

It was cutting-edge stuff at a time when Europe was still conducting a love affair with steam. The first electric locomotive had been designed by Englishman Charles Brown (1863–1924) – the 'Brown' of the Zürich company – and in 1891 he demonstrated how it could be used on a 280 km (170 mile) route.

With its abundant supply of hydroelectricity, it was perhaps unsurprising that electric trains were developed in Switzerland.

In 1920, the Gotthard tunnel was electrified. After early hitches caused by the collected fuel smuts inside, the long-snouted 'crocodile' locomotives, designed for flexibility around tight bends with swivel bogies and a buckle-proof rod drive, began operating on the line and remained the engine of choice for some 60 years.

# CORKSCREW TRACKS TAME THE MOUNTAINS

SOMETIMES THE SWISS DECIDED to go around the mountains rather than through them.

It was an era when engineering solutions were coming thick and fast. But still man's ingenuity was taxed, having to overcome testing hurdles including glaciers, lakes and rivers, gorges, ravines and the elements.

After the Gotthard tunnel there was a drop of some 2,000 feet that had to be negotiated so that trains could make an onward journey. To make the gradient as shallow as possible, the line was built in circuitous loops in order to corkscrew down the valley.

From the inside of the train, landmarks appear on one side of the carriage and, soon afterwards, on the other. The effect is bewildering.

From the outside, the layout looks like a giant model layout, with a train vanishing in one direction, only for its nose to appear again soon afterwards around another bend in a different direction altogether.

In addition to standard lines, there is also a sprawling narrow gauge network through the Alps, built at reduced width to help overcome the perennial problem of gradients and bends. The most famous is the Rhaetian Railway.

The first length of line was laid thanks to the efforts of Dutchman Willem Jan Holsboer, who ran a hotel in Davos at a time when the lofty resort, favoured by those who suffered chesty tubercular complaints, was served only by horse-drawn carriages.

*Swiss railways adapted to deal with slopes and snow, creating thereby some of the most spectacular rail trips in the world*

The Landquart to Davos service began in 1890 – although it was a further two decades before it was extended any further. Despite its limitations, a delighted Holsboer indicated his desire to increase the network.

It grew in 1904 when the 67 km (42 mile) long Albula railway between Thusis and St Moritz, with its 144 viaducts and bridges and 42 tunnels, was finally completed.

The narrow gauge Bernina railway was opened in sections from 1908, finally linking St Moritz with Tirano in Italy. Plagued by financial difficulties, the line was eventually taken over by Rhaetian Railways in 1943.

## Wait a second – it's Swiss time

It wasn't just a case of building railways; it was also a matter of linking lines and gauges both nationally and internationally.

Switzerland is the turntable of Europe, with great volumes of passenger and freight traffic passing through in all directions every day.

Good timekeeping is fundamental to the Swiss way of life – watches have been made there since 1550. After the Second World War, stations were provided with clocks that ticked for 58.5 seconds then stood still for 1.5 seconds to 'bring calm in the last moment and ease punctual train departure', according to Hans Hilfiker (1901–1993), designer of the Swiss railway clock. Fifty years on, those clocks are being replaced but punctuality is still highly rated. Even a train delay of four minutes is considered a serious matter in railway management.

The secret of success apparently includes a computer-generated timetable; building a buffer into a train's timetable to help resolve unforeseen hold-ups; and a commitment to running a world-beating public transport system.

So spectacular are the latter two lines that they were listed by UNESCO, which paid tribute to the way the railways had 'overcome the isolation of settlements in the Central Alps early in the 20th century, with a major and lasting socio-economic impact on life in the mountains'.

Technically, architecturally and environmentally, the lines were 'outstanding', said UNESCO, adding that they were 'in harmony with landscapes through which they pass'.

47

# SKI TRAINS TO ST MORITZ

ST MORITZ

ENGADINE      SWITZERLAND
6000 ft.

LIPS & CO · BERN

SWITZERLAND BECAME A SUMMER FAVOURITE with English tourists in the last half of the 19th century as a peaceful alternative to Germany, France, Austria and Italy, countries that were all periodically involved in skirmishes.

Alongside less robust souls, who believed refreshing mountain air and spa waters had health-giving properties, there was a small army of alpine hikers.

However, one far-sighted hotelier in St Moritz artfully changed the profile of the nation's tourist industry. He tempted outdoorsy British tourists, who were typically young aristocrats, to return in the winter months. If they did not like what they found, he said, he would pay their return fare. The adventurous types took him up on his offer – and the era of winter sports began.

Skiing had been part of everyday life in northerly areas for centuries, primarily as a practical mode of transport. Without heed to its history, the British saw it as a sport.

Sir Henry Lunn (1859–1939), a former Methodist minister, began Co-operative Educational Tours to Switzerland in 1893, which offered both religious retreats and snow sports. He was also behind the Public Schools Alpine Sports Club.

After starting travel agents Lunn Poly in Horncastle, Lincolnshire, Lunn based himself in Mürren, Switzerland. When his friend Sir Arthur Conan Doyle visited, the writer confided that he wanted to devote his time to psychic research but was unsure how to divest himself of his enormously popular creation, Sherlock Holmes.

'Push him off the Reichenbach Falls,' suggested Lunn, before taking Conan Doyle to the site. And as far as readers were concerned that's just how the pipe-smoking detective apparently met his end.

Winter tours were first organised by Thomas Cook during the 1880s. By 1908, the firm's brochure made winter sports, now firmly in vogue, sound irresistible.

'Winter sport exhilarates and rejuvenates; it generates a glow of pleasure in the mind which acts powerfully upon the whole physical organisation, while all the time the nerves and muscles are directly braced up by the keen, dry air, tempered by bright, genial sunshine.'

> **'Winter sport exhilarates and rejuvenates; it generates a glow of pleasure ...'**
> Sir Henry Lunn

At the time, a room in less fashionable Engelberg on an accompanied tour cost £9.10s.

According to *Bradshaw's*, tourist season tickets in first, second and third class were available on Swiss railways for periods of 15, 30 or 45 days.

Lunn's son Arnold devised both slalom and downhill skiing and encountered great battles with purists who felt it should be a Norwegian-style horizontal sport. The events were included in the Olympics for the first time in 1936, with British athletes including Arnold's son Peter giving a sideways salute to the Games' host, Adolf Hitler.

## Braving the Cresta Run

With an influx of athletic young men to the burgeoning Alpine resorts, there was pressure to find new and challenging entertainments.

In 1885, casting envious eyes at the prestigious toboggan race in nearby Davos, five people on the outdoor amusements committee of the Kulm hotel in St Moritz resolved to create a better run. It took nine weeks to build but was, by common consensus, the most exciting downhill sport of the day.

Two years later, competitors began going headfirst down the Cresta Run, with its ten corners and steep sides. The same year, the original Swiss toboggan underwent numerous improvements, a process that continues today.

The course is still made each year entirely from iced snow. The record for at least part of the course stands at more than 82 mph, considerably faster than the trains that fetched tourists to Alpine resorts in 1913.

# AMSTERDAM TO NORTHERN FRANCE

IN BELGIUM, THE STORY OF RAILWAYS is one of success and catastrophe.

In 1913, Belgium had 50 per cent more railway tracks in use than neighbouring Holland, signalling that in its 80-year existence it had become a competitive European power despite its diminutive size.

Industrialisation, ably assisted by the network of railways, brought prosperity for its government and people. But in 1914, after Belgium was invaded by Kaiser Wilhelm II's troops, those same railways helped an enemy army gain a foothold. Ultimately, some Belgians sought to destroy the railway rather than see it spirit an enemy to swift victory.

As the Germans had intended, the Netherlands stayed neutral in the First World War, so its railway system, although less extensive, remained intact. According to one traveller in 1904, a second-class carriage on Dutch railways was upholstered in plush velvet and was fitted with an umbrella stand, a hat peg and a lavatory.

It was refinements like these that were swept away in the railway carriages that operated in countries fighting the First World War. As governments requisitioned locomotives and rolling stock, civilians got used to a more rudimentary railway service that was altogether a far cry from the excitement of a golden age of travel throughout Europe in the final decades of the 19th century.

# DUTCH DITHERING ON THE RHINE LINE

LIKE FRANCE, THE NETHERLANDS had an extensive and established network of waterways upon which commerce and travellers had always relied.

With the advent of railways some of its population wanted to stay abreast of this barnstorming technology. Another vocal lobby saw no need for such an expensive, intrusive new system.

Thanks to a happy arrangement of rivers and canals, all the major ports on the North Sea coast were already linked with the industrialised Ruhr in Germany. Barges were bigger than ever, taking ample quantities of freight, while people and the mail travelled by *trekschuiten*, horse- and sail-powered vessels that covered about seven kilometres an hour and offered considerably more comfort than a coach. From the tow path, an attached horse with rider pulled the barge while aboard a skipper checked its direction. In the early 19th century, there were 100 *trekschuiten* departures a day from Amsterdam in all directions.

Yet inland waterways weren't always ideal. In the winter they froze, while in the summer lack of rainfall left them so shallow that craft could only proceed slowly and half-filled with cargo.

Boats on rivers might be hampered by lack of width, by rapids or even by waterfalls. Those on canals might face charges for using locks. Afloat, there was little chance of escaping any number of taxes and tariffs imposed by landowners or regional authorities.

A powerful lobby defended the well-used waterways in the Netherlands, in which money had been invested for centuries, at the expense of railways

For any of these reasons, the journey between Amsterdam and Cologne using rivers and canals, a distance of some 300 km (186 miles), could take two weeks.

As it happened, one Dutch army officer witnessed the opening of the Liverpool–Manchester railway in 1830.

William Archibald Bake (1783–1843) was impressed with what he saw and drew up plans for a railway linking Amsterdam and the Ruhr, running parallel with the Rhine. When the blueprint was unveiled in 1834, he declared: 'I want to transfer this wonder of human ingenuity to the soil of the Netherlands so that it may act as a mighty driving force for lifting up commerce and industry.'

Unfortunately, there were insufficient numbers feeling the same way. The Dutch soil was too soft to support railways, detractors said, and the investment too precarious. Another factor was the country's waterways, which also provided a natural barrier to railway construction. Even if it had wanted to step in, the Dutch government was crippled by debt and didn't have the money to finance such a scheme.

It was a private company that underwrote the first railway to open in the Netherlands, with a British-built engine, *De Arend*, running between Amsterdam and Haarlem. The line opened in September 1839, and eventually got to Rotterdam in 1847 after a delay caused by greedy landowners demanding exorbitant prices for land needed for the track bed.

Bake's plan wasn't forgotten, though, and finally, in 1838, one of its biggest advocates, the Dutch king William I, ordered that it should be implemented.

## Gothic grandeur – Amsterdam's Central Station

As the 19th century drew to a close, the fortunes of the Dutch government had turned and a building scheme to renovate Amsterdam began.

Not least among the new developments was the Central Station, started in 1881 on the soggy banks of the IJ river. This huge Gothic building needed more than 8,000 wooden piles or stakes driven into the ground, making three artificial islands to prevent damage by the shifting sands beneath. Its Dutch designer Petrus J. H. Cuypers (1827–1921), who also styled the Rijksmuseum, chose red brick and a richly ornate facade. The engineer Adolf L. van Gendt (1835–1901) was responsible for ensuring sufficient trains would be accommodated, while the station's cast-iron roof measuring 40 metres (131 ft) was one of the last items made by Andrew Handyside (1805–1887), who ran a prolific foundry in Derby, England, and had recently supplied the roof for London's Olympia.

Despite the best efforts of all those involved, the boom in railway traffic quickly outgrew the station after it opened in 1889 and it was expanded on several occasions.

# DUTCH DOUBLE UP ON GAUGE

WORK FINALLY BEGAN on the Rhine railway that Bake had proposed in 1834. Bake himself wasn't involved. Shrewdly, he had started a foundry in Leiden that was poised to produce items necessary for the new Dutch railways.

The man responsible for executing the blueprints was Bernard Goudriaan (1796–1842), chief engineer of public works, and he looked to Britain for inspiration.

Perhaps unfortunately, it was to the views of Isambard Kingdom Brunel that he subscribed. Brunel believed that trains would be swifter, smoother and altogether more comfortable if they were built to a 7 foot gauge. It was this width that Goudriaan chose for the Rhine railways rather than the narrower gauge instituted by George Stephenson.

Other European railways had taken a lead from Stephenson and Goudriaan found himself isolated, much as Brunel and his cohorts were, with a potentially superior system but one that lacked popular support. Adding further expenses to an already costly project, Goudriaan made the decision to change to the commonly used gauge even before the railway reached Prussia in 1856. (In Britain, change was implemented gradually, until the broader gauge finally disappeared in 1892.)

Still, the Rhine railway did have the look of Brunel's Great Western Railway in the shape of the rails, which in cross-section looked like a hat, and the composition of the bed upon which they were laid.

There were the usual difficulties with purchasing land. Navvies rebelled when they went unpaid during bad weather. And, as the open-ended expenditure rose, it was decided to transfer the project from state to private hands, with the majority of stock in the control of English investors.

Goudriaan brought locomotives from Gorton, near Manchester, England, taking delivery of handsome green engines that were copied in Dutch workshops after their arrival. The move helped to inspire a slow-burning industrial revolution in the country, which for many years preferred sail to steam.

Nonetheless, *Bradshaw's* praises the Dutch for being a people 'owing not only their wealth and high commercial position but even the very land to their own labour and enterprise'. The guidebook is referring, of course, to the draining of the swamp land that plagued Holland, first by windmills and, by the middle of the 19th century, by steam turbines, creating farmland.

Passengers – by 1913 with a choice between the state-owned Dutch Railways or privately owned Netherlands State Railway – were further forewarned by *Bradshaw's* that trains ran according to Amsterdam time, which was 20 minutes before Greenwich Mean Time. And there was no free luggage allowance for travellers on its 2,000 miles of track.

## Peace Palace at The Hague

In 1913, the Peace Palace was opened in The Hague, built with money from a man who used to work on America's railways.

Andrew Carnegie (1835–1919) was born in Scotland but emigrated with his family to America when his father became jobless. It wasn't working on railways that made Carnegie his fortune, but running a string of steelworks at a time when the US needed the metal for skyscrapers, among other things.

Despite a passionate belief in workers' rights, Carnegie's reputation was tarnished when a dispute at his plant was harshly suppressed, resulting in nine deaths. It's one of the reasons that Carnegie sought to give away the millions he received when he sold his company to J. P. Morgan in 1901.

Before his death he had parted with $350 million, some of which paid for the Dutch building that houses the International Courts of Justice and The Hague Academy of International Law. As a consequence, he was bitterly disappointed when his aspirations for peace were so quickly dashed by the onset of the First World War.

# VICTOR HUGO'S HURRICANE RIDE

BELGIUM'S RAILWAY NETWORK expansion was second only to Britain's in the mid–19th century, quite an achievement for a country that only came into being in 1830 after acrimoniously severing ties with the neighbouring Dutch.

As a country it was blessed with abundant coal stocks and busy North Sea ports. But its agenda for the swift introduction of railways was set by the control the Netherlands still exerted over the rivers that ran through Belgium.

*Belgium's great achievement, in launching Europe's first railway service, was celebrated by its people*

In May 1835, Belgium became the first country on the Continent to run a steam train service. It was between Brussels and Malines, with King Leopold I among the passengers on the 30-carriage train. A Stephenson engine led the way at a sedate speed.

French author Victor Hugo (1802–1885) became a convert to railways in August 1837 during a trip to Belgium, anxiously in awe of their power. He

described a trip on this line after it had been extended to Antwerp, taken at nightfall when his train passed another going in the opposite direction. 'It was the most terrifying thing – these two bursts of speed flying past each other at apparently double their real rate; you could see neither carriages nor passengers, just black and white shapes in a sort of whirlwind … each train had 60 carriages so over 1,000 people were carried off by the hurricane.'

> **'It was the most terrifying thing – these two bursts of speed flying past each other at apparently double their real rate ...'**
> Victor Hugo

The rapidly industrialising Belgians would not be satisfied until their small country was smothered with lines. First, their eyes were on the prize of the 'Iron Rhine', a link with Cologne which began operating in 1843. Then there was the task of linking every major town to the network. In 1848, there were over 725 km (450 miles) of track in operation. By 1884, the system was six times bigger, producing what was generally recognised as Europe's densest network.

And, like Britain, Belgium produced some eminent locomotive engineers. Among them was Egide Walschaerts (1820–1901), who patented a new system of steam distribution in 1844; Alfred Belpaire (1820–1893), who introduced distinctive larger-than-usual square-topped fire boxes in 1864; and Jean-Baptiste Flamme (1847–1920), designer of two new and powerful engines (the type 10 Pacific and the type 36 2-10-0).

The next period to about 1870 was marked on the one hand by comparatively slow growth in state lines but on the other by a switch to private enterprise with foreign capital, mainly English.

Belgium was strategically placed between Britain, northern France, the Netherlands, Luxembourg and Germany and, despite escalating tensions, still marketed itself as a holiday destination. *Bradshaw's* said: 'Belgium offers great attractions of noble medieval architecture, a wealth of painters' art and a wonderful modern industrial development.'

One advertisement for Ostend called it 'the queen of watering places' with 'the finest sands on the continent'. It boasted of one million visitors who could expect a daily symphony concert, 25 days of horse racing a year, motor races, lawn tennis, pigeon shooting, yacht races, a battle of flowers, regattas, bicycling, children's races, fancy dress balls, polo, golf, football, paper hunts and gymkhanas. There would have barely been time to take the recommended thermal cure in the Trinkhalle of the Parc Leopold.

## Chocolate box

Like other European countries, Belgium has been making chocolate for centuries, latterly using cocoa from its African colonies.

In 1912, Jean Neuhaus made history in Brussels when he created the praline, a crisp chocolate shell with a soft inner filling. Three years later his wife Louise created the 'ballotin', an elegant presentation box that made Belgian chocolates the must-have gift of the decade. Thanks to railways, the sweet treat could be exported with ease across Europe and the world, establishing an important domestic industry that still flourishes today.

# EUROPEAN RAIL: HARBINGER OF CONFLICT?

*Across Britain and Europe railways raced to the front line. Both sides wanted men and machinery in position as early as possible in the hope of winning a quick victory*

THE RACE FOR PRE-EMINENCE in Europe that resulted in the First World War began decades before.

Yet still there were some who never thought Germany would bear arms against Britain or Russia. Kaiser Wilhelm II was, after all, a cousin of the British King George V and Russian Tsar Nicholas II. Dozens of other marriages had been made among Europe's royal families, intended to strengthen links between them.

At least one eminent historian blamed the railways and their rigid timetables for driving diverse countries towards armed struggle. A. J. P. Taylor (1906–1990) argued that, previously, mobilisation had been merely a show of strength. However, in the First World War mobilisation involved ferrying troops by train and, once begun, the process was doomed to an inevitable and bloody conclusion.

He explained it like this.

> **'All the mobilization plans had been timed to the minute, months or even years before, and they could not be changed. Modification in one direction would ruin them in every other direction ...'**
> A. J. P. Taylor

'All the mobilization plans had been timed to the minute, months or even years before, and they could not be changed. Modification in one direction would ruin them in every other direction. Any attempt for instance by the Austrians to mobilize against Serbia would mean that they could not then mobilize against Russia because two lots of trains would be running against each other.

'The same problem was to arise later for the Russians and in the end for the Germans who, having a plan to mobilize against France, could not switch round and mobilize again against Russia. Any alteration in the mobilization plan meant not a delay for 24 hours but for at least six months before the next lot of timetables were ready.'

It's not a theory that's won universal support but it illustrates how the age of trains had now radically altered modern warfare.

Trains got men and their equipment to the front line on an industrial scale. In Britain, for example, some 20,000 men, 1,200 horses, 210 bicycles, 20 motor cars and 600 other vehicles were delivered to Southampton by rail in a single day two weeks after war was declared on 4 August 1914.

But Britain's men and armaments had to await transport across the Channel. Already on the Continent, Germany and the Austrian empire combined had more locomotives than France, Russia and Belgium put together, and more carriages and wagons. According to the Belgian vice-consul, trains packed with troops were leaving Cologne every four minutes. There were plenty of men to transport. In 1913, *Bradshaw's* estimated the German army on a war footing would be some three million strong.

## Departing for the Front

From 1916, the countryside of northern France became enmeshed in a system of narrow gauge tracks that carried men and equipment, including barbed wire and poison gas, to the front line.

At the outbreak of hostilities French and British railways were taken over by their respective governments. The rest of France endured a skeleton service as all serviceable locomotives and covered wagons headed for the war zone. Shipments of locomotives and carriages came from Britain, too.

But a British government report in 1916 revealed that despite every effort the transport system in northern France was at breaking point.

The 600 mm (1 ft 11 in) gauge railways, which linked railhead, artillery dumps and the trenches, were one way of alleviating the pressure on the main lines. Before the end of the war, more than 1,300 km (800 miles) of track had been laid. However, its proximity to the fighting meant it was prone to damage by enemy shells.

But carrying troops was not their only role. Soon there were fully equipped ambulance carriages, made in Britain, craned on to ships and attached to locomotives in France.

The gun carriages of large pieces of long-range artillery were also made to travel on rails. That meant these giants – like the Germans' Paris gun with its 34 metre (110 ft) barrel and 120 km (75 mile) range – could be transported into position with ease while other guns, like the howitzer branded 'Big Bertha', had to be dismantled.

Armoured trains were also now being made. Dubbed 'mobile pillar boxes', they had heavy metal coats and were armed with machine guns, but the two that were built in Britain didn't see active service.

With so much dependence now on the railway system, queues of trains that went back for miles were commonplace before large-scale offensives.

# RAILWAYMEN AT WAR

RAILWAYS WERE PART of everyday life during the First World War, but sometimes their role turned out to be more pivotal.

As an opening gambit the Germans had the Schlieffen Plan, using trains to bring a concentration of forces to the French border. The aim was to sweep through Belgium and Luxembourg, invade northern France and, following a speedy French surrender, regroup on Germany's eastern borders to then take on Russia.

As it happened, there was stronger resistance from the vastly outnumbered Belgians than had been anticipated. Much of the country's relevant railway network was blown up by Belgian patriots, hindering the German advance.

The first waves of quick-moving German troops heading for the French capital soon ended up 80 miles ahead of their nearest railway and were hampered by having to use horse-drawn transport for supplies.

Meanwhile, the French were assembling more men from the south using a rail network in which all lines conveniently led to Paris. British forces were also en route by rail. It meant that, although French troops withdrew at the Marne at the end of August, there were enough well-supplied men to form a new front that would successfully defend Paris.

German troops celebrate the capture of French guns. Both sides were able to deliver artillery swiftly to the front line, and despite hopes for a speedy end the war became a bloody stalemate

The French government, together with numerous national art treasures, headed for a temporary home in Bordeaux, alongside thousands of Belgian and French refugees, on the south-bound return trains.

Afterwards, the Western Front soon stabilised between two major railways: a German-controlled line coming out of Flanders through Lille and the Ardennes and a French one coming down from the Channel ports via Amiens and Paris. With both sides relatively well provided with food, arms and men, it was no surprise the war drifted on for so long.

The British contributed numerous locomotives to the war effort but also relied more heavily on motor transport than the French. The folly of this was exposed at the Battle of the Somme, which began in July 1916, when unseasonal rainfall turned the roads into swamps. Fleets of lorries with their solid rubber tyres ran into difficulties and, as a result, the artillery suffered a shortage of shells.

When the British tried to switch tack and invest in more locomotives, they discovered that UK manufacturers were frantic with French orders.

By 1918, all the railway lines in northern France were in a state of poor repair. Despite the number of skilled railwaymen who joined the war effort from Britain – and a number sent from the UK since – there was a forced reduction in maintenance, which was matched by a shortage of coal. It was a similar story for the French, Germans and Austrians.

## Armistice in carriage 2419

One particular railway carriage assumed significance after being used to sign the armistice that ended the First World War.

A restaurant carriage (No. 2419) previously used on the Orient Express service was stationary in the forest of Compiègne when the document that stilled the guns after more than four years of bitter fighting was signed at 5.10 a.m. on 11 November 1918. Punitive reparations – including the surrender of 5,000 railway locomotives in working order – were inflicted on Germany.

Later, it became a symbol to Germans of what they considered to be their wrongful humiliation and, following the invasion of France in 1940, the roles were reversed as the French surrendered in the same carriage, which was later shipped back to Berlin.

As the Second World War headed towards a second victory for the forces ranged against Germany, the SS burned the carriage to ashes. A replica has since been made.

However, with American support, the Entente powers managed one final push against the Germans – with lorries playing as significant a part this time as trains. A battle of logistics – of which the train was a major factor and which the Central Powers only narrowly lost – finally decided the outcome of the war.

# 2

**MADRID** TO **GIBRALTAR**
**TURIN** TO **VENICE**
**DRESDEN** TO **KIEL**
**COPENHAGEN** TO **OSLO**
**PRAGUE** TO **MUNICH**
**BORDEAUX** TO **BILBAO**

AT THE BEGINNING OF 1835, mainland Europe didn't have a single railway to its name. Just 15 years later, steam locomotives ploughed through cities and countryside, leaving a sooty trail in their wake. Accompanying railways was industry, usually already in evidence but now given a boost. Alas, a goodly proportion of it centred on armaments. In any event, the lives of the richest aristocrats, who made and lost fortunes in railway investment, and the poorest peasant, now shackled to manufacturing in towns rather than feudal estates in the countryside, were changed forever.

Having a fully functioning railway network soon became a matter of national pride, although some countries embraced the railway revolution more effectively than others. In Germany and Italy, still years from unification, those driven by a vision of nationhood believed railway lines were a pivotal part of a self-governing future and expansion progressed quickly. Not so in Scandinavia, where nature's barriers initially held back railway development.

Spain struggled for many years. Shortage of cash was one of the reasons, opening the door for financiers from France and Britain. In the mid-19th century, these two countries had largely outgrown costly conflicts and preferred to influence events in neighbouring lands through a new kind of capital gain. King Edward VII's travels across the Continent by train both as Prince of Wales and king helped to ease the inward path of the British, who were awash with money from successful speculation in domestic railways and the £20 million paid by the government to 46,000 slave owners following Abolition.

As the decades wore on, European countries garnered their own engineering experience – initially sourced in Britain – and accrued sufficient wealth in most cases to finance their own growth. It left imperial nations like Britain and France watching nervously as the industrial and economic advantage they once held was whittled away.

# MADRID TO GIBRALTAR

AT THE END OF THE 15TH CENTURY, Spain was one of the most powerful nations on earth. From its ports, great explorers set sail to claim hitherto unknown lands. With territorial discoveries came new benchmarks in science and the arts. As the country finally reclaimed its cities from the occupying Moors, it entered what was considered *El Siglo de Oro*, a golden age.

By the 19th century, however, Spain was in the doldrums. Prosperity had dwindled and economic lethargy was such that one of its last remaining colonies, Cuba, had a railway before Spain itself. Nor did the eventual arrival of the railways greatly enhance the industrial output of a country, as foreign investors moved in to corner the best of the newly opened markets.

From the end of the 19th century there was prolonged unrest among workers, who were feeling the hardships brought about by stagnant trade. Signs of the nation's turmoil started spilling over, not least with the 1906 assassination attempt on King Alfonso XIII on the day of his marriage to British princess Victoria Eugenie Julia Ena. As she was a granddaughter of Queen Victoria, her marriage had been brokered by King Edward VII. Wedding guests included the future King George V.

The couple had already overcome numerous objections from both families, with Ena, as she was known, converting to Catholicism to silence many critics, including her future mother-in-law. However, even the extensive voluntary work she did in hospitals and for the Spanish Red Cross could not reverse Ena's negative public image.

Three years later came rioting after Spaniards, angry at being conscripted for a war in Morocco, took to the streets to protest. A general strike in 1917 was followed by a coup in 1923. The royal couple left Spain in 1931 when a Republican government took power and separated, with Ena finally making a new home in Switzerland.

Five years after that, Spain was torn apart by civil war. Among the numerous victims was the insubstantial railway network destroyed in three years of bitter internal warfare.

# SPANISH TRAINS AND CIVIL STRIFE

IN 1913, SPAIN WAS STILL CONSIDERED PRIMITIVE in European terms as far as trains and railway coverage were concerned. There are stark words of warning in *Bradshaw's* for the unwary traveller: 'First class carriages are tolerably comfortable, second class carriages are wanting in comfort, third class carriages are unsuitable for British travellers.'

The guidebook went on to say that railway speed was slow, rarely more than 15 miles per hour. And it would be some decades before the pace of railway travel noticeably increased in Spain.

It wasn't only railways where infrastructure was wanting. The roads were notoriously potholed, adding hours to carriage journeys.

Behind it all was a lack of investment caused primarily by political unrest. Spain suffered an extended civil war in the 19th century after Isabella II was crowned. She won the support of Spanish liberals but conservatives supported her uncle, Don Carlos. The Carlist Wars, as they are known, flared up periodically over decades – occasionally involving foreign powers – until 1876, two years after Isabella's son Alfonso XII became king.

The politically precarious position of Spain wasn't the only issue, either. There was such a scarcity of domestic capital that even banks had only modest sums to invest. Also, the terrain of the peninsula was hardly conducive to an extensive railway-building programme. Its central plateau is blocked at almost every side by a number of hill and mountain ranges, as well as broad rivers scything here and there through the landscape.

However, in 1855 the government decided to welcome foreign investment as a means of expanding the railways, offering 99-year leases to anyone who would build lines and provide rolling stock. Ultimately, this meant that railway lines were built piecemeal rather than with any rational outcome in mind. There was plenty of focus on the capital, Madrid, but precious little on the industrial areas that badly needed a helping hand.

But at least a railway network finally got underway, with Madrid's first line opening in 1851. (The route to Aranjuez was later known as the Iron Road, denoting its importance during the belated industrial revolution that finally galvanised Spain.)

Behind the building initiative which continued throughout the 1850s was mostly French money, although German and English investors later alighted on Spanish railway projects. Two French banks were responsible for creating key railway companies. The Madrid–Zaragoza–Alicante Railway, better remembered as MZA, was financed from 1856 by the French bank run by James de Rothschild. He was already a major player in the French railway company that ran the busy service from Paris to Boulogne-sur-Mer, where ferries were perpetually docked in preparation for cross-Channel voyages to England.

The other company, known colloquially as Norte, was financed from 1858 by journalists Isaac (1806–1880) and Émile (1800–1875) Péreire, the founders and operators of the Paris–Orléans Railway. They used money garnered through small investors who put their money with Crédit Mobilier, founded by the brothers. Passionate about railways, Émile Péreire said: 'It is not enough to outline gigantic programmes on paper. I must write my ideas on earth.'

Alongside another two companies, they competed to cross the typically empty interior of Spain with noble intentions, to promote public wealth. In reality, establishing a railway system had serious disadvantages for Spain's businesses and people. George Stephenson made a gloomy appraisal of the prospect for railways in Spain when he visited in 1845 at the request of an engineering company: 'I have been for a whole month in the country but have not seen during the whole of that time enough people of the right sort to fill a single train.'

H. M.– M.
MADRID
ESTACIÓN DEL MEDIODIA

## The grandeur of Atocha

Madrid's first railway station has gone on to be its largest and remains its most remarkable after a modernisation project. It was opened in 1851 and was later refashioned after a fire, in metal and brick. It is pictured here in 1910.

Still, when Spain became committed to a programme of high-speed trains, Madrid's prestigious station didn't meet the necessary specifications. Rather than pull down the grand and historical building it was emptied of railway paraphernalia to become a shopping mall with a covered tropical garden containing giant trees, turtles and birds.

# THE TROUBLE WITH SHERRY

IN MOST COUNTRIES, TRAINS WERE AN ANTIDOTE to urban hardships and rural poverty and they recorded a clear and immediate economic benefit on arrival.

In Spain it was not necessarily the case. In the 1850s and 1860s, railways swallowed up public money that could have bolstered other enterprises. Moreover, foreign and domestic railway operators found the traffic on the newly opened lines was so limited that costs were barely covered, making it difficult to service any loans that had financed their construction.

The sherry-producing region of Jerez is a fine example of how railways could skew an established trade, in sometimes unexpected ways.

Jerez de la Frontera, which is inland, was linked by train to El Puerto de Santa María on the coast in 1854, this being the third railway line in Spain and the first to open in Andalusia. The town was famous for making sherry, a fortified wine that was particularly popular in England.

The main purpose of the newly opened service was to connect the sherry makers and the ships that would export their product, so the train operated regular collections. Thus this small industrial locomotive was a tremendous boon for the entrepreneurs, who had been lobbying for just such a connection since 1829. But there were other unintended consequences.

Until that point, Jerez products had been costly, as a result of low yields from vines thanks to the local soil type, and high labour requirements and taxation.

However, the ease of railway transport – coupled with vine diseases that wrecked a number of grape harvests – led to the adulteration of sherry with cheaper wines by some unscrupulous producers struggling to stay competitive.

**'... these wines have not proved serviceable or usable; their peculiar earthy and tarry character being impossible to overcome ...'**

Sometimes, alcohol brewed from potatoes was added. There was even evidence of cheap wine being shipped from Spain to London and being returned as 'sherry' after being doctored there.

A British consul report dated 1865 highlighted the issue.

'During the past year large quantities of wines have been introduced into the district from Malaga and Alicante, but these wines have not proved serviceable or usable; their peculiar earthy and tarry character being impossible to overcome as, although mixed with other wines but in small quantities, the unpleasant flavour and smell is always distinguishable to a judge of wine.'

Eventually, people began to think of sherry as an unwholesome or even dangerous drink, a perception that had direct ramifications on trade in Jerez. After 1873, sherry producers launched a campaign hoping to reduce the elevated levels of tax applicable to the drink because it was fortified, as compared with French wine – another negative for the buyer.

## Lucky escape for the royal couple

Political instability led to several plots to assassinate King Alfonso XIII (1886–1941) during his reign. The most notorious attempt on his life took place on the day he married Princess Victoria Eugenie (1887–1969).

After the wedding ceremony at the Royal Monastery of San Jerónimo on 31 May 1906, anarchist Mateu Morral tossed a bomb disguised in a bouquet on to the royal party as they drove through the streets. About 30 people and numerous horses were killed. The royal couple survived because the bomb bounced on overhead tram lines, but Ena's dress was splattered with blood. Apprehended by the authorities, Morral shot himself rather than face trial.

As for those who picked the harvest, they saw their wages plummet as cheaper supplies of wine from elsewhere poured in. Although there are no reliable figures, it's thought that the area in Spain devoted to growing vines doubled between 1800 and the mid–1880s in response, shackling more labourers to the land.

To improve sherry's quality, the Association of Sherry Exporters was established in 1910.

Sherry had brought financial advantage to that corner of southern Spain for centuries prior to the arrival of trains. In Jerez, there's scant evidence of a hoped-for transformation in trade, given the very modest increase of 12,000 in the population during the half-century leading to 1900, when a figure of 63,473 was recorded.

# MR HENDERSON'S RAILWAY

AT THE SOUTHERN TIP OF SPAIN lay Gibraltar, the overcrowded British garrison which had uncertain relations with its much larger neighbour.

In the summer, officers and their wives longed to escape the heat by retreating to the Spanish hills. But, without a railway, the trip was rendered nearly impossible thanks to poor roads and the threat of bandits.

However, Alexander Henderson (1850–1934), a businessman who made a fortune from railways in Britain and South America, decided things would change. The result was a 172 km (107 mile) railway line between the coastal town of Algeciras to the hilltop fortress of Ronda, which opened fully in 1892 and was nicknamed 'Mr Henderson's Railway'.

In fact, although it was Henderson – who was chairman of Britain's Great Central Railway for 23 years, a major shareholder in the Manchester Ship Canal and later became Lord Faringdon – who financed the project, it was built thanks to a collaboration between engineer John Morrison, Gibraltarian Captain Louis Lombard and Frenchman Charles Lamiable.

For a failed previous initiative, Lamiable had drawn up plans to cross the difficult mountainous territory between Ronda and Bobadilla which now came into their own.

It was Lombard who piqued Henderson's interest when they met in South America, probably telling him the rights for the line were easily accessible through a London company. And it was Morrison who turned the blueprint into a reality for the Algeciras (Gibraltar) Railway Company Ltd.

After its first piece of track was laid on 1 September 1888, British consul Alexander Finn predicted it would provide a valuable link to the rest of Europe and would enhance Gibraltar's economy thanks to the export of wine, olive oil, cork, livestock, pigs, fruit and minerals.

Its single-storey stations, with fringed wooden canopies and flower beds, looked like quintessentially English halts. Drivers of Manchester-built locomotives on the single-track line carried a hoop if they had right of way, which was handed to the stationmaster at the next stop, who would in turn give it to a returning train. Without possession of the hoop, the driver was not permitted to go forward.

With his local nous, Lombard knew the Spanish wouldn't countenance a rail link through Spain with Gibraltar. To get over this hurdle, he began a ferry service between Algeciras and Gibraltar in 1894 that chimed precisely with train arrivals and departures.

At the other end of the line, there was a link to the Córdoba to Málaga service, which itself had connections with Madrid, enabling visitors from London to reach Gibraltar overland for the first time.

Henderson's money also built two smart hotels, one in Ronda and one in Algeciras – generally agreed to be the best and most expensive in Spain

## Tragedy at Ronda

Ronda is famous for its Puente Nuevo, or 'new bridge', built on three levels across a steep gorge and standing at a lofty 98 metres (321 ft). A first bridge in the location, completed in 1735, collapsed six years later killing 50 people.

This bridge was built in 1793, almost a century before the Forth Railway Bridge. Two other bridges are older and lower, and were built by the Moors when they occupied the region. The last section of line to be completed ended at Ronda in 1892.

– to cater for the vast numbers of well-heeled visitors who came from around Europe and from Gibraltar. It was at one, the Reina Cristina, that the Conference of Algeciras was held in 1906 to decide the future of Morocco after a dispute arose between its colonial power, France, and Germany.

The dispute was over who wielded most influence and nearly brought the two countries to the brink of war. It created a gulf between France and Germany - while cementing French and British diplomatic relationships.

The line, thought to have cost in the region of 45 million pesetas, was expensive but it undoubtedly transformed the lives of local people too, for thanks to the new railway they could transport their produce more easily and no longer lived in fear of being robbed by bandits who roamed the isolated paths.

The only railway line in the region that led to a harbour - and for years the only harbour with a crane - it helped to transform the economy of Algeciras, which in turn made John Morrison a famous and popular local figure. The Spanish government also used the harbour and its crane to transport goods to Ceuta.

The line was sold to an Andalusian company in 1913, as was the shipping company whose name then changed to Compañía de Vapores del Sur de España.

# TUNNELLING THE ROCK

Although Spain opposed the British building railways on Gibraltar there was nevertheless an extensive construction programme in the dockyard that included two railways. Today a cable car takes visitors up the distinctive peak of Gibraltar

WHILE THE SPANISH FIRMLY OPPOSED a railway link to service Gibraltar, the British had different ideas and at one stage had not one but two lines running around 'the Rock'. The best known was the one that ran from the dockyard, although an industrial one operated simultaneously for a while.

The dockyard railway was installed during an extensive refurbishment of facilities that was agreed at the turn of the 20th century. One Australian newspaper account dated 1904 outlined the scale of the work.

'Practically a new dockyard and harbour are being called into existence, involving an immense variety of work, both temporary and permanent, including the building of breakwater, docks, quays, retaining walls, stores, factories, boiler shops, and a pumping station, the displacing of the sea and reclaiming of the land, dredging, blasting, quarrying, railway construction, concrete block making, drainage, water supply, lighting and much else.'

'Practically a new dockyard and harbour are being called into existence ...'

Staffordshire-based W. G. Bagnall Ltd had supplied the first 13 locomotives from 1895 for the Admiralty. These were used alongside at least four others brought in by the London-based contractors Messrs Topham, Jones and Railton.

To bring quarried rock from one side of Gibraltar to the other, workers needed to drive a railway tunnel through the Rock for about three-quarters of a mile. It was nothing new. Tunnels had been made in the Mediterranean outpost centuries earlier and would be again, such was its strategically vital position.

Men wielding pickaxes and crowbars, and using gunpowder, burrowed into the limestone during a four-year siege of Gibraltar which began in 1779. The aim was to achieve height superiority so that British guns facing the Spanish and French forces in the north would have a significant advantage. By 1790, around 1,200 metres (4,000 ft) of tunnels had been constructed inside the Rock.

This time tunnelling was easier, thanks to advances in technology and tools, and the space needed for the metre-wide gauge was only limited. The quarried rock emerged from the tunnel to be crushed, with wagons mounting an incline and tipping their load into the

## The secret cave

More tunnels were excavated during the Second World War, bringing the total to some 50 km (31 miles). Spain was under the control of Fascist dictator General Francisco Franco, and the British were sure he would ally with Hitler and Gibraltar would be invaded. In fact, Franco and Hitler could not agree on terms. Nonetheless, the British made a contingency plan for the fall of Gibraltar, involving the digging of a secret cave into which six men agreed to be sealed with supplies for at least a year. The aim was to stay hidden and monitor shipping in the Strait of Gibraltar. The volunteers, an executive officer, two doctors and three wireless operators, were ultimately never called upon and the chamber was sealed until being found by cavers in 1997.

mechanised compressor. In turn, that would fill wagons waiting below and the crushed rock was taken away to make concrete for use in building work.

The workforce comprised 4,000 Spanish labourers drawn from nearby towns.

In 1908, work started on another system of tunnels to transport water by rail from catchment areas on one side of the peninsula to the population on the other. Again the tunnel was small, just big enough to accommodate one of the French-made Decauville wagons. Evidence of this railway system remains to this day.

It's thought the last steam locomotive to reach Gibraltar dockyard arrived in 1920 and was also the last to be scrapped, in 1959. However, there's evidence diesel engines operated there too during the Second World War.

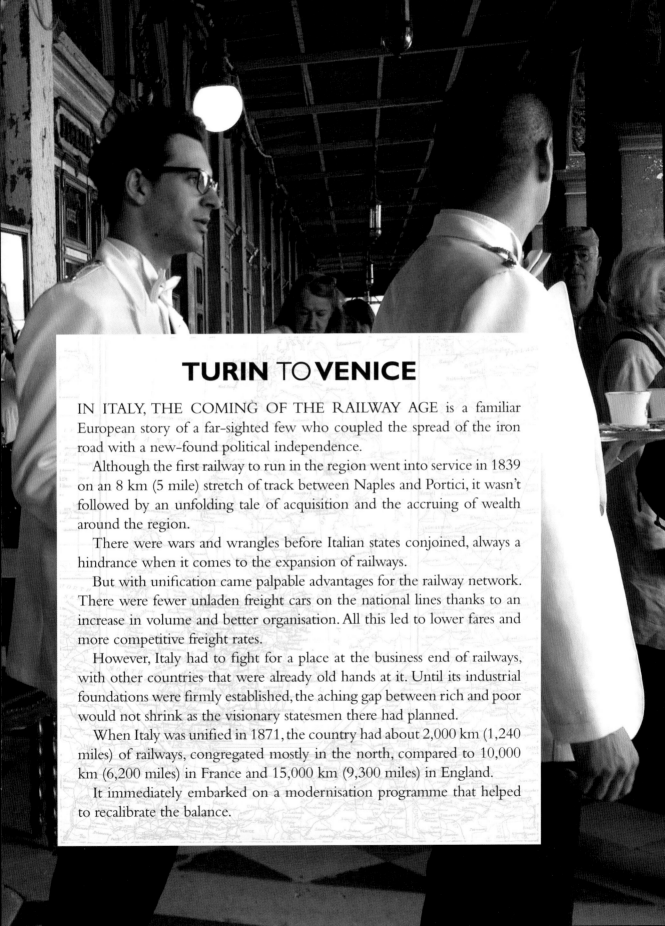

# TURIN TO VENICE

IN ITALY, THE COMING OF THE RAILWAY AGE is a familiar European story of a far-sighted few who coupled the spread of the iron road with a new-found political independence.

Although the first railway to run in the region went into service in 1839 on an 8 km (5 mile) stretch of track between Naples and Portici, it wasn't followed by an unfolding tale of acquisition and the accruing of wealth around the region.

There were wars and wrangles before Italian states conjoined, always a hindrance when it comes to the expansion of railways.

But with unification came palpable advantages for the railway network. There were fewer unladen freight cars on the national lines thanks to an increase in volume and better organisation. All this led to lower fares and more competitive freight rates.

However, Italy had to fight for a place at the business end of railways, with other countries that were already old hands at it. Until its industrial foundations were firmly established, the aching gap between rich and poor would not shrink as the visionary statesmen there had planned.

When Italy was unified in 1871, the country had about 2,000 km (1,240 miles) of railways, congregated mostly in the north, compared to 10,000 km (6,200 miles) in France and 15,000 km (9,300 miles) in England.

It immediately embarked on a modernisation programme that helped to recalibrate the balance.

# MARVEL BENEATH MONT CENIS

ON CHRISTMAS DAY 1870 A LANDMARK IN ENGINEERING WAS REACHED, deep in the bowels of a European mountain. So extraordinary was the news – dispatched to London by telegram – that it knocked the siege of Paris by the Prussians from the headlines.

The telegram read:

'The working parties in the opposite headings of the Mount Cenis Tunnel are within hearing distance of each other. Greetings and hurrahs were exchanged through the dividing width of rock for the first time at a quarter past four o'clock on Christmas afternoon.'

'The working parties in the opposite headings of the Mount Cenis Tunnel are within hearing distance of each other.'

For centuries mountains hindered communications and trade. After the Mont Cenis tunnel was completed engineers knew there was now little that could block the path of progress in the realm of railways

It was the first of the Alpine tunnels to be bored, stretching 13.7 km (8½ miles) from Modane in France to Bardonecchia in Italy, and finally opened in 1871. This was the most significant of the 29 tunnels on a 60 km (37 mile) double track that finally linked the two countries.

Despite the hard graft of numerous Italian labourers, it was a French project led by Germain Sommeiller.

Until then travellers between the two countries relied on a Napoleonic road through the mountains, a route subject to Alpine snowdrifts that made it dangerous or impassable.

The technological boldness of the decision to go ahead with an underground railway track was matched by the skill of surveyors who accurately plotted the course of the tunnel. When the two gangs met that Christmas, they were just two feet out of alignment in terms of height,

## Mail train to Susa

Before the tunnel came into use there was a temporary British railway scaling the Mont Cenis pass, to speed the passage of mail to India.

In 1865, engineer John Barraclough Fell (1815–1902) won a temporary grant from the French and Italian governments to run a mountain railway with a carefully designed track bearing a central line, to tackle the gradients. Ultimately mail, freight and passengers made use of the line, which began in St Michel, France, and ended at Susa in Italy. When the Mont Cenis tunnel opened this mountain railway closed, after just three years in operation. Its specially designed rolling stock went to Switzerland for more mountain ascents.

while both sides met almost perfectly in terms of width. The estimated length of the climbing route was just 13.7 metres (45 ft) less than the actual length, revealing the considerable talent possessed by these novice mountain tunnel surveyors.

Starting in 1857, the 4,000 workers were using hand-held tools for more than three years until refinements to the newly developed pneumatic drill made it suitable for the task. For the first time four or five blows could be wielded against the quartz-veined rock every second, or several hundred every minute.

After around 40 minutes, a hole with a depth of about 75 cm (30 in) was created by each one in a bank of drills. Debris, washed out with a hose, was taken away by wagons. When the rock had been punctured by about 80 holes, the drilling equipment and hoses were packed away as explosives were set. Diggers retired behind a strong wooden barricade and did not move forward again until compressed air had pushed out the resulting smoke and gas.

Work sped along so quickly that the estimated opening date of the entire line was reduced by nearly five years, which was fortunate for Sommeiller who lived just long enough to see most of the project completed. Still the cost was at least £3 million, although the contractors acknowledged that, thanks to the experiences gained and the machinery now available, the costs of future projects would be reduced.

# STRENGTH IN UNITY FOR ITALY'S RAILWAY

IN FRAGMENTED ITALY, THE RAILWAY became a symbol of unity and an implied greatness that surely lay ahead for any newly born nation.

One of its pioneering politicians, the aristocratic Camillo Benso, Count of Cavour (1810–1861), of Piedmont, saw the possibilities early on when he visited Britain in 1835 to observe the London to Birmingham line being built.

He deemed railways to be more important than the advent of the printing press, with greater economic benefits and a more significant effect on national consciousness. In 1846, he predicted: 'The locomotive is destined to diminish the humiliating inferiority to which many branches of the great Christian family are reduced.'

Cavour favoured free trade, free speech and a secular rule; libertarian values that he saw squashed in the revolutions that swept Europe in 1848 and were now notably absent from many of the states in Italy outside Piedmont.

'Now that Italy is made we must make the Italians,' said Cavour in 1860. He believed a railway network would help unite the disparate states

The battles for a railway network were hindered not only by the number of states, under the heel of one empire or another, but also by the Pope in Rome.

Pope Gregory XVI, who died in 1846, was firmly against the spread of railways – which typically helped new and competing philosophies to starburst across the Continent. A joke circulating at the time of his death had the Pope walking a long and dusty road to heaven. 'If only you had built a railway,' said St Peter. 'You would be in paradise by now.'

From 1852, Turin-born Cavour was prime minister in Piedmont, a state which was ruled by King Victor Emmanuel II, who was a fellow enthusiast for trains. Consequently, it was no coincidence that, two years later, the first inter-city main line from Turin to Genoa opened. It was paid for by money loaned from other nations, primarily Britain.

Within five years, Piedmont had constructed some 600 miles of railway track, part of a calculated plan drawn up by Cavour. In 1859, he contrived a war with Austria, having previously secured the support of the French. The Piedmontese army and its 120,000 French allies could by now manoeuvre troops easily into position by rail, which helped them secure two significant victories. It was the first mass movement of soldiers on trains in history.

Cavour had to relinquish Savoy and Nice to fulfil previously agreed obligations to France, but now unification was within sight as Tuscany, Parma, Modena and Romagna, previously subject to Austrian or French influence or control, joined with Piedmont. The fiery Giuseppe Garibaldi (1807–1882) had conquered the south and many Papal States on the peninsula, and in 1860 he agreed to turn these territories over to the Piedmontese king.

Unfortunately, Cavour did not live long enough to see the cities of Venice and Rome, ruled by Austria and France respectively, enter the Italian fold in 1871. But that citizens of newly unified Italy could travel between each of its major cities by 1866 on 2,752 miles of track served as an epitaph to the man who laid its foundations.

## Tickets to adventure

Novelist E. M. Forster perhaps had Turin in mind when he said: 'Railway termini are our gates to the glorious and the unknown. Through them we pass out into adventure and sunshine.'

Built from 1861, Turin's Porta Nuova station was grandly appointed so as to befit the capital city of a modern country. Unfortunately, before its completion in 1864, the capital had switched to Florence. Nonetheless, that left Turin with a station that's particularly remarkable for the royal waiting room – Italy had a royal family until the end of the Second World War – which is still furnished with paintings, chandeliers and mirrors. Even passengers using the divided departures and arrivals area were treated to frescoes depicting the crests of 135 Italian cities and showing their distance in kilometres from Turin.

# THE STEPHENSONS' LEGACY

Porta Nuova station, late 19th century. Rolling stock had to be imported to Italy when the first rail networks got started

PERHAPS CURIOUSLY, TURIN'S PORTA NUOVA STATION – originally known as Central Station – bears a plaque honouring George and Robert Stephenson, the British father and son who brought the dream of steam railways to fruition.

It's a measure of how much store Italians set by the power of the railway the two men created, credited in part with unifying Italy. According to the plaque, the Stephensons 'perfected the locomotive, opening new trade routes to the advantage of the brotherhood of peoples'.

That British engineering had substantial influence in Italy is beyond doubt. Robert Stephenson (1803–1859) travelled there in 1839, eventually becoming the supervisor for a new railway between Florence and Pisa. His company also provided locomotives for Italy.

But did the supply of locomotives by foreign companies keep Italian manufacturing on the back foot for the second half of the 19th century? There's evidence that the industrial revolution which inevitably followed in the wake of railways across Europe stalled after an incoming tide of overseas railway-related trade.

At first, importing rolling stock for railways was a necessity. In 1867, before Italy was fully unified, the Minister of Public Works listed projects on the stocks. Apart from 'introducing that wonderful instrument of civilisation the locomotive into the most remote corners of the land', there was a need for new roads, irrigation projects, the introduction of the telegraph, the improvement of the postal system, a fleet of steamships and more.

All of this was urgent, he said, 'not so much for the benefit of public welfare and national wealth itself but rather as a result of the nation's need to ensure its independence … in order to quickly forget ancient quarrels and divisions and to build a solid foundation for national unity and strong government'.

Engineer Giovanni Ansaldo (1814–1859) had been quick to seize the opportunities, opening up in a fledgling railway industry.

With encouragement from Cavour, he took over a recently failed factory, Taylor and Prandi, in 1852, and marked a new era by building two steam locomotives that had been commissioned by the Savoy government to operate between Turin and Rivoli.

Between 1855 and 1858, a further 20 locomotives were delivered, by which time the factory employed 480 workers. Eight years later, it had a workforce of 1,100 people making not only engines but rails, bullets and roofs for railway stations.

But this had been something of an isolated success story and, anyway, could not meet the burgeoning demand. Figures show that between 1861 and 1864 only 231 locomotives were bought from Italian manufacturers by their government, which amounted to just 17.8 per cent of the total.

### Arch critics in Venice

It was known as 'the Austrian bridge'. But the arched causeway that connected Venice with mainland Italy was built by Italian engineers, using Italian labour. Its construction took more than four years, with a fleet of 60 vessels transporting materials to the route. After it opened in 1846, Venice was linked to Milan by train. But the causeway was hated by champions of Venice, such as art critic John Ruskin (1819–1900), who loathed its modern connotations.

Despite its associations with Austria, Venice was finally relinquished by the empire following its defeat by Prussia in 1866. The island city, which had once enjoyed a maritime empire, became part of the newly founded state of Italy.

# NETWORKING ITALY: BREDA'S RAIL REVOLUTION

An Italian-built locomotive designed by Otto Busse of the Danish Railways DSB, but made by Ernesto Breda's company in 1900. Renovated in 1930 with a large boiler, it could reach speeds of 100 kph (62 mph)

TO SOME IN THE NEWLY FORMED ITALY, both British manufacturers and home-grown industrialists were jointly responsible for the slow start being endured by the economy.

As one disgruntled Italian observer explained:

'The reason why the locomotive industry did not make any great progress was not that we did not know how to build them but rather that railway management hardly ever turned to Italian producers to satisfy their requirements and thus never gave them any encouragement to develop production any further.

'If our industrialists were to be given a continuous series of orders then not only would they be able to produce all the locomotives required at a fair price but in this way they would soon be able to compete with their foreign competitors.'

Finally, there was a step change when Ernesto Breda (1852–1918), born the same year Cavour became prime minister, started his own engineering works.

In 1882, he went abroad to investigate how railways and the associated industries were run in Germany, Holland and Denmark. When he realised that Italian industry was a pale comparison, he began his own business in 1886 in Milan, after taking over the failed company Elevetica.

His bread-and-butter work was to produce armaments. But his ambition was to supply the ever-expanding Italian railway network with steam engines at a time when England, Germany and America were the big players. In fact, he first entered the international arena in a small way in 1887 when he produced 21 locomotives. His business received a boost in 1891 after winning a contract to supply 22 locomotives to Romania.

He also made wagons, carriages and trams.

On 1 July 1905, the Italian railways were nationalised, unifying the criteria for design, and afterwards orders began to boom. Out of more than 1,000 locomotives then ordered by the government more than one-fifth came from Breda's factory.

By 1907, the company celebrated the delivery of the 1,000th locomotive built in Milan and, to mark the event, he instituted a week's paid holiday for workers who had been with him for more than five years. Breda's business continued to thrive, enabling the company to build houses for employees from 1910, having already introduced pensions and savings plans.

Between 1905 and 1914, the number of locomotives made in Italy bought by the government reached 2,124, or 77 per cent of the total.

At last, the brake on the national economy provided by foreign influence and investment had been released. The industrial census carried out in 1911 put the numbers at more than 14,000 factories and 248,118 workers.

> **'The reason why the locomotive industry did not make any great progress was not that we did not know how to build them ...'**

## Queen of the locos

By the turn of the 20th century, Italian railway engineering factories were turning out trains that would become familiar and fondly remembered sights on the country's lines for years afterwards. They included some built for speed and others for durability. In 1900, the RA 3701 steam locomotive reached 126 kph (78 mph) in tests. A dozen years later, it was the GR 685 steam locomotive that was attracting attention, winning the soubriquet 'Queen of Locomotives'. But the industry also produced workhorses like the GR 740, built from 1911 to 1923. Particularly suitable for steep lines, some 470 were built with the last going out of service as late as 1990.

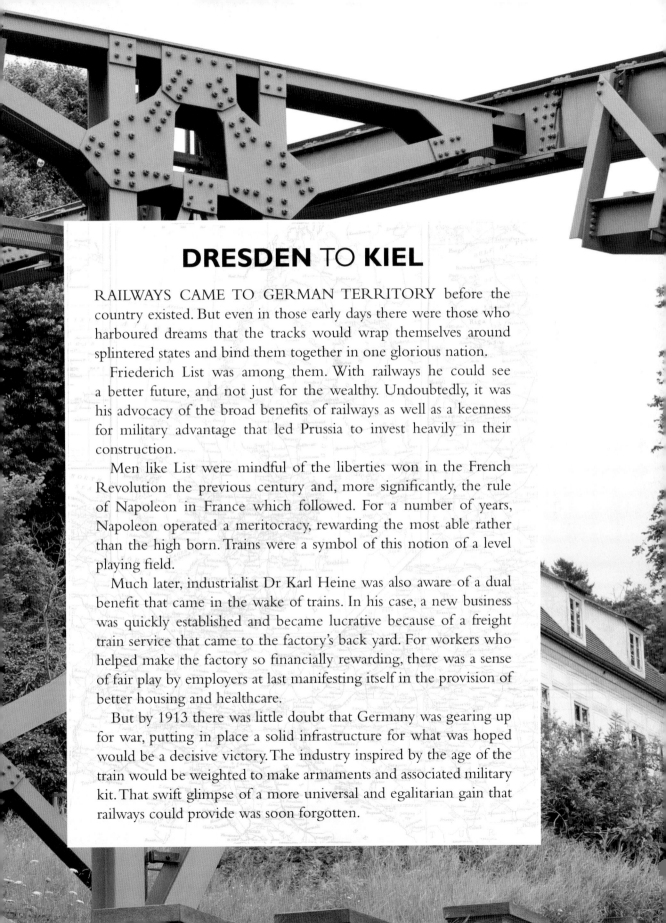

# DRESDEN TO KIEL

RAILWAYS CAME TO GERMAN TERRITORY before the country existed. But even in those early days there were those who harboured dreams that the tracks would wrap themselves around splintered states and bind them together in one glorious nation.

Friederich List was among them. With railways he could see a better future, and not just for the wealthy. Undoubtedly, it was his advocacy of the broad benefits of railways as well as a keenness for military advantage that led Prussia to invest heavily in their construction.

Men like List were mindful of the liberties won in the French Revolution the previous century and, more significantly, the rule of Napoleon in France which followed. For a number of years, Napoleon operated a meritocracy, rewarding the most able rather than the high born. Trains were a symbol of this notion of a level playing field.

Much later, industrialist Dr Karl Heine was also aware of a dual benefit that came in the wake of trains. In his case, a new business was quickly established and became lucrative because of a freight train service that came to the factory's back yard. For workers who helped make the factory so financially rewarding, there was a sense of fair play by employers at last manifesting itself in the provision of better housing and healthcare.

But by 1913 there was little doubt that Germany was gearing up for war, putting in place a solid infrastructure for what was hoped would be a decisive victory. The industry inspired by the age of the train would be weighted to make armaments and associated military kit. That swift glimpse of a more universal and egalitarian gain that railways could provide was soon forgotten.

# PROSPERITY AND POWER – GERMANY'S RAIL DIVIDEND

GERMANY'S FIRST LONG-DISTANCE TRAIN served the cities of Dresden and Leipzig after 1839, both in the kingdom of Saxony.

One of the driving forces behind the project was Friedrich List (1789–1846), who became known as 'the father of German railways'. Of course, his death came years before Germany was unified, but his influential opinions helped fashion a mindset in favour of rapid railway expansion for industrial rather than military purposes.

German-born List had lived in America before arriving in Leipzig to act as US consul. It had been in the US that he first encountered railways in action, immediately appreciating the transformative effect they would have in his homeland.

List acknowledged that railway networks could be used as a means of national defence, but his interest lay in other areas. Thanks to their 'civilising potential', he was convinced they brought essential talent, knowledge and skill to connected cities.

With the extensive supply network provided by a railway, cities and towns would no longer be subject to famine, while the tracks would be the foundations for new economic wealth. There was, he said, a 'reciprocal relationship which exists between manufacturing power and the national system of transportation, and that the one can never develop to its fullest without the other'.

Moreover, he felt railways encouraged the spirit of nationhood and he hoped that they would go some way to creating a unifying bond between the numerous Germanic states.

In fact, none of the privately run railways particularly wished to help their neighbours and, even after confederation and nationalisation, there remained a measure of antipathy between regional railways.

With some justification, List suspected Britain of trying to corner new technologies – 'to make the rest of the world, like the Hindus, its serfs in all industrial and commercial relations'.

His hopes for a customs union between the German states and for tariff protection to shield newly wrought industrial progress from predator nations like Britain came to nothing during his lifetime.

But List was among many who believed that the classless nature of train services would ultimately hasten social and political liberalisation to finally end the long-established power of the aristocracy. These were views that reflected a growing desire for democracy around Europe that culminated – unsuccessfully – in a series of revolutions in 1848.

Plagued by financial worries, he committed suicide two years before there were uprisings around the Continent.

## A funicular health trip

More than 55 years after that first inter-city line opened, another connection was built, this time heading out of by now industrialised Dresden into the clean air of the pine-forested hills beyond.

In 1888, Dr Heinrich Lahmann (1860–1905) opened a sanatorium in Weisser Hirsch, a settlement set apart from Dresden, where he advocated his beliefs in a vegetarian diet and the curative values of physiotherapy and hydrotherapy. He preferred fresh air and exercise to pills and his message won broad support among progressive thinkers of the era.

Having been planned in the 1870s, the funicular finally went into service in 1895, transporting more visitors in pursuit of better general health than had ever visited the resort before. Electrified in 1909, the funicular operated on a 1,000 mm gauge and climbed 547 metres (1,795 ft) at a gradient of 29 per cent.

It was the competing philosophy of free trade, powerfully advocated by Britain's Adam Smith (1723–1790), that led to 16 locomotives being exported from Britain for the new Leipzig line. They were shipped to Saxony in pieces accompanied by John Robson, a driver on the Liverpool–Manchester railway, who supervised their reassembly.

Despite its idiosyncrasies – the trains would not take children and the ticket office didn't open until shortly before departure – the advent of the railway in Dresden would have thrilled many Britons and Americans who regularly visited the city known internationally for the quality of its art and music, and sometimes dubbed 'Florence on the Elbe'. Endorsing that view, *Bradshaw's* insists: 'Dresden cannot be excelled'.

From the outset, railway builders like those responsible for creating Germany's first long-distance railway between Dresden and Leipzig had to bridge roads and rivers, improving existing construction technologies to do so

# SEEKING THE LIE OF THE LAND

THE BUSINESS OF RAILWAY CONSTRUCTION was still in its infancy when the Dresden to Leipzig line was built from 1837. It was fortunate that the ground between the two cities was without a major incline, although they were 113 km (70 miles) apart.

Surveying the track was a key part of ensuring any railway project's success. The art of surveying wasn't unknown before the coming of the railway age. Canals needed to be properly surveyed before being built, so civil engineers had been responsible for getting the sums right on major investments of this nature for some time.

Tracks had been laid before the arrival of trains, too, along wagonways built to take the friction out of horse-drawn transports. A horse was usually still needed – unless there was a downhill stretch – but the wheels of the cart it pulled rolled on plated wooden tracks and, prior to that, on stone.

So a body of expertise about the technical detail required had been building for decades, but it was held mainly in British libraries and companies. As a consequence, it was usual in the early years of European railways for British experts to be brought in to execute projects, and the Leipzig railway was a prime example of this.

Although he had little fondness for railway work, James Walker (1781–1862) began surveying it, spending two weeks trying to find the flattest lie of the land to economise on earth shifting, which would all have to be done by hand. Walker is better remembered for his work on lighthouses and harbours around the British coast.

## Ticket pleas

A curious legal case occurred after a passenger collapsed at Dresden's railway station in 1885. The man keeled over after buying his ticket but before boarding his train, dying before anyone could fetch help.

Afterwards, the man's family sought a refund, the journey never having been taken. Following a flat refusal by the railway company, the case ended up in court. A judge ended the costly wrangle by deciding the family were entitled to a refund, less the price of a platform ticket which was due to the railway company. The costs of the case were not disclosed.

He handed the project on to John Hawkshaw (1811–1891), who himself was more of a canal man. Nonetheless, Hawkshaw set about travelling the route on foot to map in painstaking detail where bridges, crossings, cuttings and tunnels might be needed to avoid gradients, bogs, streams and rivers.

Afterwards, there came British engine drivers, coach builders and, inevitably, navvies, who found plenty of work on the Continent during the early days of the railway. The Leipzig–Dresden Railway Company board, formed of a dozen local men, brought in the expertise.

When the line finally opened, it was a British driver at the helm of a locomotive called *Robert Stephenson*. The presence of the British was not always appreciated by a German populace being stirred by a new-found nationalism. However, there were benefits too. Thomas Worsdell (1788–1862) established a manufacturing base in Germany during a four-year spell as locomotive, carriage and wagon superintendent for the Leipzig railway. A form of railway mania soon infected all the German states, eager to reap the benefits.

Keen to have its own prestigious network, the Prussian government guaranteed the investments of those who put money into railway construction. As investors had nothing to lose, funds flowed freely into the German railroads. This rapid expansion meant home-grown talents were fostered and highly valued.

Slowly, the business of railways cascaded away from the British and into the laps of a new generation of industrialists. By 1850, Germany could provide everything needed for its railway industry from its domestic steel production.

# HOME-SPUN SUCCESS IN LEIPZIG

FROM TODAY'S PERSPECTIVE, LEIPZIG appears to have lacked the necessary stature to be a prestigious terminal of the first major railway link in the German states, with a reputation linked more to music than industry.

Although published more than 70 years after the event, *Bradshaw's* nonetheless goes some way to answering the conundrum. 'Leipzig is a town of great commercial importance,' it says. 'It is the centre of the book and fur trades of Germany, the seat of the supreme law courts of the Empire and its university is ancient and renowned.'

By now it was also the centre of Germany's cotton industry, thanks entirely to the arrival of the train. In the 19th century cotton was a key international industry, with the US and Egypt supplying it raw and England and Switzerland exporting processed thread.

German industrialist Dr Karl Heine (1819– 1888) created a new neighbourhood through land reclamation that would become a new manufacturing hub.

Although the cotton mills in Leipzig were grimly imposing, there was plenty for workers to look forward to out of working hours, with new leisure, health and education facilities

On 21 June 1884, the Leipziger Baumwollspinnerei was registered as a company. Crucially, the site had a railway siding – and soon it would have a network of smaller industrial railways – to transport raw materials in and goods out.

A year later, the first factory had been built and contained five spinning machines. A year on, there were 30,000 spindles at work. Other factories were subsequently built, increasing capacity enormously.

And alongside the capacious industrial buildings came houses for workers, a training school, a company fire brigade and a canteen. Before the turn of the 20th century a public baths had been added to the complex, along with a nursery for children, a park, health centre, shops and clubs and societies.

With a shortage of manpower, people migrated from all over Europe to the *spinnerei*. The quest for supplies of raw cotton inspired Germany to

## Märklin's model railway

The age of the train ushered in a new consumerism which included children's toys. Among them there were working model railways, the first of which was made in Germany in 1891 by the manufacturer Theodor Märklin.

Although toy trains and models had been made previously, they were either operated by clockwork or had no moving parts. It was Märklin who introduced a range of tin-plated engines and accessories, in three different sizes. There was now an opportunity to buy model railways in sections and build up a collection of items. Rival producer Stefan Bing, also in Germany, soon followed suit.

So perhaps it is fitting that the world's biggest model railway is in Hamburg, Germany. In addition to trains running on 13 km (8 miles) of track, the layout features fire engines, police cars, 200,000 figures and an airport. Everything is controlled by 40 computers and a workforce of 260 people. It's the result of some 500,000 meticulous working hours spent to ensure that life in miniature runs smoothly, and accordingly it's become one of the country's top attractions.

seek new African colonies, another contributing factor to the international tensions prior to the First World War.

There were spats between workers and clashes with the management. But productivity continued to rise and the enterprise was extremely profitable.

In 1907, 20,000 bales of cotton were processed into 5 million kilos of thread by 1,600 workers putting in a ten-hour day in what was the biggest cotton mill on the Continent. At this point the industry had reached its zenith, although it continued to operate for decades afterwards.

Built in 1784, the Kiel Canal was remodelled twice in quick succession, with this gondola being added to the newly raised railway in 1913

# MAKING WAY FOR THE NAVY: THE RENDSBURG BRIDGE

ANOTHER COMPONENT OF GERMANY'S WAR CHEST was the Kiel Canal. Thanks to the local train service it was made ready for conflict in 1914.

It was the canal, of course, rather than the rail service that loomed large in the minds of the German government. The prospect of a short cut for the German navy between the North Sea and the Baltic, rather than sailing the elongated route around Denmark, fell to the Prussians after Schleswig-Holstein was annexed in 1866.

In 1784, the Eiderkanal was built to link the two coasts, narrow and shallow but nonetheless useful for transporting shipping for some years.

Eyeing an opportunity, it was decided to build a better canal between the mouth of the Elbe river and Kiel harbour, severing the peninsula above and using part of the existing route. Kaiser Wilhelm I laid its foundation stone in 1887.

In the subsequent eight years, some 9,000 navvies heaved an estimated 80 million cubic metres of earth out of the channel that would form the Kiel Canal. But in solving one problem the canal builders created another. The existing railway line needed to be accommodated, so two parallel swing bridges were also built in order that the Neumünster to Flensburg railway service could continue uninterrupted.

At the time, railway lines had right of way over shipping so, when a train came through, ships using the canal had to queue while the bridge was in place. It was a source of some frustration to fast German navy ships, which anyway had insufficient room to overtake merchant shipping.

## The Magdeburg disasters

Curiously, Magdeburg has been the venue for two of Germany's worst rail crashes. The first occurred on 22 December 1939 when a train bound for Cologne made an unscheduled stop at Genthin station. When the driver of the Berlin express ignored a stop signal his train powered into the stationary one, destroying the rear three coaches and killing 132 people. A further 109 people were seriously injured, although there's doubt about the veracity of the figures as Nazi chiefs may have reduced them to minimise the scale of the disaster. On 6 July 1967, a double-decker train ploughed into a fuel tanker on a level crossing at Langenweddingen. The resulting fire claimed many lives, with a final death toll of 94. The accident happened after a telegraph cable that had expanded in the summer heat became caught on the manually operated level crossing gate. As its operator lifted the gate to free the snagged wire the tanker went on to the lines, into the path of the oncoming train.

Accordingly, further fresh plans were drawn up to extend and improve the canal. These included a new, high bridge which would no longer hinder the progress of shipping. During a seven-year programme, the canal was made some 160 metres (526 ft) wide and 11 metres (37 ft) deep, with roomy and efficient locks. As *Bradshaw's* noted in 1913: 'The largest warships may pass through.'

The railway bridge was erected between 1911 and 1913 by Friedrich Voss (1872–1953), head of the Ministry of Public Works, one of three viaducts he built over the canal. He incorporated a spectacular climbing 360-degree loop of track so that the train could reach the improved height of the bridge, and a gondola beneath to carry foot passengers. The distinctive box girder section of the bridge measures 2,486 metres (8,156 ft).

As far as the British government was concerned, the Kiel Canal improvements were part of a chain of measures aimed at extending the reach of German naval power.

The waterway was finally opened on 25 June 1914, three days before the assassination of Archduke Franz Ferdinand in Sarajevo, the acknowledged trigger of events leading to the First World War.

# COPENHAGEN TO OSLO

SCANDINAVIAN COUNTRIES WERE RARELY VISITED by British travellers before the First World War. The Edwardians took some interest in Denmark, as it was the home country of Queen Alexandra. However, most visitors only went further north as part of an onward journey to Russia.

No passports were needed for Denmark, Sweden or Norway, perhaps a sign of how unprepared those countries were for visitors. Yet Bradshaw's could envisage some possibility of Norway at least becoming a tourist destination of note. 'If Norway is not an advisable resort for absolute invalids the healthy, hearty, good tempered tourist, the sportsman and the admirer of natural beauty who is willing to bear and forbear and even occasionally to rough it will be amply rewarded,' reported the guide.

Of course, Norway maintained an enduring link with the guide's creator George Bradshaw, as he died in Oslo. The guide he so painstakingly created continued after his death with the same name and attention to detail. Thus, his fame continued to escalate while chunky editions protected by a yellow dust jacket were still sought and bought decades after he was laid to rest in the cemetery adjoining Oslo Cathedral.

If there was a reluctance to build trains in smaller countries like those in Scandinavia it was on the grounds of cost. With a mix of state-owned and private railway networks becoming established in the mid-19th century, there was inevitably a levy on the public purse. And these were countries where ensuing benefits were not guaranteed.

Despite the arrival of railways, Denmark retained an economy primarily led by agriculture, with the processing of meat and dairy products assuming importance. Industrialisation was limited to Copenhagen and its environs.

Sweden's manufacturing boom came as late as the First World War and centred on its natural resources, including wood and pulp. For Norway, a key plank of its economy remained fisheries, as well as foreign trade and maritime services. Unrelated to the arrival of railways, a blip in its previously successful economy came in the 1890s and was caused by a wave of emigration.

# RAIL TRAVEL IN THE FROZEN NORTH

*Extremely cold winter weather was just one of the difficulties facing railway builders in Scandinavia*

BEFORE THE ADVENT OF RAILWAYS, there were difficulties even building roads around Scandinavia. Not only were its communities isolated by fjords, forests or extremely cold weather, but Denmark, Sweden and Norway were variously united or divided by occupation and treaty.

Given some political uncertainty and that all those countries had extensive coastlines, waterways and islands, boats would be equally as important as trains for quite some time – and even when trains had been introduced the train ferry became a pivotal feature of many journeys.

A first foray into railway building by the Danish ended badly. Having built a line that linked Altona and Kiel – at that time in the Duchy of Holstein – in 1844 a war 20 years later put Kiel squarely into the German Confederation and the line was lost to Prussia.

More prudently, a line from Copenhagen to Roskilde was chosen as the next construction project three years later, and obviously retained by Denmark. Norway built its first line with help from Robert Stephenson in 1854 and, two years later, Sweden forged a link between Stockholm and Gothenburg.

Further north still, Finland, part of the Russian empire at the time, opened its first rail link in 1862 using the broad gauge that Russia favoured.

Denmark's progress continued, with her comparatively flat landscape causing few difficulties for track layers. Likewise, Finland had remarkably few natural barriers to a rail network.

But it was a different story in Norway, which had hostile northern territories to breach. Labourers in the tunnel that would link Oslo to northerly Bergen were cut off from the outside world by wintry weather in 1902 for weeks at a time. Exposed in the open, men could only work safely for three months a year. Bergen wasn't linked to Norway's network until 1909, after which it became part of the most commonly used route for Britons travelling to Russia, who crossed the North Sea by ferry from Newcastle and used the train for the rest of the journey.

Norway didn't achieve independence from Sweden until 1905, by which time many of its railway lines were linked to Swedish towns but didn't connect Norway's settlements to each other. Another building programme was needed to remedy this, which included a 1½-mile coal train line on the Norwegian island of Spitzbergen which, when it opened in 1917, was the most northerly line in the world.

Swedish railway builders also did battle with the elements to establish the Lapland railway north of the Arctic Circle, a remote line the purpose of which was to bring iron ore from Sweden to the ice-free port of Narvik in Norway for export. The Malmbanan, as it is properly known, is surely one of the most desolate lines ever built, reaching across miles of tundra. It was completed in 1903 and didn't join the Norwegian rail network, even though it passed through that country.

## Narrow gauge – 'harmony and proportion'

Although Norway's first line was built to the standard gauge, later ones were constructed with narrow gauges in a bid to economise on costs.

Engineer Carl Pihl (1825–1897) chose a 1,067 mm (3 ft 6 in) gauge for two isolated lines to attain what he called 'proper harmony and proportion'. The lines opened in 1862 with the use of British locomotives. By the end of a first wave of railway building in Norway in the 1880s, there was nearly 400 km (250 miles) more narrow gauge track in use than standard gauge. However, the government realised that the two systems had to be integrated and conversion began on the Bergen line, which had been planned as a narrow gauge, before it opened. Still, the last narrow gauge railway was built there as late as 1924. Much of it was converted by occupying Germans in the Second World War, with the job being completed by 1960.

# VLADIMIR LENIN AND THE SEALED TRAIN TO SWEDEN

*On Lenin's sealed train dashing through Swedish countryside the talk was of revolution – and a smoking policy among passengers*

BY 1917, PUBLIC ANTIPATHY TOWARDS the First World War had reached epic proportions in Russia, where poverty and food shortages were endemic.

A provisional socialist government, which took control in February that year, had kept Russian soldiers fighting at the front, to the fury of exiled Communists. Swiss-based Lenin now wanted to return to his homeland to end the bloodshed of what he saw as a capitalist war. As a consequence, he approached the German government to ask for safe passage, using the argument that German soldiers would be released from the conflict on the eastern front as a direct consequence of his return.

In today's terminology, Lenin was an extremist. The Germans were delighted by the prospect of Russia's early exit from the war, but concerned that Lenin could spread his revolutionary message before he got to the border. The answer was a sealed train that would race through Germany to Sweden and Russia, permitting Lenin and his accompanying cronies only limited exposure to others, a hitherto unknown refinement on using the train as part of a military strategy.

Lenin embarked on the train at a border town on 8 April, where supporters who were horrified by his collaboration with the Germans begged him to stay. Unmoved, he boarded the train without a word, being transported alongside a considerable stash of German money to finance his activities.

Accompanied by his wife Nadezhda Krupskaya and about 30 others, as the train raced through Germany he gazed out of the window at towns and villages populated only by women and boys. A chalk demarcation line prevented him from approaching the German soldiers who guarded him.

Lenin made notes, discussed socialist theories and read. But he was frequently disturbed by the arguments of smokers and non-smokers, and about who had priority. Lenin loathed the habit and came up with a ticketing system to govern one of the carriages. Still, the bickering continued.

In Sweden, which remained neutral during the First World War but maintained a close relationship with Germany, there was a warm welcome. As the train approached Stockholm, press photographers and Swedish Communists crowded on to the platform. Inside the waiting room, which was bedecked with a red flag, the mayor hosted a breakfast smorgasbord.

Austrian Karl Radek (1885–1939), who was among Lenin's party, wrote about their joyful response in 1924.

'We poor fellows, who in Switzerland had been accustomed to have no more than a herring for our dinner, looked at this enormous table with innumerable hors d'oeuvre: we rushed at it like a swarm of grasshoppers and completely emptied the table, to the astonishment of the waiters, who were used to seeing only civilised people at the Smörgas table.'

He also insisted on taking Lenin to a department store to prepare him for his return to Russia. Lenin had been wearing mountain boots studded with protective nails and was persuaded to buy shoes and trousers – but flatly refused to get a new coat.

Perhaps as part of the agreement with the Kaiser's government, Lenin denied German trades unionists an audience. although once he had crossed the border he spoke to Russian soldiers he encountered.

American critic Edmund Wilson (1895–1972) later wrote about what happened when Lenin arrived in Beloostrov.

'There was a demand for Lenin to speak and the train crew, who knew nothing about their passenger except that he was somebody special, picked him up and carried him into the buffet and stood him on a table.'

But when the conductor came along to tell the locomotive crew it was time to go, Lenin cut short his speech and the train departed for St Petersburg, or Petrograd as it was then known. Lenin's radical agenda prevailed in Russia, setting the country on course for more than 70 years of Communist rule.

> **'We poor fellows, who in Switzerland had been accustomed to have no more than a herring for our dinner ...'**
> Karl Radek

## That runaway thrill

A different kind of railway history exists in Tivoli Gardens, the pleasure park founded in Copenhagen in 1843. It's one of the oldest working rollercoasters in the world, and has thrilled generations of passengers by reaching speeds of 50 kph (31 mph) along a 720 metre (2,362 ft) dipping track. The rollercoaster was installed in 1914 in a make-believe mountain, giving it the feel of a 'runaway' train.

The history of rollercoasters has been traced back to Russia, where people sat on ice blocks, using straw or fur as a seat, and sped downhill until being brought to a halt on a bed of sand.

Later, railway companies in the United States allowed passengers to ride gravity-controlled stretches of line for a small price at weekends, thus establishing a pleasure principle for fast track-borne rides.

# THE BALLS TO BUILD RAILWAYS

BALL BEARINGS ARE THE UNSUNG HEROES of the modern age, with all their hard work going on behind the scenes and without acknowledgement.

When the ancient Egyptians built pyramids, they rolled hefty stones to their chosen site on logs to reduce friction.

It's an example of a raw concept that later emerged in the shape of a ball bearing, although not until the Industrial Revolution got underway in Britain. One of the first known examples was found at the Sprowston postmill near Norwich, built in 1730. When it was destroyed by fire in the 1930s, investigators found large cast-iron rings among the mill workings containing some 40 cast-iron balls measuring 57 mm (2¼ in) in diameter.

The purpose of the ball bearings was to have the windmill work better, give the sails a smoother action and make the machinery less prone to breakdowns.

As industrial mechanisms grew more complex, so the humble ball bearing assumed greater importance. It was used in the development of railways in axles and rolling stock, ultimately helping to make rail travel more comfortable and to lessen the chance of derailments. And ball bearings weren't just in railway trappings themselves but in the machinery that made them.

Ball bearings are iconic among engineers but their sterling work is little known among the rest of the population

Cast iron gave way to steel but difficulties in mass producing ball bearings that were the precise size and strength required by industry had yet to be overcome as manufacturing companies usually made their own.

Now it was time for specialist firms to come to the fore – like the Hoffmann Machine Company, which began in New York and opened a branch in Chelmsford in 1898, making one million steel balls a day a decade later.

It wasn't only in Britain that this process was unfolding, however. In Sweden, plant engineer Sven Wingqvist (1876–1953) was concerned about shortcomings in the steel ball bearings in the textile plant he operated. By 1907, he had developed a self-aligning, double-row ball bearing which he patented. It was to be produced in Gothenburg by AB Svenska Kullagerfabriken or SKF, a new company that went on to become a giant of Sweden's industrial scene. Twenty years later, SKF began car production under one of the company's trademarks, Volvo, derived from the Latin for 'I roll'. Eventually, SKF parted company from the car manufacturers, but continued to make ball bearings.

As they are unseen and soundless, it's easy to forget just how important ball bearings are to industrial societies. As a measure of their worth, the Americans drew up a plan to destroy a ball bearings factory in Germany during the Second World War, believing its destruction would bring the entire Nazi war effort to a halt. In fact, after sustaining high losses in the aerial bombing campaign, the Americans abandoned the notion, so the theory was left untested.

## Bradshaw brings it all together

By the time he contracted cholera on a trip to Norway, George Bradshaw (1801–1853) was known throughout Britain for his railway guides. His role in railway history had been significant. As the railways expanded through private enterprise, he used his experience as a cartographer and printer to catalogue the services available to customers. In 1839, when his first guide appeared in print, there wasn't even a standardised time used by the railway companies, many of which were hostile to his efforts. They saw no reason why passengers should not use their own published timetables, to the exclusion of all other services. Bradshaw bought shares in numerous railway companies in order to present his case for more joined-up thinking. In 1847, the first Continental guide was published, a tome that grew exponentially with the size of the European rail network.

By the time the 1913 edition was published it was some 1,000 pages long, filled with descriptions, directions, timetables and scores of advertisements from hotels hoping to snare the interest of British tourists.

# HYDRO POWER AND THE FIRST ELECTRIC TRAINS

FOR SWEDEN AT THE TURN OF THE 20TH CENTURY, hydroelectricity was the fuel of choice for its new-found industry.

With a plentiful number of rushing rivers, Sweden exploited early technologies that had developed through the 19th century when water was being used to power turbines.

Electricity garnered from the energy created by falling water had first powered a single lamp in a country house in Northumberland, England, in 1878. Four years later, the first hydroelectric plant to serve customers opened in Wisconsin, starting a trend in the USA and Canada. In 1895, the world's largest hydroelectric development of the time, the Edward Dean Adams Power Plant, was built at Niagara Falls.

While North America indisputably became world leaders, Sweden and Germany took up the mantle in Europe.

The Swedish State Power Board was founded in 1909 to manage investments in hydro power as the industry grew at record pace, bringing about advances in the technology of transmission lines and significant price reductions in fuel costs. Activities were consequently increased on the northerly Luleälv river to enable the first major electrification of a railway in the world to occur.

*From above, the power of this Swedish hydroelectric power station is better gauged, created as the calm waters on the right are pushed through the dam*

## The missing link

After the last ice age 7,000 years ago, the land bridge between Denmark and Sweden flooded. Undaunted, modern civil engineers decided to recreate the link with a tunnel and bridge, both collectively known as the Øresund Bridge.

Plans for a link had been mooted for decades before the ambitious project got underway. It was finally opened for road and rail traffic in 2000, becoming the world's longest cable bridge. The journey from Denmark begins with a 3,510 metre (2.2 mile) underwater tunnel that emerges from the water on to an artificial island. After that it progresses with a 7,845 metre (4.9 mile) bridge across the final strait to Malmö. Although expensive tolls for drivers have deterred some, the loans that built it were expected to be paid off within 30 years.

Work began on the Malmbanan line, used to carry iron ore freight, in 1910 and took more than a decade to complete. By 1920, electric motors powered almost four-fifths of Swedish industry.

After the Gothenburg to Stockholm line was electrified in 1942, passengers could for the first time make a journey of more than 1,000 miles by electric trains, from Malmö in the south to Riksgränsen, 200 km (124 miles) north of the Arctic Circle. This was at a time when most of strife-torn Europe remained dependent on steam.

Sweden continues to generate hydroelectric power, and 2010 figures revealed the country to be the biggest user of hydropower in the European Union and the tenth biggest in the world.

It was a different story in Denmark, which had no access to either water power or coal. When diesel engines had finally overcome some enduring power-to-weight ratio issues that hindered their use in locomotives, Denmark chose these to haul carriages and freight. The process of switching to diesel power began as early as 1927 but wasn't completed until 1970.

This lengthy timeframe wasn't because there was an enduring fondness for steam among the Danes – although King Frederick IX of Denmark was such an enthusiast that, at his funeral in 1972, his coffin was towed to its final resting place in Roskilde under steam. Instead, there was a natural reluctance to dispense with fully working steam engines before they were either worn out or obsolete.

# PRAGUE TO MUNICH

IN ONE OF HIS NOVELS, CHARLES DICKENS vividly describes a train travelling with a head of steam: 'Roaring, rattling, tearing on, spurning everything with its dark break . . . shrieking, rolling, rattling through the purple distance.' By Victorian times these were the only rail-running vehicles known in Britain.

Yet early railways didn't necessarily have steam locomotives on their tracks. Wagons or carts were towed by ropes and pulleys, a static steam engine or, more usually, horses – and these were a common sight in industrial areas.

Nor was there any immediate desire to change from this system to locomotives when the early models travelled barely faster than a galloping horse.

In ten years, the speed of the fastest trains had doubled and then investment – which was no small undertaking – in railway lines more recognisable to our modern world became attractive. Despite the large amounts of money involved, speculating on railways in the early days as they began to spread was rarely a bad idea. New lines, their locomotives and the companies that ran them had a habit of attracting industry and its associated wealth.

At the turn of the 20th century, the German railway system was the world's second largest, extending to some 64,500 km (40,000 miles). This indicates how buoyant its economy was, and that Germany was vying for pre-eminence in Europe.

Germany's fortunes would duly change in the course of the 20th century, as would those of steam trains. New technologies eventually signalled the end of the age of steam, although those locomotives that remained in working order have been kept pristine and revered by enthusiasts. Oskar von Miller was motivated by similar emotions when he realised a technological heritage was slipping away. As a result, one of the biggest science museums in the world was established.

# SPA TRAIN TO PILSEN AND THE BOHEMIAN RAILWAYS

WITH THE AUSTRIAN EMPIRE IN CONTROL, there were soon trains snaking across Czech lands. The first steam railway there was named for the Austrian emperor Ferdinand I and V (1793–1875) but was better known as the Northern Railway. Naturally, perhaps, it began in Vienna but its route ended in Prague.

Commercially, the key railway in Czech history was the one that connected Prague to Pilsen in 1862. Ironically, it was built not to spur on an already burgeoning economy in Pilsen but to bring wealthy Austrians to the spas beyond at Karlovy Vary and Mariánské Lázně.

Its net effect was nonetheless to transform Pilsen, where a steelworks begun in 1859 would soon be taken over by Emil Škoda (1839–1900) to become a bicycle, car and, later, locomotive builder.

Škoda installed industrial railway lines that connected his works to the national network to assist in the delivery of raw materials and the distribution of items when they were made. During wartime, this assisted in the swift dispersal of the armaments made there.

Within 30 years Škoda was the town's biggest employer,

With Europe suffering persistent wars during the 19th century there was a buoyant market for the armaments produced at the Škoda factory

but the Dual Monarchy's national railway was also high profile. After establishing the largest rail repair shop in the empire at Pilsen's busy railway junction it became the second biggest employer.

And that in turn led to the growth of the Pilsen beer trade. After the excellent communications at Pilsen were established, the golden beer made from locally grown hops could be enjoyed by railway workers in their spare time – and across Europe by discerning drinkers. As luck would have it, the beer and steam engines that transported it both benefited from the soft water supplies found at Pilsen. The water was deemed partially responsible at least for the popular taste of the beverage, while it kept the internal workings of the steam engines clean from the 'fur' associated with hard water use.

So the arrival of the railways transformed Pilsen, with its 1786 population of 5,000 bulging to 100,000 by the end of the First World War.

## Horse power on the Budweis line

The story of railways had a surprisingly early start in Bohemia where a 130 km (80 mile) railway was built by 1832. It was a railway without a locomotive, however, as the tracks that linked Budweis, in what is now the Czech Republic, to Linz in Austria were designed for horse-drawn transport.

When it opened it was by some distance the world's longest railway connection. It was designed by Prague-born Franz Anton von Gerstner (1796–1840), who had visited England in 1822 and left as intrigued by how railway lines could be laid as by the steam engines that would one day pull trains.

Gerstner was the son of physicist and engineer Franz Josef Gerstner, who had himself suggested the link years before. Despite a lack of written evidence at his disposal about the construction of railway lines, Gerstner the younger set about his task using tried and tested physics equations to tackle the inclines.

Initially, the line was built for the transport of salt, at the time an expensive commodity, to the North Sea via the Danube river. But it was also used for passenger services, providing a smoother ride than equivalent coach services.

Gerstner went on to work in Russia and finally visited America, ostensibly to investigate the detail of the railroad there on behalf of the Russians. In fact, it was probably in an effort to resurrect a career that had been sidelined after showing initial promise.

For two years he travelled North America, assiduously making notes on railway operations. After his untimely death, assistant Ludwig Klein assembled them into a book that later became a standard text for students of American railways.

DIE LUDWIGS-EISENBAHN
zwischen Nürnberg und Fürth.

Diese Eisenbahn, die erste in Deutschland, welche mit einem Dampfwagen befahren wird, ist durch das patriotische Zusammenwirken der Actionaire, durch die un-ermüdliche Thätigkeit der Directoren, u.durch die Umsicht eines gewandten Baumeisters im Lande EINES Jahres ins Dasein getreten, so dass sie am 7ten December 1835 feierlich eröffnet werden konnte. Zwei Städte mit ansehnlicher Bevölkerung sind sich dadurch so nahe gerückt, dafs sie gleichsam nur noch EINE bilden. Der Vaterlands-freund begrüßt das schöne Werk mit frohen Hoffnungen u.freuet sich schon im Geiste der Zeit wo die Ludwigs Eisenbahn ihre Arme weiter ausbreiten wird, um Städte und Länder segnend zu verknüpfen.

# KING LUDWIG'S FLYING SCOTSMAN

GERMANY'S RAILWAY AGE DAWNED IN NUREMBERG in 1835 with the opening of the Bavarian Ludwig Railway, named for a king who had precious little curiosity about this innovation. Although King Ludwig gave permission for the project, he did not travel on it until eight months after it was opened.

Perhaps he was cautious of the extensive British input. At the request of the newly formed Royal Privileged Ludwig Railway Company, George Stephenson provided advice, locomotives and a driver in the shape of William Wilson.

The Scots-born engineer accompanied the crated locomotives from north-east England to Nuremberg, via Rotterdam and Cologne along the inland waterways. He helped assemble the locomotives, providing guidance for a future generation of railway engineers, and drove the first train on 7 December 1835.

Stephenson had guaranteed Wilson's services to the Bavarians for eight months, stipulating for him a 12-hour working day. But when the contract finished Wilson showed no signs of wanting to return home.

He had achieved a hero's status in Nuremberg for his 'safe' driving on the steam engine and initially his obligations to the 6 km (3.7 mile) line were just two trips a day. The rest of the timetable was fulfilled by horse-drawn transport, as imported coal to power the locomotive was costly and difficult to transport there.

Passengers who opted for the mechanised journey preferred to see 'the tall Englishman [sic]' in a top hat at the helm, and there was a corresponding fall in profits if he did not appear on the platform.

But his commitment to the line seriously compromised his health. Standing daily in the elements, together with the regular inhalation of smoke, weakened his constitution. It wasn't until the winter of 1845 that drivers were issued with leather coats to replace woollen ones, and protective roofs for drivers' compartments were a further eight years away.

And the conviction among customers that Wilson was better or safer than his German co-workers was misplaced. After three years, *The Mechanics' Magazine* reported on its progress and revealed that 'no life has been lost on the railway, no serious accident of any kind has occurred and the railway has received no material injury'.

Furthermore, passenger numbers amounted to 1,357,285 when the population of both Nuremberg and Fürth totalled no more than 60,000, implying that each citizen had made seven journeys each year.

The line was costly, exceeding its initial budget by something like a third. Track layers were inexperienced and the price of land was pushed relentlessly upwards by landowners. Initially, only newspapers and beer were transported by rail until more general freight was added in 1839. However, within 20 years the dividends for shareholders stood at a healthy 12 per cent.

As for Wilson, he died in 1862 in Nuremberg, with his funeral attracting hundreds of mourners.

## Paul von Denis

The straight tracks that carried the Ludwig Railway, running parallel to the road, were the work of Paul von Denis (1795–1872). Already he had gathered considerable expertise by visiting Belgium, France and England – where he met George Stephenson.

Afterwards he built other important lines in Bavaria, including one that linked Munich and Augsburg. By 1856 his skill at railway projects was so honed that he took only five years to build a 61-mile stretch of track when seven had been scheduled. By the time he was 70, he was credited with building almost 1,000 km (621 miles) of railway. Denis favoured Stephenson's standard gauge, but his speed of construction is partly accounted for by his preference for single tracks which inevitably curbed the volume of traffic that could use them. At the end of 1881 the Bavarian state system consisted of 73 lines with a combined total of 2,668 route miles. Of this, only 178 miles were double-tracked.

# RUDOLF DIESEL'S RAIL REVOLUTION

STEAM ENGINES DEVELOPED NOT JUST FOR TRAINS but for all kinds of engineering uses. Although they were an innovation that provided a eureka moment for Europe's rapid industrial development, there were also a host of disadvantages, primarily in terms of pollution.

One man helped to change that, although he didn't live to see the engines he designed hauling coaches and wagons. Rudolf Diesel (1858–1913) was born in Paris of Bavarian parents. When Prussia besieged the French capital in 1870 the family were forced to leave and Diesel was ultimately sent back to his parents' family in Augsburg to continue his education.

He spent some time at the Royal Bavarian Polytechnic in Munich and a machine works in Switzerland before returning to Paris to work with one of his professors on a refrigeration plant.

But the able-minded Diesel wasn't content with one modern triumph. He began work on a new generation of steam engines but was nearly killed when one exploded. Following his recovery, he changed tack again and investigated new ways with thermodynamics. The result was the diesel engine, in which

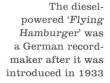

The diesel-powered 'Flying Hamburger' was a German record-maker after it was introduced in 1933

hot air ignites diesel oil with the resulting combustion the source of its power.

He didn't start on the idea completely from scratch. Work had already been done on a similar theme by British inventor Herbert Akroyd Stuart, but Diesel's patents were granted from 1892 because he could prove he'd made additional changes.

Initially, it was used in manufacturing, on submarines and in ships. By 1912 an estimated 70,000 diesel engines were working around the world, most being static in factories.

The success was enough to make him a millionaire. Yet on 29 September 1913 he apparently threw himself from the deck of the post office steamer *Dresden*, somewhere between Antwerp and Dover, and drowned.

With international tensions running high, conspiracy theories were rife. When his death was announced there was speculation that he was murdered, being en route for talks with the British government. However, his bank balance was almost empty while a cross on that day in his diary appeared to indicate he planned to commit suicide.

Further modifications were made to the diesel engine before it could be incorporated in trains. Finally, two primary issues, its size and its transmission difficulties, were resolved and it was used in America on a locomotive for the first time in 1925.

After the Second World War, use of locomotives became much more prevalent until lines for electrification were installed. In 1933, the diesel-powered *Flying Hamburger* entered service in Germany – so called for its brown central stripe sandwiched between a wheaty yellow – setting a new world record for rail when it achieved a speed of 214 kph (133 mph) in 1939 between Berlin and Hamburg.

Fittingly, perhaps, one of Diesel's original engines, before they were used in railways, is on display at the Deutsches Museum in Munich.

## Saving science

Munich's science and technology museum is the product of one man's quest to preserve the rapidly unfolding story of man-made triumphs.

Electrical engineer Oskar von Miller (1855–1934) was aware that while artefacts from history and art were being cherished, objects that made the modern world were overlooked or even discarded. As a consequence, he proposed the foundation of the Deutsches Museum to house a plethora of relevant items.

By 1903 the Association of German Engineers had lent its support and the city council had donated Coal Island in the Isar river as a venue. Nonetheless, it took until 1925 for the museum's permanent home to be completed. It was officially opened by Miller on his 70th birthday. Nine years later he died there after suffering a heart attack. Today, the Deutsches Museum has 100,000 exhibits on three sites that tell the story of today's world and attracts more than a million visitors every year.

On 1 September 2009 the Winton train, named for Sir Nicholas Winton, pulled out of Prague station to mark 70 years since the start of the Second World War

# KINDERTRANSPORT

A JEWISH COMMUNITY WAS RECORDED IN PRAGUE from the 10th century, contributing to a subsequently vibrant intellectual life. Throughout the centuries, they were subjected to spells of anti-Semitism, to lesser or worse degrees, from a Christian population keen for a scapegoat.

One of the city's most famous sons, writer Franz Kafka (1883–1924), frequently scrutinised issues like alienation and brutality in his work. But even he could not have imagined the terrible fate that lay ahead for the Jews, just 15 years after his death.

In 1938, Germany annexed parts of Czechoslovakia, receiving a warm welcome in some quarters which were populated by ethnic Germans. It left the Jewish community everywhere exposed to the radical anti-Semitism that pervaded the regime. Before the Second World War erupted, one British man used the railways to save hundreds of Jewish children from certain death.

Nicholas Winton was a 29-year-old stockbroker when he visited Prague in December 1938, alerted by some British embassy friends in the city to help at refugee centres. When he realised the bleak outlook that faced the Jews there he set about organising the evacuation by train of as many young people as possible.

Leaving two colleagues behind in Czechoslovakia, he returned to London to raise the £50 needed for each traveller, gather the necessary documentation – forging it when he had to – arrange accommodation for the flood of young immigrants and raise awareness of their plight. With families in Czechoslovakia pleading with the British to take their children to safety, the demand was overwhelming.

Winton and his friends managed to organise eight trains out of Prague which headed through Holland to a northern port, for passage to England. A ninth was prevented from leaving German territory on 1 September 1939 after the invasion of Poland and the outbreak of war. Those who did make their escape arrived at Liverpool Street station with name or number tags around their necks, to meet Winton and others who duly despatched them to their new homes.

Nothing was known publicly about the mercy mission until 1988, when Winton appeared on a British TV programme called *That's Life*, after his wife Grete shared a scrapbook she found in the attic with the BBC. Unbeknown to him, the television audience consisted entirely of those who owed their lives to him. Always humble, he not only celebrated the 669 children he saved but regretted the loss of those on the last train that he did not.

He was knighted in 2003 for his humanitarian work. When Winton died in 2015, aged 106, the stories of those he saved – most of whom he outlived – were once again retold.

## 'Winton's children'

Aged 17, Nina Klein saw her mother for the last time on the platform of Prague's station. Hastily, her mother shoved a diamond ring into her hand and told her to bargain for her life with it if necessary. Nina kept the ring under her tongue for the entire journey and wore it for the rest of her life. She died in 2009, having returned to Czechoslovakia, then moving to Australia and finally the US.

Fourteen-year-old Hanna Beer left her mother in Prague on 15 May 1939 and joined her father and brother, already in England. After the family discovered her mother died in a concentration camp, her father committed suicide. Much later, her brother did too. She discovered she was one of 'Winton's children' after watching a Czech-made film in 1999.

Ernst Steiner was 12 when he left Prague, to live in a children's home run by Jewish women in London's East End. Subsequently evacuated to avoid the London blitz, he later joined the Jewish Brigade to fight the Nazis and finally emigrated to Israel.

Peter Sprinzels, who lost his mother and grandmother in the Holocaust, emigrated to Australia to become a biochemist and a grandfather of four before his death in 1989.

# BORDEAUX TO BILBAO

AS TRAINS BECAME MORE NUMEROUS around Europe there was less significance attached to crossing national borders. Usually, frontiers passed in a blur as the train sped to its destination. When passengers crossed from France to Spain, however, it wasn't just the language that changed. The train they travelled in had to be swapped because both countries had different railway gauges.

It may well be one reason why Britain's King Edward VII opted to stay in France – but it's much more likely that the promise of fine regional wines kept him there. He once said: 'One not only drinks the wine, one smells it, observes it, tastes it, sips it and – one talks about it.' He chose to go to Biarritz in the spring, where he would spend time reading official papers and playing bridge with his mistress Mrs Keppel.

Railway entrepreneur Émile Péreire established nearby Arcachon as a winter retreat for those seeking restorative breaks. According to *Bradshaw's*, 'the exhalations of the pines with the sea air render the Ville d'Hiver a very healthy quarter. Climate temperate at all seasons.'

However, *Bradshaw's* is very specific about when visitors should go to the Pyrenees, with summer and early autumn recommended for the climate.

'Along the Pyrenees the scenery is ruggedly magnificent, forest, torrent, broken and towering mountains, with health resorts crushed in gorges or perched on ridges where the curative springs are most accessible,' *Bradshaw's* gushes.

It's thanks to scenery like this that Spain, playing catch-up with its wealthier neighbour as regards a railway network, had not only broad gauges on its main lines but also narrow gauges, to cope with steep inclines and precipitous descents.

There were narrow gauges too installed for industrial use, especially in the industrialised north-east.

# WINE TRAINS AND THE PORT OF BORDEAUX

LONG BEFORE THE ADVENT OF THE RAILWAYS Bordeaux enjoyed a busy commerce with wine at its heart.

With its thriving port and inland waterways, the city was ideally placed to ship quantities abroad in a trade fuelled by demand from the Dutch, the English and the Catholic Church.

It was fine wines that were bottled and sold, typically sweet and heavy ones that travelled well, as voyages and onward transport took some time. The more expensive bottles also better absorbed the high taxes levied in France and by other countries.

Of course, there was plenty of other wine produced that could not be classed as 'fine'. High transport costs meant these were only consumed locally. Anything remaining in the cellar on the eve of a subsequent harvest was ditched. During years of an abundant harvest, this could amount to an enormous quantity of very drinkable wine, to the detriment of the grower's income.

The railway between Paris and Bordeaux, via Orléans and Tours, was finally completed by 1853. Here at last was an opportunity to send litres of cheaper wines to Paris and beyond. Parisians had long enjoyed wines produced in the north, but the wetter climate made them expensive or unsophisticated.

Thanks to the proliferation of railways and a corresponding boom in trade, Britain was also lowering its taxes and favouring a free market, which was a bonus for the region's wine makers, who responded by planting up every hillside and field.

But just as the future seemed rosy, harvests were decimated first by mildew and then by phylloxera, a vine-killing aphid. It took years to recover from the blights and finally French growers had to graft their own vines on to US rootstock which had proved resistant to phylloxera.

The figures were daunting for the industry. In 1875, France, always Europe's biggest wine producer, had an output of 78 million hectolitres. In the following decade, the highest annual amount was 25 million hectolitres short of that peak, while the lowest figure recorded during that time was a humble 23 million hectolitres.

Costs were remaining the same, as mechanised grape-crushing methods that squeezed pips as well as pulp frequently harmed the flavour of some wines. Even in the mid-1880s, many wineries had farm workers treading the grapes to ensure this didn't happen.

As the amount of wine produced dropped, unscrupulous dealers adulterated the French product with cheaper wines bought in from Italy or Algeria. But the dark chapter eventually closed and by the time production was once again soaring there were specially made railway wagons that carried huge oak vats between producer and newly mechanised bottling plants.

It is on these foundations that today's successful wine industry has been built. Today about 70 million cases of wine are produced annually in the five districts that make up Bordeaux, by 9,000 producers. Nine-tenths of the wine made there now is red. Thus a trade begun by the Romans in classical times continues.

## Eiffel's Bordeaux masterpiece

Engineer Gustave Eiffel (1832–1923) is forever linked to the tower in Paris that bears his name, the world's highest building when it was opened in 1889 and the first made of iron.

It wasn't an immediate hit, with many Parisians believing it 'vulgar', but its construction beckoned in a new generation of skyscrapers that changed skylines around the world.

The tower was built at the height of his career, but 30 years previously Eiffel left his mark in south-west France, building the wrought-iron bridge at Bordeaux that carried rail traffic across the Garonne river. It was the first major contract he had supervised and, in its day, the building work was innovative and the configuration of girders appeared remarkable. Eiffel went on to install an enormous roof, 56 metres (184 ft) wide, at one of the Bordeaux stations.

Other work to his credit includes the Statue of Liberty in New York, a viaduct across the Douro in Portugal and Pest railway station in Hungary.

# ESCAPE TO BIARRITZ: KING EDWARD VII'S OPULENT TRAIN

FOR KING EDWARD VII (1841–1910) THE AGE OF RAILWAYS helped him to become the 'uncle' of Europe. With a keen interest in foreign affairs, a yearning for better health and a 12-wheeler royal saloon parked in a shed at Calais that could be hitched to any suitable locomotive, he frequently travelled around the Continent both for the business of diplomacy and for pleasure.

It was not unusual for monarchs of the day to have their own royal rail carriages. Indeed, his mother, Queen Victoria – who first travelled by train in 1842 and thereafter refused to have its speed exceed 40 miles per hour during daylight hours – had her own at Calais also.

The decor was considerably more comfortable than that on public services of the era. In the king's private coach there were armchairs, thick pile carpets and toilets. Accompanying him on the train were 30 servants and his beloved fox terrier, Caesar.

As the Prince of Wales, he had become the focus of British society thanks to his love of good living and extravagant high spirits at a time when the

*In 1909 King Edward VII was still well enough to enjoy a beach walk at Biarritz*

Queen was considered dour and remote. He carried this reputation as a bon viveur with him overseas and his favourite resorts became instantly fashionable among the aspirational aristocracy.

Every March as king he made his way to Biarritz by train to stay at the opulent Hotel du Palais, before spending some weeks cruising in the Mediterranean. Indeed, it was at this hotel in south-west France that he officially named Herbert Asquith as British prime minister on 7 April 1908.

That Asquith had to make a trip to France to kiss the sovereign's hands for the purposes of protocol and to accommodate the king was subject to some criticism in the press back in Britain. But there's no doubt that the king took a genuine interest in government at home and an active role in promoting Britain around the world.

Recently, there's been a suggestion that he was the unwitting architect of the First World War because of the series of agreements and treaties he drew up while he was monarch which ultimately propelled Britain into the conflict. He had no affection for his nephew, Kaiser Wilhelm II of Germany, and believed another nephew by marriage, Tsar Nicholas II, to be weak. Certainly, all the diplomatic ties he contrived were intended to keep Britain at the top of the international pile.

He didn't use the train just for holidays, when he would typically travel as 'the Duke of Lancaster', or for talks. Concerned about his weight and a range of other illnesses, he often directed the royal train to spas around Europe, sometimes mixing business and pleasure by conducting discussions in luxuriously appointed baths.

The king died ten days after leaving Biarritz, allegedly whispering 'goodbye' to the resort he adored before his departure.

> ## Assassin at large
>
> There were also unhappy associations with steam trains for King Edward VII. In 1900, when he was travelling through Belgium to Denmark by train he was the target of an assassination attempt by a young Belgian anarchist protesting against the Boer War. And after his death his body was taken from Paddington station in London to Windsor by train before his burial at St George's Chapel.

The king is pictured returning home from Biarritz for the last time, after murmuring a farewell to the city from his hotel window

For decades
passengers
travelling between
France and Spain
had to leave one
train to join
another, after
Spain chose to use
a broad gauge.
However, tearing
up the railway
was an expensive
proposition

# NARROW-MINDED SPAIN GOES IT ALONE

ONE OF THE EARLY MISCALCULATIONS of the Spanish railway companies was to choose a broad gauge rather than the standard one that proliferated in Europe.

It seems Spain opted for the wide measurement as long ago as 1844 after an early feasibility study, influenced by the views of Isambard Kingdom Brunel (1806–1859) – who built broad gauge railways in Britain – was sent to the Spanish government.

One long-held theory is that it was chosen to prevent an invasion by train from neighbouring France, which would have been unable to send locomotives down the differently constructed line.

In *Bradshaw's*, passengers are warned they will have to change carriages at Irun on the frontier although, it points out, the French and Spanish trains park alongside each other to make the switch as easy as possible. It was more problematic when it came to freight, which had to be turned out of one wagon and into another.

The width, measuring 1,668 mm (5 ft 5½ in) compared to the standard gauge of 1,435 mm (4 ft 8½ in), was equal to six Castilian feet, an old-style measurement, and is sometimes known as the Iberian gauge as it is compatible with neighbouring Portugal. Russian lines are also broader than normal.

There were some plus points. Broader gauges promoted a more equal distribution of forces on two rails, which made wagons and carriages more stable. There was an increase in capacity inside wider trains, which in turn could achieve high speeds – although smaller rolling stock was cheaper to make and the rails needed less bracing.

There was a concern among the broad gauge lobby that narrower gauges needed more maintenance as pressure fell on one rail.

However, it was a numbers game that ultimately won the argument for the standard gauge. With more train companies and countries adopting it, the few that didn't use standard gauge became more isolated. According to his biographer Samuel Smiles, George Stephenson could see this unfolding early on. When he was quizzed about what gauge should be chosen for lines being made in two different parts of England he advised using the same width. 'Though they may be a long way apart now, depend upon it they will be joined together some day,' he said.

Britain uprooted broad gauge track but Spain stuck with it. Domestically, debate about which was preferable raged for decades. One Spanish analyst, Jesús Moreno, rued the choice made by George Stephenson back in the earliest days of locomotive construction, to stick with the gauge used when trucks were towed by horses. It was, says Moreno, picked as a result of misguided pragmatism rather than informed analysis.

If there were advantages to wide gauge railways they disappeared with the advent of diesel and electric trains. Technology finally provided an answer in 1968, after which a train could slowly drive through a special 12 metre (39 ft) long assembly point for an automated gauge change. When modern high-speed trains were introduced into Spain, a choice was made to use the standard gauge for its track.

It has left Spain with three well-used gauges: broad, standard and narrow gauge built for agriculture and industry but now used for passenger transport.

## Farewell to broad gauge

Changing a route's gauge meant the withdrawal of rolling stock as well as uprooting the track itself, which might explain why Spain has fought shy of ripping up major segments of its network. In Britain, the last stretch to be converted was between Exeter and Truro in 1892, and one account of the extended process describes the response of some the labourers involved:

'Some of them had never seen the sea before; one man, indeed, was overheard to express some indistinct ideas about the time of the tides being controlled from the general manager's office at Paddington, and was told instead that the times were fixed by the Admiralty!

'Friday was the final day of the full size gauge and crowds of people assembled at various points along the line to witness the passing of the last broad gauge train. The countenances of the drivers were serious and at stopping stations farewell salutations were regretfully exchanged.'

## HAULING COAL: THE LOST WORLD OF *EL HULLERO*

San Sebastián's railway station is also marked by the work of Gustave Eiffel, who built the canopy that still protects passengers on platforms

LYING BETWEEN FRANCE AND SPAIN is the Basque region, distinct in terms of language and culture from the two huge countries that surround it.

It's also distinct in terms of railways, with its own network run on a metre gauge from Bilbao that extends for 181 km (112 miles). A train that has always been known as *El Topo*, or the mole, connects France and San Sebastián. Another links stations around the Bilbao region, and from there it's possible to catch a Spanish train, travelling on a similar gauge, to the Atlantic coast.

There's a long history of narrow gauge railways in the region, born of its industry. Now there's a concerted effort to make a virtue of the unusual rail size. The Basque railway offers inter-city and urban options, while there are also tourist trains that now run where industrial engines once pulled heavy loads.

**'In this valley [in northern Spain] you will find archaeological remains, historical relics, unique landscapes, vistas only possible from the *Hullero* ...'**
Juan Pedro Aparicio

Novelist Juan Pedro Aparicio (b. 1941) takes credit at least in part for this transformation. In 1980, he rode on *El Hullero*, the train that pulled coal between the old Castilian capital of León and the port at Bilbao, which was closing after a century of service.

Aware that Britain and France had made disused narrow gauge railways into iconic attractions, he said:

'If Spain were a less uncouth place the route … would be one of the most important tourist attractions in the country; the *Hullero* would be one of Spain's major tourist trains.

'In this valley [in northern Spain] you will find archaeological remains, historical relics, unique landscapes, vistas only possible from the *Hullero*, places that are integral to this country's origins, and which have remained exactly as they were more than a thousand years ago.'

His tales of sharing a railway stew – water, beans and chorizo cooked over the steam train's coal fire – with its crew before the industrial line closed inspired a campaign to save it. The train carried not only coal hewn from the picturesque Picos de Europa mountains, but also workers from outlying villages who were the industrial muscle of the era.

The railway yard in Bilbao that was used by *El Hullero* is now long gone, with the famous Guggenheim Museum standing where steam locomotives used to be.

But other historic track journeys in the Basque region have also survived. There's the scenic railway at San Sebastián, built in 1928 when a clifftop casino was closed in the wake of anti-gambling legislation, on a Swiss mountain theme and designed by German engineer Erich Heidrich.

The track runs for 400 metres (1,312 ft) and achieves a maximum speed of 50 kph (31 mph). Thanks to its curious side friction design, the two carriages which each carry 20 riders really do become airborne at times and a brakeman rides between the cars to properly control cornering and the descents. (It was Heidrich, from Hamburg, who built a similar scenic railway at Great Yarmouth in 1932, where he stayed as its operator until the start of the Second World War.)

A funicular that dates back more than 100 years and tackles gradients of between 32 and 58 per cent takes riders to the scenic railway from the town's beach. Meanwhile, further inland there is the Rhune railway, which dates from 1924 and scales a Pyrenean mountain. It takes 35 minutes for the rack railway to complete its journey at a speed of 9 kph (5.6 mph).

### Gondola travel in Bilbao

Bilbao also boasts the oldest hanging transporter bridge in the world. Better described as a gondola, it was built in 1893 across the mouth of the Nervión river and initially operated by a steam engine. The Vizcaya Bridge, from which the gondola is suspended, is made of iron and twisted steel cables high enough above the waterway to avoid disruption to shipping. It's braced by 50 metre (164 ft) pillars at either side.

Today, there's room for six cars and many more passengers who dangle over the water for just 90 seconds during the 164 metre (538 ft) journey.

**3**

**TULA** TO **ST PETERSBURG**
**ROME** TO **TAORMINA**
**WARSAW** TO **KRAKÓW**
**LA CORUÑA** TO **LISBON**
**HAIFA** TO **THE NEGEV DESERT**
**LYON** TO **MARSEILLE**

THE WORTH OF RAILWAYS TO THE ECONOMICS of industry was soon proved, with raw materials and freight shipped around the continent with increasing speed. As the volume of freight went up, rates came down. However, the enhancing effect on tourism wasn't immediately apparent outside the well-trodden path to the South of France.

And in Spain, it wasn't the sunny south coast that initially benefited but the wind-swept north-west corner where visitors began to establish an early tourism 'beat'. And it was here, in Rome and in the Levant that railways aided those thousands who travelled for religious purposes. Pilgrims could more easily reach the magnificent Santiago de Compostela Cathedral, visit iconic Catholic sites in Rome or travel from Jaffa to Jerusalem, while devout Muslims could (eventually) board a train that facilitated their religiously significant trips to Mecca.

Poland, prior to its independence, and Italy both saw their railway systems used by an army of emigrants heading for a new beginning in the US.

All European countries were exercised by the state versus private ownership question. Eventually, most opted for state. France tried to get the best of both worlds by compelling privately run railway companies – who enjoyed profit guarantees from the government – to bend to the state's will. A short-lived, ill-judged and bad-tempered programme it may have been, but the result was, with finance raised by the sale of bonds, the construction of many rural lines that might otherwise never have been built to help more remote communities.

With its own peculiarities, Russia was late to the start line when it came to building railways. But once the country had got up a head of steam, it embarked on a remarkable construction project that would link its wealthy western provinces with the distant Pacific coast, eclipsing the achievements of more advanced railway nations.

# TULA TO ST PETERSBURG

WHEN IT CAME TO LAYING DOWN RAILWAY TRACK, Russia was slow off the mark. There may have been a prevailing sense that the country was a hopeless case, too vast and unpopulated to make train travel viable. However, the Tsar and his government were to learn some stark lessons about its strategic advantages. During the Crimean War, which began in 1853, Sevastopol was besieged by the French and the British, who soon imported a railway line to improve supply lines.

At the time, there were only 700 miles of rail track in the whole of Russia and none of it was in the vicinity of Sevastopol. Its defenders had to rely on a solitary road leading north. Defeat in 1855 escalated the importance of railways for the Russians and, by 1881, they had built 14,000 miles – a figure that continued to rise given that new lines were inevitably long-distance ones.

Without realising it, Tsar Alexander II created a huge number of potential passengers when he ordered that serfs be emancipated in 1861. They would be track layers, too. In one way or another, railways became a significant feature of daily Russian life.

Since their inception, railways have found a role in literature, especially that from Russia. Tolstoy's associations with the railway are well documented here. It also features in Boris Pasternak's 1957 novel *Doctor Zhivago* as a symbol of time and fate. Notably in the story, trains – like relationships – frequently broke down.

Two-thirds of the railways were nationalised by 1914, a move that normally brings greater benefits for poorer people. But that wasn't enough to stop millions of peasants rebelling against the ruling elite, not once but twice in 1917.

# PRIVATE MONEY AND PEASANTRY – THE KEY TO RUSSIA'S NEW RAILWAY

ALTHOUGH IT WAS ON EUROPE'S PERIPHERY, Russia was nothing like its Continental counterparts. Much bigger and flatter than its western neighbours, it was ruled more autocratically. When it came to building railways, its population comprised a tiny percentage of aristocrats, to provide the necessary finance, and a huge proportion of peasants, who would be the industrial muscle.

Those differences were thrown into sharp relief when it came to establishing passenger train services, the first of which ran in 1837.

Before that, Russia relied on its canals and rivers for long-distance transportation. But in the north the freezing weather put paid to this for at least half the year. Even in the south the waterways could be frozen for months rather than weeks; nor were there many roads available to use as an alternative. Civil engineers dealing in roads, canals or rail were confronted with one inescapable truth – that any transport system designed to serve the far-flung corners of the Russian empire was going to be both time consuming and expensive to build.

Nothing daunted, Austrian engineer Franz Anton von Gerstner wrote to Tsar Nicholas I (1796–1855) in 1835 proposing that he, Gerstner, should supply Russia with a railway network. Although the Tsar was anxious to avoid any drain on the state's coffers, he finally gave his approval and plans for the first experimental line with a six foot gauge between St Petersburg and Tsarskoe Selo, the site of a presidential palace, were drawn up.

Russia's aspirations quickly grew from the first line between St Petersburg and Tsarskoe Selo to the monumental undertaking of the Trans-Siberian Express

## Steam versus serfs

With the impetus for railways sorely lacking in Russia, the opportunity for the nation to become a leader in the field was missed. For Russia had its own locomotive pioneers in the shape of father-and-son team Yefim (1774–1842) and Miron (1803–1849) Cherepanov.

Like George Stephenson, they were from poor backgrounds and had a passion for steam engines. From 1829, they built 20 at the factory where they worked in the Urals. Although he was a bonded labourer, Miron even visited Stephenson in Britain to learn more about locomotive technology.

However, his employers at the Demidov factory in the Urals saw no merit in having a railway. Tracks were all well and good, but they believed wagons could be hauled by the numerous serfs they employed rather than a locomotive – even if sometimes those workers had to be helped by a horse.

There being no patents system in Russia, there was little the Cherepanovs could do to capitalise on their work, the role of the Demidov family who effectively owned them notwithstanding. But the 4.5 km (2 mile) railway system with a locomotive that they built, which operated between a Demidov factory and a mine in 1833, was a first in Russia.

ПАРОВОЗ Е.А. и М.Е. ЧЕРЕПАНОВЫХ 1833-34

Gerstner initially struggled to raise funds through a stock company, for the Tsar was adamant that private companies should take the financial risk. He also had to import heavy machinery, as well as rails and rolling stock. But one resource that was available was abundant manpower, and manual workers drawn from villages set to clearing land and building embankments, bridges and stations.

Special care was taken by Gerstner with the tracks, which were made more robust than usual to withstand winter snow.

On 3 November 1836 a locomotive pulled five carriages up and down a completed 5 km (3 mile) section of line. Among the passengers was the royal family. The official opening of the line came a year later, when Gerstner himself piloted a new engine up the 26 km (16 mile) line, which perhaps did not significantly assist trade and industry in the area but silenced a number of critics, most of whom had money tied up in canal projects.

There was plenty
of interest in
railways after
St Petersburg
and Moscow were
linked by rail

# STRAIGHT TO ST PETERSBURG
# WITH AMERICAN KNOW-HOW

IN 1842, AFTER SEVEN YEARS OF DELIBERATIONS, the Department of Railways was established by Nicholas I with a rail link between Moscow and St Petersburg as its task in hand. Late to the table Russia may have been, but it was now embarking on the creation of one of the longest lines in existence at that time. The route, some 647 km (403 miles), was relatively flat, but there were few Russians with sufficient experience to supervise the project. Accordingly, American engineer George Whistler (1800–1849), painter James Whistler's father, was brought in. It's he who is thought to have selected the width of five feet for the gauge before his death from cholera in St Petersburg.

At least Whistler and his successors had plenty of manpower for the project. Although there are no proper records, it is believed 50,000 serfs laboured on the construction of the railway, with one in ten dying of diseases like typhoid and dysentery. Few will have been paid.

For years it was said the route, which was uncommonly straight, was the result of the Tsar using a ruler and pencil on a map after becoming exasperated by lengthy talks about where it should be plotted. A bend at

Novgorod was thought to be where the pencil followed the outline of one of his fingers.

Certainly, there were hold-ups caused by Nicholas I wanting to be involved in the minutiae of the scheme. But it's possible that planners chose the most direct path, tackling swamps and forests where they found them.

Despite a new-found enthusiasm for railways, the Tsar still preferred to spend his money on military hardware. Ultimately, it took nine years to gather the wherewithal to complete the railway, which cost twice as much as initially expected. However, when it was finished it was well used by passengers, with nearly 2,000 people a day making the 22-hour trip, as well as freight, including livestock. (New generation trains that operate between the two cities today complete the journey in just four hours.)

Although the Tsarkoe Selo line was different,

## People's palaces for the metro

An expanded railway system brought a greater population to Moscow, where plans for a metro were discussed as early as 1902 to relieve city centre congestion. In fact, it was 1935 before the first 11 km (7 miles) of underground track was opened, serving 13 stations. And it was the stations that got attention worldwide. Rather than utilitarian hallways and platforms, the Moscow metro was marked by marble, mosaics and granite decor, or sometimes modern iron and glass, but all built on a mighty scale and dubbed 'palaces for the people'.

For 20 years the grand structures continued to be built in considerable style until the extravagance came to an end in the mid-1950s with the slogan 'kilometres at the expense of architecture'. While city commuters might not notice the mirrors and chandeliers that still bedeck some stations, they remain an extraordinary sight for tourists.

Russia afterwards adopted the five foot gauge, probably mindful of a perceived risk of invasion if the standard gauge was used. A programme that would rapidly extend the network now swung into action. Engineer Pavel Melnikov (1804–1880), a chief architect of the Moscow to St Petersburg link, was made Minister of Transportation in 1865.

He'd already published Russia's first book about railway construction, rooted in his observations on a tour of America's railways, and had pioneered new methods of building railway wagons. Thanks to his groundwork, Russia's railway network, a modest 5,000 km (3,000 miles) in 1866, was ten times bigger by the turn of the 20th century.

# TROUBLE ON THE TRANS-SIBERIAN

AS RAILWAY CONSTRUCTION GATHERED MOMENTUM in Russia, the notion of linking the western cities with distant easterly ports came under discussion. In favour of the idea were those who highlighted the rich potential of minerals and agriculture in Siberia. There was a precedent in America, where railway lines had forged into the wilderness and quickly inspired new settlements and the creation of industry. Private companies from Europe also eyed the possibilities with interest.

A busker entertains passengers during the lengthy cross-continent trip

Those against pointed out the distance was nearly 9,300 km (5,750 miles), dwarfing every other known railway scheme. Nor was the climate of Siberia conducive to establishing new towns and cities, while the landscape the line would cut through included desert, tundra, permafrost, mountain and forest.

Still, in 1886 Tsar Alexander III (1845–1894) was persuaded the nation should undertake this task and gave the go-ahead to use funds from the Russian treasury, not least so that the eastern flank of his empire could be better protected.

Three surveying teams went out into the heart of the thinly populated Russian interior in preparation for the first labourers. In 1891, Alexander's son, the future Tsar Nicholas II got construction underway in Vladivostok, Russia's easterly port.

Exiled prisoners and soldiers joined the effort to make up a shortfall in labourers as the project became a matter of national pride. Although they used mostly hand-held tools rather than imported technology, the cost was still a crippling 855 million roubles.

Incredibly, much of the single track line was completed by 1903, with builders achieving a rate of some 600 km (373 miles) a year. Little of the terrain was easy in construction terms, but the region around Lake Baikal – a huge freshwater lake known as 'the blue eye of Siberia'– was exceptionally difficult, and here a ferry was used until a loop around its shores was completed in 1905.

This astonishing speed came at the expense of quality, with lightweight rails laid on unseasoned sleepers, and the track soon needed improvements. Partly because of this, the journey from Europe to the Pacific took a month.

The Trans-Siberian Railway brought about a raft of new problems for Russia: in 1905, Japan, unhappy about encroachment so close to Korea, attacked. Far too confident about the capacity of the new railway, Tsar Nicholas II engaged in hostilities – and lost. There was chaos on the Trans-Siberian line after a revolt by disgruntled soldiers coming home from the conflict saw them hijacking locomotives.

In January 1905 there were problems the other end of the country too, as soldiers turned their guns on a crowd calling for reforms. The event was branded 'Bloody Sunday' and resulted in some short-lived concessions.

This first revolution against the Tsar was successfully suppressed – but it wasn't the last.

## Abdication on the train home

By the spring of 1917 there was widespread dissent in Russia, among soldiers at the front and workers in the factories. After Cossacks refused to fire on demonstrators, it became clear the authority of the Tsar had been terminally undermined.

After discussions with politicians in the Duma, or parliament, the Tsar agreed to abdicate. He signed the necessary papers inside a carriage of his imperial train, parked in sidings at Pskov, on 15 March 1917 as he made his way home from the front line.

The document read: 'Internal popular disturbances threaten to have a disastrous effect on the future conduct of this persistent war. The destiny of Russia, the honour of our heroic army, the welfare of the people and the whole future of our dear fatherland demand that the war should be brought to a victorious conclusion whatever the cost.'

He abdicated in favour of his brother, Grand Duke Mikhail, who had no appetite for the role, and Russia was ruled by a provisional government. The Tsar and his family were held captive at Ekaterinburg as a Bolshevik government usurped the socialist parliament. When a Czech contingent of the White Army approached in July 1918, guards shot the royal family, their doctor, a maid and two waiters.

# DEATH ON THE TRACKS AND THE GENIUS OF TOLSTOY

When Tolstoy died at Astapovo station thousands gathered to mourn the writer, who was seen as a 'father' to the peasants

FOR LEO TOLSTOY (1828–1910), railways provided an inspiration for one of his greatest novels. *Anna Karenina* begins with a railway crash that sets in motion a series of events that cause her previously well-ordered existence to spiral out of control. The novel culminates in the suicide of the main protagonist, under the wheels of a train.

According to his biographer Henri Troyat, Tolstoy was struggling with a planned work on Peter the Great when he recalled an incident the previous year that had made a tremendous impact. A neighbour had begun neglecting his mistress, also called Anna, after becoming beguiled by his children's governess. When Anna discovered his plans to marry the teacher, she ran off carrying a bundle of clothes and wandered the countryside before throwing herself in front of a freight train.

Before her death in 1872 she sent a note to her former lover, telling him: 'You are my murderer. Be happy, if an assassin can be happy.'

A day later, Tolstoy went to Yasenki station, where the tragedy happened, to observe her body while the police investigated. Said Troyat: '[Tolstoy]

tried to imagine the existence of this poor woman who had given all for love, only to meet with such a trite, ugly death.'

A story formed in the writer's head about the frailty and fecklessness of men and the passion, often misguided, found in women. When *Anna Karenina* was published five years later, the writer had begun with the line, 'All happy families are alike; each unhappy family is unhappy in its own way.'

And these were prophetic lines as life began to imitate art for Tolstoy. For years he had been happily married to Sophia, the mother of his ten surviving children. But the couple became increasingly hostile when Tolstoy began contriving his personal philosophies on spirituality, some of which alarmed the more conventional Sophia.

He became convinced she was after his money. She distrusted his 'disciples', who helped perpetuate the new spirituality that put him at odds with the Russian Orthodox Church.

Despite being 82, Tolstoy decided to leave her, slipping away in the night and travelling third class on a train to visit his sister in a nunnery. For ten days Tolstoy's disappearance was the subject of national headlines. When he turned up it was in the stationmaster's house at the remote Astapovo station. That's where he died, succumbing to pneumonia, as his family, journalists and Russian secret police gathered.

It's by no means certain that Tolstoy wholly approved of trains, unlike some in his generation who clearly did. Perhaps curiously, given the circumstances, shortly before his death he said: 'Remember that you're not standing still but moving, that you're not at home but on a train which is carrying you towards death.'

## Reward and punishment aboard Trotsky's train

After the October 1917 revolution by Lenin and his Bolshevik forces, the so-called White Army that opposed them gathered, mostly in the south. In charge of the opposing Red Army, Leon Trotsky (1879–1940) travelled between front lines on an armoured train from 1918 until the war was won. Later, he said: 'The train linked the front with the base, solved urgent problems on the spot, educated, appealed, supplied, rewarded and punished.' Inside, there was a printing press that produced a newspaper, a telegraph, a radio, a library, a garage containing two cars and a bath. Fifteen of the 120 men usually aboard the train – discernible by the black leather gear they wore – died after disappearing in battle. Trotsky remained with the train for more than two years, until the battle against the Whites was won.

# ROME TO TAORMINA

JUST EIGHT YEARS AFTER BRITAIN'S FIRST RAILWAY SERVICE ran between Liverpool and Manchester, trains began rolling on the Italian 'boot'. The first train in modern Italy is credited to a king of one of its former independently run states. Ferdinand II had surely never seen a locomotive in action before, so his motivation for agreeing to the project must have been a mix of curiosity and the notion of leaving something of himself to history.

But after this flying start it was slow going, travelling by rail in Italy. Not all the existing states prioritised railways, nor had the money to do so. Ironically, the one place that undoubtedly did have the finances, Vatican City, finally built a train but never used it.

Then, when the network gradually stretched around southern Italy, it was badly run with an international reputation for slovenliness. Before the 1913 *Bradshaw's Guide* was published that had all changed, thanks to the energies of one far-sighted man, who could envisage the advantages of a timely rail service to rich and poor alike.

By the time of the First World War, the railways of Italy could be divided into two systems: principal lines owned and worked by the state, and secondary lines owned and worked by many independent private companies. The latter acted as feeders for the principal lines and early hitches that beset the juvenile system were finally ironed out.

# THE TRAIN NOW STANDING AT VATICAN CITY

BEFORE IT BECAME CAPITAL OF A UNITED ITALY, Rome had its first railway, opened in 1856 and extending for 20 km (14 miles) to the resort of Frascati. Inevitably, as a capital city and a major centre for tourism since the days of the Grand Tour, undertaken by British luminaries such as John Keats and Percy Shelley, expansion in its network would continue. But it did so only slowly, with a mere three major links established by 1870.

The southern half of Italy was so racked with poverty that even the nation's newly declared king, Victor Emmanuel II, was reluctant to move to Rome in 1871, despite the range of antiquities it had to offer.

But the story of Roman railways is unremarkable compared to the curious case of the Pope's train in neighbouring Vatican City. When Rome joined with other states to form Italy, it earned the enmity of the Pope and that hostility lasted for more than 50 years.

Finally, the Lateran Treaty was signed in 1929, which normalised relationships. Article 6 included the provision of a railway in Vatican City, which had previously been bypassed. The treaty further permitted Vatican railway carriages to travel on Italian railways.

Pope Pius XI was keen to have a station that befitted its significant location and the result was a grandly appointed building some 61 metres (183 ft) wide, lavishly decorated with marble. Inside, there are eight green columns, all obtained from a single block of marble carved from a mountainside, installed for decoration rather than structural purposes. When the Pope saw it, he exclaimed that it was 'the most beautiful station in the world'.

*Although a locomotive puffed in at its opening, the Vatican station was rarely used*

However, he never travelled on the line, or through the sliding iron gates attached to an elegant archway bearing his coat of arms that defined the border of Vatican City, or along the Gelsomino Viaduct built to carry the railway tracks into Rome. Although there was talk of a papal train, none appeared and the tracks remained largely silent.

In fact, the first pontiff to travel on the Vatican railway was Pope John XXIII, who made the journey in 1962, almost 30 years after it opened, using the Italian presidential train. Later, Pope John Paul II travelled on the line twice, but still it remained devoid of railwaymen and rolling stock.

It's been infrequent goods deliveries that enliven it. Thus, the sumptuous station designed for dignitaries was discreetly turned into a goods office.

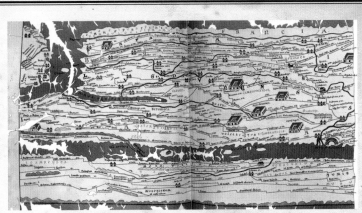

## Did the Romans build rail routes?

Among the legacies left by the ancient Romans was the concept of a straight, broad, paved road. Engineers, surveyors and legions of soldiers built roads in Rome, in Pompeii – later preserved under burning pumice stone when Mount Vesuvius erupted – and all over the empire.

Roman roads brought similar advantages to railways centuries later. They were used for quick progress by the military, for trade, and to aid swift communications. Typically, the roads were raised slightly and solidly built to withstand bad weather.

There's a theory that the builders of Roman roads influenced the construction of railways, as George Stephenson is said to have favoured the standard gauge for its traditional use on the tramways that existed in the era before railways. Those tramways are thought to have been built on old Roman routes, with a width that enabled two chariots to pass. No one knows whether there's truth in such speculation – or whether all horse-drawn carts down the years bore a similar width.

# THE FRENCH CONNECTION BRINGS ITALY'S FIRST RAILWAY

An oil painting captures the thrill and the fear generated by Italy's first train

IN ITALY, IT WAS ONCE AGAIN A KING who ushered in the railway age. Ferdinand II (1810–1859), of the Kingdom of the Two Sicilies, wasn't known as a progressive leader. The year before the railway opened, he became notorious for his violent treatment of Sicilians protesting for greater freedoms.

However, from Naples the new railway came conveniently close to his palace at Portici, so it was a tempting proposition. The line hadn't been his idea. It was the brainchild of French engineer Armand Bayard de la Vingtrie, who offered to build it at his own cost in return for a 99-year lease.

When the lease was reduced to 80 years, agreement was reached and construction began. That involved building 33 bridges, no small undertaking. But on 3 October 1838, two British-built locomotives, the *Bayard* and the *Vesuvio*, hauled carriages containing 258 passengers and covered the 7 km (4½ mile) route in about ten minutes. The king, who gave the go-ahead, chose to travel in the second train after having been convinced by the experimental first journey that no threat was posed by it.

A goodly number of peasants fearfully made the sign of the cross after seeing the engine grunting towards them. Still, 58,000 people a month soon trooped through the three entrance arches of the neoclassical station to travel on the service, proving the business instincts of the French engineer were correct.

After the railway arrived in Naples a foundry was established nearby at Pietrarsa, initially making boilers for locomotives and steamships. In 1843, the king declared the workshop should be used to build and maintain steam locomotives, a facility rarely found on the Italian peninsula at that time.

The following year two British engines, the *Impavido* and the *Aligeri*, were overhauled there. By 1845 manufacture of steam locomotives got underway, albeit using imported parts. A decade later, the plant had 700 employees and no longer depended on components from Britain, building carriages and tracks as well as engines.

This occurred years before the advent of the factories founded by Breda and Fiat – although this vault into industrialisation was a somewhat isolated example, especially in the south where train construction was slow to get going. It was one of only two locomotive manufacturers on the peninsula.

In subsequent decades, the foundry at Pietrarsa had its highs, including employing 1,125 people by 1860, and its low moments as trade fell away after the Second World War. It was finally closed in 1975, after which the site was transformed into the National Railway Museum of Pietrarsa, opened in 1989 to mark the 150th anniversary of Italian railways.

As for Ferdinand, an unexpected hero of the piece, he died two years before Guiseppe Garibaldi entered Naples by train after conquering Sicily, paving a path for the Italian Risorgimento or unification.

## The boat train to Sicily

Since 1899 train passengers heading from mainland Italy to the island of Sicily have been able to remain undisturbed by the ferry crossing. That's because their railway carriages are loaded aboard a ferry for the crossing that takes about 30 minutes. The locomotive remains on firm ground while the carriages are gradually installed in the bowels of the ship, rolling in on rails embedded in the hold. Passengers can remain inside or enjoy the trip across the Strait of Messina from the ship's upper decks.

Traditionally, it's the service used by Sicilians working on mainland Italy to return home, although a decline in passenger numbers has led to cuts in services.

Only twice have train ferries come to grief: once in the First World War after a ship hit a mine and later, in 1943, another was scuttled by the Germans. That ferry was raised after the war and put back into service, and continued to operate until 1991.

Still, it remains one of the primary travel options for visitors to Sicily as plans to build a bridge, mooted since Roman times and recently the subject of costly planning, have come to nothing.

Train ferries like this were once common on the crossing between England and France. One run by Southern Railway from 1936 between Dover and Dunkirk had the receiving ship in a dock where the water level could be adjusted to permit easy loading.

# NATIONALISATION AND BIANCHI'S VISION

THE PACE OF RAILWAY CONSTRUCTION began to quicken after
Italian unification with a curious combination of private enterprise and state
support. Although Britain and America were content for cash from private
companies to fund railway expansion, other European countries including
Italy felt the ruling regime's hand was needed to steer it in the right direction.

Before his death in 1849, Charles Albert, king of Piedmont, summed up
a prevailing feeling in government which continued even after Italy was
unified. 'I am persuaded that I cannot better utilise the ever growing resources
and the flourishing credit of the royal finances than by procuring for the
people … a new and much desired factor in general prosperity.'

Nonetheless, a raft of private companies did spring up in Italy, jumping in when state money was short in 1865.

The state resumed ownership in 1876 until a (second) railways act nine years later which corralled the 10,066 km (6,250 miles) of railways into three major companies: the Mediterranean, the Adriatic and the Sicilian. Each owned its rolling stock, but all of them leased lines from the government to varying degrees. The government reaped an income from this, worked out on a sliding scale. Unfortunately, the equation chosen for this arrangement meant the more money the companies earned, the more they paid.

This compounded the usual problems associated with unmotivated private ownership and rail users were plagued with high fares, slow trains, worn-out carriages, poor punctuality and ill-paid staff. Hope that the companies would invest in new lines came to nothing as none were built.

## A private backlash

The measures taken by Bianchi had an almost immediate effect and were popular among the public. Writing in 1909, economist Filippo Tajani said:

'Everybody in Italy agrees that we shall never return to the operation of railways by companies not even if the government system should prove unprofitable to the public and should give rise to all the difficulties commonly ascribed to government management …

'We have become sceptical of the possibility of framing satisfactory and permanent [private] contracts [and] operation by the state, in the direction which it has taken in the last three years, has become very popular.'

Finally, in 1905 the railways were nationalised under the inspirational leadership of Riccardo Bianchi (1854–1936). Before taking charge of the country's rail network Bianchi had developed safer signalling and worked for both the Mediterranean and Sicilian railway companies. Despite the long-term neglect of the system, Bianchi was determined it would be better able to compete under government stewardship.

With Italy dependent on coal imports, he cut fuel costs by establishing a dedicated office in Cardiff that would find better deals. Locomotive workshops were established so that repairs could be more effectively carried out and he ordered many more tracks and new engines, wagons and carriages after securing a government loan. His presence was so galvanising that in just one year he acquired or had built 567 locomotives, 1,244 coaches and 20,623 freight carriers. Single lines were made into double track to enhance the services available and new links were built.

All this when mountains down the spine of Italy – which had inhibited the construction of east–west links – made the cost of building railways double what it was in the US. Nor were revenues very high, as most freight consisted of agricultural goods rather than high-value minerals. But there was an overriding feeling that southern Italy, mired in poverty, should have access to an efficient and well-priced railway system, for this was crucial to the very survival of the country.

# ROUND VESUVIUS TO POMPEII

A VISIT TO POMPEII was already on every Edwardian visitor's itinerary, given the great store set by classical civilisations at the time. Here was a Roman town frozen in time after being swamped when Mount Vesuvius erupted in AD 79. The site had lain undiscovered until the middle of the 18th century, when artefacts were found and digging unearthed more clues.

Visitors then and now use the Circumvesuviana train to reach the site from Naples. The train which, as its name suggests, skirts the volcano was opened in sections from 1885. One stretch built in 1891 took people to Pompeii, although it's the Sorrento extension, opened in 1932, that's now used for access to the ruins rather than the town station used previously.

This stylish station on the Circumvesuviana, pictured in 1930, was typical of the scenes that greeted overseas visitors making their way to Pompeii

## Sabotage on the funicular

In 1880, a funicular was opened to speed the journey of visitors to the cone of Mount Vesuvius. Although it was conceived by Hungarian tramway owner Ernesto Oblieght, built by Italians and inspired the Neopolitan song 'Funiculi Funicula', it ended up in the hands of British travel agent Thomas Cook just seven years later after lack of money had nearly closed the one kilometre service.

To reverse the fortunes of the funicular, he cut payments to local guides – who responded with sabotage.

It was shut for six months until the issue was resolved in Cook's favour. The firm went on to build an electric railway covering a distance of some 8 km (5 miles) to complement the funicular, with some sections using rack technology to tackle the gradients, which opened in 1903. The following year the holiday company built a 25-bedroom hotel, The Hermitage, where guests would be breathing air that was 'pure and transparent'. Tourists flocked to the area – for a while at least.

In 1906, Vesuvius erupted, smothering the region with volcanic ash and killing scores of people. With its top station destroyed, the funicular had to be rebuilt and opened again in 1910. Although tourists still came they were fewer in number, initially because of the First World War and then as rising nationalism gripped Italy. Thomas Cook was compelled to transfer ownership to a subsidiary company during the 1930s.

There was a further significant eruption in 1944, once again wrecking the funicular. The electric train survived and was sold in 1945 to the company running the Circumvesuviana.

*Bradshaw's* has some stern advice for those visiting. 'Four to five hours are required for even a superficial visit, two or three visits are really necessary and it is hardly worth the trouble entailed to the mere passer-by who has not previously given attention to the subject.'

When the guidebook was published admittance to the site on Thursdays was free as there were no guides available. On other days a fee of two lire 50 cents was charged and it cost a further two lire an hour for an English-speaking guide. 'Persons offering services outside the entrance should be disregarded,' *Bradshaw's* intones.

Uncharacteristically, the guidebook resorts to understatement when it says: 'It is assumed that the labour of clearing will extend to the middle of the 20th century and cost about five million lire.' At the moment final costs are unknown but there is indeed about one-third of the town still to excavate.

# WARSAW TO KRAKÓW

WITH AN ABUNDANT AND INEXPENSIVE SUPPLY of coal to feed industry, Poland proved fertile ground for the growth of a new railway industry. But initially it was not the Polish who would benefit from this, as the region they called their own was split between three empires, all keenly aware of how railways could swell their own coffers.

At least there was ambition to build railways there, for the indisputable economic bonus they would provide. And two of the three empires were persuaded by that argument. Prussia and the Austrian empire were keen to exploit Polish mineral wealth and bring it westwards. For Russia, the prospect of better links with its Polish lands wasn't an entirely attractive one as relationships with its neighbours were historically fractious and didn't look set to improve.

Despite the way the Poles were governed – and many sought the creation of an independent state – railways were welcomed as a way of expressing nationalism. Consequently, the Poles were willing railway builders and they built them well. One tribute to their workmanship is that the Galician Carl Ludwig Railway runs to this day. And the bridge over the old bed of the Vistula river in Kraków, built in 1863, is still used by railways today. The five-span bridge with brick vaults was built for a double track railway line, replacing an old wooden bridge. With numerous working steam engines, there are ready reminders in today's Poland of a proud engineering past.

One unintended consequence of the multitude of lines was how it spurred emigration among the poor. Waves of people huddled together in the dim light of oil lamps for rail journeys that lasted hours, determined to seek a new life in America. Before the advent of the train, the trek over impossibly long distances from Eastern Europe to ports in the west would have been impossible. Americans with Eastern European heritage have now become acquainted with vintage railway networks so that they can decipher the route taken by their ancestors.

A plume of smoke reveals the impending arrival of a steam train at a remote Polish station

# POLAND'S THREE MASTERS OF RAIL

FOR YEARS POLAND WAS A CAMPING GROUND for many of Europe's powerful empires after being partitioned following a series of wars. As the age of the train dawned, its territory was divided between Russia, Prussia and the Austrian empire.

Thanks to Prussian and Austrian keenness for new railways, Poland had plenty of lines heading west when it was granted nationhood at the end of the First World War. To the east, however, the map charting train tracks looked spare.

One of the most industrially vital sites in Poland was Silesia, rich in coal and minerals and under Prussian control since 1748 following the invasion of Frederick the Great. With Prussia's preference for having railways funded privately, a company called the Upper Silesia Railway Society was formed to capitalise on lines in the region.

Accordingly, one of the earliest trains was the link between Breslau (now Wrocław) and Oława, opened on 22 May 1842, pulling out of a station that had been built on the town's execution site. Eight carriages were hauled by a British-built locomotive called *Silesia*.

As the tracks were thought to need continuous supervision a number of staff were employed who lived at gatehouses spaced at every kilometre along the 26 km (15 mile) stretch. An electric bell installed at each one signalled the approach of a train. Later, manning levels were dropped as both trains and rails proved safer than first anticipated.

With the Austrians building two lines from Vienna into their own Polish territory, the competitive Upper Silesia Railway Society began to extend its services out of Breslau, eventually to reach Berlin. Numerous other lines were opened in short order until it became the largest railway company in Prussia.

In tandem with this, industry romped ahead. In 1850, the steelworks in Upper Silesia made half of everything used in Prussia, while a decade later the zinc mills were the largest producers of that metal in the world.

Prussia was engineering a leading position in Europe, aiming to eclipse the Austrian empire in power and strength.

But with the monumental number of railway-building projects – 50 companies were looking after 63 networks in Prussia by 1876 – there was a sense of administrative chaos. A directorate was finally formed to assume better control over the system. Later, a railway act in 1892 gave the green light for construction of narrow gauge lines in Poland over short distances and difficult terrain.

Russia and Austria co-operated to link Warsaw and Vienna by rail in a long-running project that finally opened in 1848. (Austria insisted it was made with a standard gauge track despite the Russian preferences for broad gauge.) The first section from Warsaw opened in 1845 with a parade of ten steam locomotives decorated with flowers, and 200 passengers in 15 carriages were joined by a military band. When the track was complete, it took 37 hours to travel between the imperial capital of Vienna and Russian-held Warsaw.

## Independence and a disparate network

Five years after *Bradshaw's* was published, the devastating First World War was over and Poland was on its way to becoming an independent nation.

Its railways had been built by former empires, all of them now vanished. Part of the legacy of that for Poland was a disparate rail network. Two of the empires, Prussia and Austria, used the standard gauge while Russia had chosen a broad gauge. So it would not be possible to use all the lines as they stood.

The layout of railways was curiously disjointed as far as the new Poland was concerned, with Warsaw being under-served and links to the Baltic difficult. Moreover, many of its existing railways were now international lines.

For Germany, the existence of Poland threatened its railway access to countries beyond, which became another reason to want rid of the fledgling nation just 20 years later.

# DESTINATION AMERICA ON A THIRD-CLASS TICKET

IN THE LANDS CONTROLLED BY AUSTRIA known as Galicia (not to be confused with the region of north-west Spain) a significant network came into being. Not only did it underpin Polish nationalism but it also served as a carrier of emigrants out of the region, en route to America.

From the first train that steamed out of Kraków station in 1858 there was relentless expansion, especially during the 1880s, despite the difficult terrain of the Carpathian Mountains. In 1871, 587 km (365 miles) of track had been completed. By 1887 the figure was 848 km (527 miles) – and counting.

Although the number of locomotives remained at around 130 – most of which were named for stations on the route – rolling stock increased rapidly to cater for an ever growing number of passengers. Numbers soared from a healthy 271,000 passengers in 1860 to a record 1.5 million people just 30 years later. Of those, just a tiny percentage travelled in first class, where there were red plush seats. About a sixth used second class, with seats covered in dark leather, while the vast majority, as many as four-fifths, sat on wooden benches in third class.

At first the aim was to connect Kraków and Lvov (now Lviv, in Ukraine), the two major cities in the region. That line

Graceful arches and glittering chandeliers are the hallmarks of Kraków's station, a stopping point on many long-distance routes across Eastern Europe

was finished by 1861. (A planned link to Pilzno was scrapped when the town council protested that the 'iron monster' would scare the animals so grievously that cows would stop producing milk.) Eventually, distances were so vast that, by the time it was finished, one section stretched from present-day Slovakia to what's now the Ukraine, which in itself measured 800 km (497 miles).

Until 1892 those railways were run by a private company, most commonly referred to as Galician Carl Ludwig Railway. It had a series of customs: that the ticket had to be purchased two hours before the train's

## Poles by any other name

No one knows just how many people emigrated to America from Polish lands because on arrival they were registered as Russian, Austrian or German. But one figure indicates that 3.6 million people left between 1870 and 1914. Apart from a perpetual lack of food and home comforts, there was virtually no education available in Galicia at the turn of the 20th century, inspiring parents to go for the sake of their children.

When serfdom was abandoned in Russia in 1861 more people than previously were able to move freely. Jewish people left after a wave of pogroms while Catholic nationalists also departed in droves. They caught trains to western European ports like Bremen, from where they would board a ship, usually travelling uncomfortably in steerage. Some left with the intention of saving a nest egg, to return to their homes in the future. The rate of emigration slowed after the First World War when Poland was created.

departure, that a gong sounded three times before it left the station and that the conductor would lock the doors on the sound of the third gong.

Significantly, the man who steered the railway to its initial success, Leon Sapieha (1803–1878), did so hoping it would aid Polish nationalism. It would be decades after his death that this dream was realised, but at least Sapieha's work ensured a generation of engineers and railway workers were established. It was these men who helped install small stations and branch lines at remote outposts. In doing so, they liberated thousands from a life of toil and hardship when the railways transported them on the first leg of an emigration journey.

The 100-year-old turntable at Wolsztyn helps to display vintage steam locomotives to visitors during special events

# LIVING THE STEAM IN WOLSZTYN

UNUSUALLY, THERE'S ONE RAILWAY STATION in Poland that would both look and smell familiar to the travellers of Bradshaw's day. Wolsztyn is home to some 30 steam locomotives, some of which still regularly grace the track to haul commuter trains.

Steam trains are a rarity on the Polish rail system today. But rather than confine those working engines that remain to a heritage track, they are put to use on scheduled services alongside more numerous electric trains. They operate from Wolsztyn on about 160 km (100 miles) of track, pulling freight as well as conveying passengers.

Poland had particular reasons for holding fast to its vintage steam engines, as there's abundant coal to power them. Although Wolsztyn remained a major, modern railway junction, it nevertheless retained an eight-stand roundhouse with a turntable, built in 1908, throughout its modernisation. The water tower is even older, dating from 1907, and there's other servicing equipment accrued during the age of steam.

As for the dozen working locomotives, the oldest was built in 1917. There's a German-built engine made in 1929 and a 1937 model from the first Polish steam locomotive factory at Chrzanów in the south of the country. For visitors, there are other models to see that don't now go on the rails, including a Prussian snowplough from 1883, a rail workshop hand-operated crane from 1913 and a freight wagon from 1911.

If passengers are disappointed to find the vintage engines are hauling more modern carriages, well, there's no need to be. There was little that was comfortable or even attractive about authentic Polish railway carriages of the era, as workers at the station – many of them British – are quick to point out.

When steam trains and their lurching carriages used to visit Łódź, it was to serve an industrial town with a booming cotton industry. The effect of the industrial

## Changing track in Polish politics

The running of the railways in Galicia became something of a family concern, in which loyalty to the business of trains trumped any political passions. Ludwik Wierzbicki (1834–1912) came from a family known for its agitation against the authorities. Nonetheless, he joined the Galician Carl Ludwig Railway in 1860, eventually entering its higher management after it was taken over by the state, to become the Imperial and Royal State Railways. Apart from his railway work, he was associated with the People's Railway School in Lvov, and with orphanage and summer camps run for the children of railwaymen.

His son-in-law Vladimir Zborowski (1860–1928) also worked for the railway and made an equally rapid ascent up its management ranks. During the First World War he was given honours by Kaiser Wilhelm II and Emperor Franz Josef for keeping the railways running.

As the war was ending, Polish rail workers rebelled and it seemed Zborowski, perceived as a patsy of the hated imperialists, had lost his job. But when the new state of Poland was created he was appointed the first president of the Polish Directorate of Railways in Kraków, despite his years of service to the former, unpopular regime.

revolution there had been to transform a town with 800 residents to one with more than 400,000 people in the 80 years leading up to the publication of *Bradshaw's*. Its industrial workers, comprising Poles, Germans, Russians and Jews, lived in squalid conditions, while the wealthy who owned factories and the like charged people before they could set foot in privately owned green parks. However, a cinema was built for workers and silent films, made from the end of the 19th century until about 1920 when talkies took over, could be enjoyed by everyone. Thus, a cinematic tradition was spawned in the most unlikely industrial backyard. And after manufacturing dwindled in the 1950s Łódź became the home of Poland's premier film school, internationally recognised for its output. Ruling Communists had intended it to be for the purposes of making propaganda. In fact, teachers and pupils watched western films barred from the rest of the population.

# DEATH TRAINS TO AUSCHWITZ

The key part played by railways in ferrying men, women and children from across Europe to their deaths at Auschwitz was overlooked for decades

IN A HISTORY FASHIONED FOR ALMOST 200 YEARS, trains have been known for propelling technology forward and spreading wealth, ideas and equality. There is, however, a dark episode in the stories of railways and that is an indelible association with the Holocaust.

Even in Bradshaw's day anti-Semitism was rife in Eastern Europe. When the Nazis took power in Germany, it was nurtured and shaped into something entirely acceptable and even expected. Like many governmental organisations, the Deutsche Reichsbahn barred Jews from getting jobs from 1933.

Five years later, after the organised violence directed at Jews during *Kristallnacht* – night of broken glass – a series of trains were organised to carry Jewish children out of Germany and occupied territories, including Austria and Czechoslovakia. The trains, which headed to northern European ports so that the children could get to Britain by ship, carried an estimated 10,000 children, three-quarters of whom were Jewish.

Later, the role of the railways became far more sinister. By 1942 the Nazi High Command had agreed to the so-called 'Final Solution', the wholesale destruction of the Jews of Europe. Concentration camps – a feature of life under the Nazi regime for years – morphed into extermination camps, where Jews and other so-called 'undesirables' would be killed on an industrial scale.

Railways were needed to bring those rounded up in France, Holland, Poland, Hungary, Czechoslovakia, Belgium and Soviet Russia to meet their deaths in the gas chambers. In March 1942, the first transport train arrived at Auschwitz.

Deutsche Reichsbahn wasn't the only railway company involved. The newly nationalised French railways helped, as did the state railways in Hungary. It's not known how much train drivers knew about their grim task. The Germans prided themselves on maintaining the utmost secrecy about their murderous intent, to facilitate a trouble-free train journey among the passengers.

However, the drivers must have been aware that passengers were being carried in wagons usually meant for animals, with only buckets provided for sanitation. Food and water were never distributed during trips that could last up to four days. Sometimes there was quicklime on the wagon floor, which burned the feet of those crammed inside.

It is known that the railway company was paid for any inbound journey to camps like Auschwitz – and sometimes for the return trip when the wagons carried stolen possessions as freight.

At Auschwitz, the train pulled up outside the entrance, next to a ramp where passengers were unceremoniously unloaded and selected for instant death or for work parties. Four out of five people were killed immediately. When Hungary was occupied, the tracks were laid inside the gates so more people could be processed.

The grim role of the train companies who capitalised on this continuing atrocity and their staff wasn't scrutinised until plans to demolish part of Berlin's Grunewald station were drawn up in 1998. As thousands had been dispatched to their deaths from there, the plans sparked widespread protests.

## Resistance and a great escape

Out of all the trains heading to Auschwitz and other camps, only one was attacked and some passengers liberated. Three young members of the Belgian Resistance armed with one pistol between them made the audacious move against a train carrying 1,631 Jews under armed guard in April 1943.

The trio used red paper to mask a lantern and imitate a danger signal, causing the driver to brake sharply. With the train at a stop, the young men used pliers to cut wire holding the wagon bolts in place. Some quick-witted deportees dashed into the night, under fire from the German guards. But the incident changed the mood among the rest and they battered the wagon doors down as the train got underway again.

Simon Gronowski, 11, was dangled and then dropped from the moving train by his mother. Despite the perils, he then approached a local policeman who helped return him to Brussels where his father Leon was in hospital. Both were hidden for the rest of the war, but his mother Chana and 18-year-old sister Ita were killed at Auschwitz.

That night, 118 people, including Simon, got away. Just 153 others survived Auschwitz.

# LA CORUÑA TO LISBON

STEAM LOCOMOTIVES HAVE OFTEN BEEN DUBBED the gift the British gave to the world. As the first country to embrace the potential, Britain was for a while the well of expertise that aspiring railway nations drew upon.

Spain wasn't the only country to welcome droves of British engineers, who arrived with a missionary zeal about their work and reaped handsome rewards. But many came to Spain and stayed – something that would not surprise the thousands of tourists who have visited the country in the intervening years.

Before the British could easily reach the far warmer south of Spain – where railways tended to be slow and used for industrial purposes – they contented themselves with its north-west corner, comparatively simple to reach by cruise liner or, later, by train via France.

There was a sense of shared heritage, with Galicia and Britain both enjoying Celtic traditions manifesting themselves in dance and music among other things. Even the weather was often similar, with storms regularly rounding Cape Finisterre, usually in the autumn but sometimes in the summer as well.

Beyond Spain lay Portugal, culturally distinct from its bigger brother on the Iberian Peninsula and another favourite destination. Portugal was – and is – Britain's oldest ally, a relationship rooted in the mutual co-operation exhibited in the Crusades against the Moors. The Anglo-Portuguese Alliance dating from 1386 has been invoked on many occasions and it was this centuries-old link that brought Portuguese soldiers to fight in the trenches of the First World War. Both countries enjoyed golden eras with conquest and colonies and historically they shared a distrust of Spain.

Britain was also Portugal's biggest market for its signature drink, port. After the railways were installed, the French drank it in greater amounts even than the British.

Yet the 'gift' from Britain in the form of the railway didn't lift Portugal out of poverty. It only increased a debt burden. Without meaning to, the arrival of trains shattered the status quo there, as those who were impaired by the country's economy sought redress.

# GALICIA AND THE BRITISH STEAM PIONEERS

WITH SPAIN SOMETHING OF A BLANK CANVAS as far as trains were concerned, it's not surprising that British engineers cropped up there to cash in. However, their history was not always a happy one. George Mould, manager of the Lancaster to Carlisle line and contractor for the Derbyshire, Worcester and Staffordshire Railway, was also in charge of the line from Santander to Madrid from 1852.

But the opening six years later was marred by tragedy after an embankment subsided and the official train ran off the tracks. At least one

Despite their presence, there was nothing in the design of the station in Bilbao serving the Santander line that gave a nod to the British

man was killed. James Livesey – who went on to become a wealthy engineer, building railways in South America and Australia – was trapped under the locomotive for an hour, while George and his son John Stephenson Mould escaped with cuts and bruises along with general manager Don Philip Sewell.

John Stephenson Mould went on to work on the railway that was to link Santiago with Pontevedra, a project beset by financial problems from its inception in 1861 until it received a government subsidy in 1873. Livesey was the consultant engineer. When it finally opened, the service was indisputably popular. In just a month in 1873, it carried 2,695 first-class passengers, 3,241 second-class passengers and 22,248 third-class passengers. The figures give some clue to the way Galician society was comprised at the time and the way railways eased the lives of poorer people whose other options were cart, mule or walking.

But the best remembered of the English engineers in the region was John Trulock (1856–1919), who became managing director of the West Galician Railway for some 40 years. Details of the early life of London-born Trulock are sketchy, although at the age of 14 he was apparently a warehouseman in an umbrella factory in Holborn.

But he joined the Spanish railway in its early years and was manager by 1883. Under his leadership the line became profitable. According to one of his descendants, Javier Losada Boedo, he sought punctuality on the service, which ran four trains a day each way, believing it a virtue, but was often frustrated by the lax timekeeping of the locals who worked for him. He made his home in north-west Spain while appearing every inch an English Edwardian gentleman in his dress code, whatever the weather.

Trulock is also remembered in Spain as the grandfather of Nobel Prize-winning writer Camilo José Cela. George Mould died in Galicia in 1874, while his son John is buried in Madrid.

According to *Bradshaw's*, the trip between Santiago and Pontevedre took two hours and 40 minutes. The equivalent trip today can take as little as 40 minutes.

## Santander's soap solution

James Livesey (1831–1925) got his first civil engineering job on the Santander line. In a memoir, he recalled: 'The first difficulty I had to deal with was the supply of water for the locomotive shops, the only available one being the overflow from the tanks of the public wash house, which consisted mostly of soap suds. Fortunately the land from the overflow stream to the shops was on the down grade; this enabled me to arrange a number of filter tanks filled with coke. After passing through half a dozen of these tanks the water was sufficiently clear for use but not for drinking purposes. That had to be fetched from a distance.'

Livesey's first son, Fernando Harry Whitehead Livesey, was born in Santander in 1860. Harry, as he was known, went on to be made an OBE in 1918 and a Knight Grand Cross of the Order of the British Empire in 1920.

# THE SAINTS EXPRESS TO SANTIAGO

TODAY, SANTIAGO IS BEST KNOWN for the stream of pilgrims who spend days, weeks or months wending their way up a series of long caminos, or paths, to this north-westerly point. Their goal is the 13th-century cathedral in the city which is thought to be the final burial place of St James, the patron saint of Spain, who preached on the Iberian Peninsula before being the first apostle to be martyred in the Holy Land.

In the Middle Ages, it was a popular pilgrimage for the Catholic devout. However, a series of wars and the presence of occupying Moors helped put paid to the practice. It was revived in the 20th century and one of the paths is called 'the English route' for its popularity among those who arrived by liner in La Coruña or El Ferrol.

If it was habitual for travellers to walk the walk by 1913 then *Bradshaw's* makes no mention of it, although the entry for Santiago waxes lyrical about the cathedral as 'the most important example of early Romanesque architecture in Spain' and 'one of the greatest glories of Christian art'.

Pilgrims basking in their achievement after a long walk on the 'camino' to Santiago

However, it's known that Galicia did enjoy a boom in Edwardian tourism thanks to Spanish businessmen and British steamship operators, who believed its Celtic heritage would harbour a special appeal. Ships run by Liverpool-based Alfred Booth (1872–1948) came into Vigo and visitors were then driven to an inland spa town or went north on the West Galician Railway to Santiago. Perhaps curiously, the trip would end with a visit to one of the sardine canneries that were typically found in Vigo.

In *Bradshaw's* 1913 guide there's an advertisement for Booth Line's Royal Mail Steamer to Vigo at a cost of £6.10s. from London for a single ticket. (According to the advertisement, the ships were fitted with Marconi Wireless Telegraphy and carried a doctor, nurse, stewardesses and musicians.)

## Queen Isabella and the Aranjuez line

In 1851, when Spain's first major railway line was opened between Madrid and Aranjuez, Queen Isabella II (1830–1904) was on the throne. Although her reign was problematic, and she was only kept in power by the army, she also presided over the opening of the first narrow gauge railway in Spain in 1852, the line that reached the Portuguese border 11 years later and the one that headed north-east to France. Spain became a republic in 1868, while the royals withdrew to Paris, presumably by means of the newly opened network. But it was a short-lived republic, with the royal family returned to the throne within a few years. By the time the Madrid to La Coruña line was belatedly finished in 1883, Isabella's son was on the throne as King Alfonso XII.

Other visitors hitched a ride to Spain with liners heading for South America, which docked in the northern Spanish ports. A popular landmark for tourists in La Coruña was the tomb of Sir John Moore (1761–1809), felled in the battle there during the Peninsular War as he fought a rearguard action against the French which allowed the bulk of his army to escape by sea. His French counterpart, Marshal Soult, was so impressed by the display of gallantry that he ordered a monument to be erected for the Englishman.

The popularity of Galicia among Edwardian trippers was short-lived, due to its dependency on ocean travel. Those who weren't put off by the sinking of the *Titanic* in 1912 were soon prevented from taking a voyage by the outbreak of the First World War.

A German-built locomotive snorts steam as it winds along the Douro valley

# THE DOURO LINE FAILS TO DELIVER

IT TOOK A DOZEN YEARS TO BUILD the Linha do Douro, running from the Spanish border in the north to Porto on the Portuguese coast. Today, most people who ride on the train which hugs the Douro river and needs 30 bridges and 20 tunnels to complete the journey would agree it was time – and money – well spent.

When the 160 km (100 mile) track opened in 1887 the journey from Pocinho to Porto was slashed from a mighty 12 days to just five hours. Yet the line was not the hoped-for panacea for the nation's problems. With its agrarian economy and lack of regular railway users, Portugal was financially penalised by the introduction of trains rather than reaping an anticipated economic harvest.

Certainly, it gave wine producers in the Douro valley a safe route for delivering produce to Porto. Until then, the only option had been the River Douro, which had a selection of natural hazards. However, improvements to the river's passage had already made life much easier for vineyards and that remained the favoured route for many.

A waterfall midway along the river had once blocked the steep-sided gorge. But from 1789 vessels could pass through it unhindered after the obstacle was dismantled. That gave greater access than ever before to vineyards further up the Douro valley – although they still had to negotiate river rapids that were capable of wrecking a boat loaded with barrels. But there were more enhancements to come in the 20th century – despite the arrival of the railway – when the river was dammed to make the waters calmer still.

Flat-bottomed boats with a long steering oar called *barcos rabelos* were used, under the skilled guidance of boatmen who navigated their tricky course from a raised platform. To return upstream, they used their broad sail or would be hauled by teams of oxen. Their capacity was limited by 1779 legislation to 70 casks.

## A question of gauge

Portugal's first railway line ran between Lisbon and Carregado from 28 October 1856. The network spread, mostly in the south where engineering work was easier.

Apart from its wide gauge tracks, Portugal also had a small network of narrow gauges that were particularly suitable for the steep hills and deep gorges of the north. When the Linha do Vouga opened with some ceremony in 1908, it wasn't the first to go into operation. But it has turned out to be the last one left running – and its future is uncertain.

In the 1930s, there were apparently still about 300 boats making regular journeys up the Douro. After that, road transport began to eclipse both boat and train. The last commercial voyage by a *barco rabelo* took place in the early 1960s.

Today modern dams have been put in place on the 900 km (560 mile) long river that would thwart the return of the *barcos rabelos*. Eight of the dams are under Portuguese jurisdiction and the remainder are Spanish. The dams both regulate the water flow and generate hydroelectricity. However, the river is still passable, thanks to a lock system, enabling popular river trips to Porto to take place. Aboard, tourists admire the trains as they weave down the valley, while railway passengers strain to catch a glimpse of the boats. A microclimate that pervades the area makes the cultivation of almonds and olives popular, too.

Wisely, the Portuguese railway builders concurred with the Spanish gauge – there was a nominal 9 mm (just under ½ in) difference between them – so there was no difficulty at the frontier. The line initially extended as far as Salamanca in Spain. But there were still a lot of overheads to meet in a country with a small population that was strapped for cash.

# A BEAUTIFUL BUT TROUBLED LAND

WITH PRIVATE RAILWAY COMPANIES STRUGGLING to stay solvent, Portuguese state railways was created in 1899. Along with other public works, railways required regular investment. This came at a time when the country's empire was in decline, leaving Portugal paupered by its financial obligations.

Nor was there a political solution waiting in the wings. As an antidote to alleged government corruption and the ensuing public unrest, King Carlos I (1863–1908) had installed a right-wing government that duly clamped down on dissidents.

It's doubtful that Britain's King Edward VII realised how poverty was paralysing Portugal when he visited in 1903, or if he spotted a brooding resentment among its people. However, five years later tensions erupted. The royal family were gunned down after having arrived in Lisbon by train, when they took an open carriage to their palace. King Carlos I was killed alongside his son and heir, Luís Filipe. Although there were many monarchists in Portugal, there was a marked indifference to the plight of the royal family. According to King Edward VII, the king and his son were murdered 'like dogs – and in their own country no one cares'. A second son, Manuel, who had been injured that day, became king but was finally ousted in 1910 during a republican revolution.

Before his assassination King Carlos I, wearing a military uniform and medals, wasn't popular among his people

By the time *Bradshaw's* guide was written, the signs of a faltering economy were starkly apparent. The book is effusive about the attractive landscapes of Portugal. 'At its best the country presents a charming variety of natural beauty; inland are mountain and valley, along the rugged coast are bold headlands of bare rock and stretches of huge sand downs broken into marsh and lagoon.'

But it warns there are whole districts where the land has been allowed to

## Labour of love at São Bento station

Some long-term projects were unfolding in Portugal, despite the difficulties. King Carlos I had laid the first stone of the São Bento station in Porto in 1900. By the time work was completed in 1916 in the French Beaux Arts style, he had been assassinated and his surviving son was living in exile in Britain. Constructed on the site of a dilapidated Benedictine monastery, it's remarkable for its artwork.

The walls in the hallway are covered, floor to ceiling, with 20,000 azulejos, or tiles, hand painted in blue and white, celebrating critical moments in Portugal's history. They were the exquisite handiwork of painter Jorge Colaço (1868–1942), born in Tangier, Morocco, the son of a Portuguese diplomat. The station is not the sole surviving work of this nature he produced in Porto. The facade of the Church of Saint Ildefonso is similarly decorated and examples of his craft survive in Lisbon as well.

'fall out' of cultivation and become poor pasture. 'In the large towns are good hotels; minor hotels should be avoided, they are generally dirty and otherwise unsatisfactory.'

While the British sovereign was legal currency, a new monetary unit, the escudo, was evidently struggling. According to *Bradshaw's*, it was mostly paper money in circulation. 'Gold has almost disappeared and even silver coins are scarce.'

# HAIFA TO THE NEGEV DESERT

IF IT WERE NOT FOR THE FIRST WORLD WAR, it's doubtful anyone outside the Muslim world would have known about the existence of the Hejaz Railway. It sidles through some of the most unpromising scenery towards two cities, Medina and Mecca, which bear huge importance for Islam and from where Westerners are entirely or partially banned.

However, as the war unfolded an Englishman later dubbed 'Lawrence of Arabia' made his home among the Bedouin tribesmen of the region as a guerrilla war was waged against the controlling Turkish troops. His adventurous exploits captured the public's imagination and his tactical brilliance was universally praised. Furthermore, his obvious regard for the Arabs he fought alongside contrasted sharply with the usual colonial attitude that prevailed at home, that the peoples of occupied territories were unequal to an Englishman.

Another railway was far better known, the one that took pilgrims from the port of Jaffa to the holy city of Jerusalem. Without proper docking facilities, the traveller who arrived at Jaffa in Bradshaw's time had to slither from a big ship into a small craft to make land.

There were two other significant differences from the modern city. *Bradshaw's* describes Jerusalem like this: 'The aspect of the city is depressing; the uneven streets are narrow, ill paved and dirty, rubbish and decay are everywhere. The sites sanctified by association are obscured by tawdry surroundings.'

That's a world away from one of today's biggest tourist cities. Also, those who went before the First World War would find little evidence of antipathy between the great faiths. That was seeded by the British when the First World War came to an end.

# CONQUERING THE DESERT – THE HEJAZ RAILWAY

Le grand pont de aman sur la ligne de Hydjaz

The Hejaz Railway, with a train crossing a bridge at Amman in Jordan

AFTER THE EUROPEAN ARM OF HIS EMPIRE disintegrated, the ruler of the Ottomans wanted to build a prestigious railway that would help him shore up his tottering regime in the Arab territories that remained under his control.

The 1,778 km (1,105 mile) route chosen by Abdul Hamid II (1842–1918) was from Damascus to Medina, which is the burial place of the Islamic prophet Muhammad. The first mosque in the world, built by Muhammad, is also here, although the original was destroyed by lightning long ago. With Medina deemed the second most holy city in Islam after Mecca, only the city outskirts are open to non-Muslims.

But the practical problems were immense. The railway would have to be built in relentless heat through barren desert comprising volcanic rock and windswept sand. Early European railway builders may have had a catalogue of difficulties but a chronic lack of water wasn't among them. Here there was precious little either to refresh the navvies building the railways or for the construction process – although when the rains occasionally arrived they turned sandy river beds into raging torrents. The provision of water for drinking, cooking and mixing mortar remained a problem throughout.

Money was another issue, with the Ottoman empire left struggling to pay a mammoth reparations bill to the Russians imposed in 1878. But, keen for the project to be an Islamic enterprise, Abdul Hamid didn't want foreign and rival empires to play a part, so he looked to Muslims for financial backing. As caliph, or leader, of all Muslims his call for cash resonated.

There was unlikely to be any industrial premium from the railway to pay back loans, although the railway would transform the trip for Muslims taking the religion's obligatory hajj pilgrimage as the journey from Damascus previously took 40 days. Moreover, the railway benefited from tracing the flat and direct route that had been carved out by pilgrims over centuries.

Construction began on 1 September 1900, the 24th anniversary of Abdul Hamid's succession. A gauge of 1.05 metres (41 in) was chosen so that it was compatible with an already existing line run by the French, and engineers decided to put the line on an embankment to mitigate the dangers of occasional flooding.

Every successive year, a ceremony was held on that same date to open the sections of line built in between times, with those completed sections quickly up and running to bring in revenue. By 1906, 30 locomotives were using completed lines.

> ## Blame the coal and driver
>
> In 1905, Lt Col F. Maunsell, who was British military attaché in Constantinople, issued a report after making a journey on the Hejaz Railway once the line had been constructed as far as Ma'an.
>
> 'The [Turkish] naval sub-lieutenant who drove our train down to Ma'an was an excellent fellow but perhaps he knew more of the sea than of engine driving as, owing partly to his inexperience and partly to the tubes becoming choked by the inferior Turkish coal used, the steam gave out when we arrived in the desert, some 20 miles from Ma'an.'
>
> Unable to raise sufficient pressure to get underway once more, the train and its passengers had to wait until a rescue locomotive was dispatched.

German Heinrich Meissner (1862–1940) was put in charge after a series of inexperienced Turkish engineers were dismissed. The services of foreign workers were also eventually brought in to replace Ottoman army conscripts.

However, working conditions remained primitive, with poorly fed men living in small tents. Without fundamental human comforts, those navvies would be subject to diseases including cholera and typhoid. To keep his workforce motivated, Meissner introduced cash incentives to boost morale, but only the introduction of medical services much later enhanced general health.

In his book about the Hejaz Railway James Nicholson observes: 'Although for political reasons the line was never extended to Mecca the achievement of reaching Medina, deep within the Hejaz, was enough to confound the sceptics who had misjudged the strength of Ottoman resolve and underestimated the will of the frail but determined Sultan.'

While branch lines came later – like the one to Haifa, begun in 1903 to give access to the sea – the main line to Medina was finally opened in 1908, with the official ceremony culminating in the laying of a foundation stone for what was proposed as the Hamida mosque. A year later, Abdul Hamid was deposed and the new building project, intended like the railway line to immortalise him, became known as the Al Anbariya mosque.

The Suez Canal
depicted in 1869,
the year it was
completed

# BRITISH SPIES AND THE
# DOOMED AQABA RAILWAY

WITH BRITAIN POISED TO GO TO WAR with Germany in 1914,
there were some colonial concerns to be addressed. What, for example, would
happen to the Suez Canal, the waterway that linked the Mediterranean to the
Red Sea, which was opened in 1869? Built by the French, the British were
initially aloof about the project. But in 1875 the Egyptians sought a necessary
cash injection by selling their shares in it and Britain came forward as the
buyer. The French remained the major shareholders.

   Not only did the Suez Canal offer a short cut for the maritime journey to
India, but it also made it quicker to reach the Persian Gulf at a time when oil
was assuming greater significance than ever before. The relationship between
Britain and the Ottoman empire had been tested in 1906 when there were
plans to extend a branch line of the Hejaz Railway to Aqaba in the north-
east – too close to Egypt and the Suez Canal as far as Britain was concerned.

Ultimately, plans for the line were scrapped.

Now Britain didn't know if the ailing Ottoman empire would stay neutral in the event of a war. Certainly, the nation had an undeniably close relationship with Germany. If the Turks did turn out to be enemies, would Britain and France be able to defend the Suez Canal?

To find out, a mapping team was sent to discover more about the desert on the Arab peninsula that bordered the Red Sea. It was done in cahoots with the Palestine Exploration Fund, set up in 1865 to investigate biblical archaeology but prone to collaborations with the Royal Engineers and the War Office, especially in the years leading up to the First World War.

As early as 1870 the PEF quarterly review noted that an expedition by Captain Charles Warren, quite apart from its archaeological merit, was 'a very important reconnaissance of central Jordan'. Among the team this time was Thomas Edward Lawrence (1888–1935). No stranger to the region, Lawrence visited in 1911 as a young archaeologist, travelling on the Hejaz Railway between Haifa and Damascus on his way to a dig at one of the ancient cities.

He gained a working knowledge of Arabic, and a love of the people and the place that led him to request the later

## Carve-up in the Middle East

During the First World War, Britain made pledges to co-operative Arab states, implying they would receive independence after victory was achieved. At the same time, however, Britain, France and Russia agreed to have 'spheres of influence' in the Middle East.

This contradiction in terms was further complicated when, on 2 November 1917, foreign secretary Arthur Balfour declared the British government's support of a Jewish homeland in Palestine – albeit stressing the civil and religious rights of existing non-Jewish communities there

It would be impossible for Britain to fulfil all those obligations. At the defeat of the Ottomans, the British and the French carved up the area on a colonial basis, creating countries that only in the future would be known as Syria, Israel and Lebanon.

posting there. Afterwards, he always credited Prince Faisal of the Hashemites, later the king of Syria and Iraq, whom he met in 1916, with giving him a prominent role in the rebellion.

As it happened, the Ottoman empire had secretly agreed to back Germany and became directly involved in the war in October 1914. In February 1915, an army of 15,000 Ottoman and German troops attacked Suez, but it was by now suitably defended and they were duly repelled.

# LAWRENCE OF ARABIA AND SABOTAGE ON THE HEJAZ

In Bedouin garb, Lawrence carried out guerrilla attacks on trains and track

WITH THE OUTBREAK OF WAR, years of simmering unrest throughout the Ottoman empire – fuelled by several years of political instability – finally erupted. At the heart of the conflict was the Hejaz Railway, a seam through the landscape built strategically out of range of any British warships parked in the Mediterranean Sea.

Thanks to the railway, Ottoman troops were initially well supplied as they struggled to suppress rebellious tribes allied to the British cause in the Middle Eastern desert. Disruption and destruction on the railway became pivotal to the success of what became known as the Arab Uprising.

Momentum changed over two years, as tribes continually shifted their allegiance. Bedouins, with little use for the railway, had always feared 'the iron donkey' would encroach as far as Mecca and deprive them of income gained until now from hiring out camel caravans. They also suspected it was built entirely so that the Turks could maintain a better grip on the region.

Thus, when it came to launching attacks on the railway to hobble the Ottoman army they were generally receptive to the idea. Uncharacteristically, they agreed to assistance from the British – who had established a Red Sea base – which famously came in the shape of Lawrence. By his own admission, Lawrence wasn't the only foreign fighter whose contribution counted. Bimbashi (Major) Herbert Garland, of the Egyptian army, blew up a troop train in February 1917, the first of a series of attacks causing a derailment along the railway.

The following month Lawrence led a full-scale attack on the railway and the garrison it supplied, setting in motion an oft-repeated sequence of destroying the railway – then blowing up the train sent to mend the shattered tracks. Locomotives that had been blown off their tracks and abandoned for years afterwards – even after the railway line itself had stopped functioning – were known as 'Lawrence's trains'.

As a result of the actions of Lawrence and others, an estimated 25,000 Turkish troops were kept fully occupied in the region. But the rebellious Arabs and their British allies didn't have it all their own way. A Herculean effort by the Turks kept the railway running despite the numerous guerrilla attacks by Lawrence and others. Realising their supplies of food and water depended on the railway, small parties of troops regularly left the stations where they sheltered to inspect the tracks. Other men went in search of trees, used as fuel for locomotives when coal ran short. The men repaired tracks and rolling stock with alacrity, reinforcing wagons that only ventured forth under armed escort.

So although the Turks lost Mecca early on, their troops did mount a successful defence of Medina. From Medina large numbers of replacement rails were brought into use, stored there for a proposed extension to the railway. When these ran short, station sidings were lifted. In the summer of 1918, Lawrence discovered a new method of blowing up railway lines that left them so misshapen they could not be reused. Despite the resilience of Turkish soldiers in the desert, their valiant efforts came to naught.

## Desert raider who loved the Arabs

Pictures of him wearing full Arab dress, at the time seen as unorthodox behaviour for an Englishman, captured the public's imagination and after the war he was lauded as 'Lawrence of Arabia'. A private edition of his book, *Seven Pillars of Wisdom*, was printed in 1926. Lawrence changed his name and retreated anonymously into the ranks of the armed services. He died in a motorcycle accident in Dorset, only months after leaving the Royal Air Force.

After his death, Lord Allenby paid tribute to him, saying he had a 'genius' for leadership. 'He was the mainspring of the Arab movement and knew their language, their manners and their mentality. He shared with the Arabs their hardships and dangers. Among these desert raiders there was none who would not have willingly died for his chief ...

'He was a shy and retiring scholar, archaeologist, and philosopher swept by the tide of war in to a position undreamt of.'

# RELIGION ON THE RAILS: FROM JAFFA TO JERUSALEM

TO LINK THE BUSY PORT OF JAFFA with the world's spiritual capital, Jerusalem, was an irresistible proposition dwelt on by many. As early as 1838, Moses Montefiore, the British philanthropist, suggested building the line and returned to the idea several times over the next 25 years. By 1864 it was engineer Charles Zimpel coming up with proposals, followed a decade later by a fellow German, Conrad Schick.

With the French, British, Germans and Austrians hoping for strategic benefit and three major faiths – Judaism, Christianity and Islam – jostling for position, the ruling Ottomans had plenty to consider before giving the go-ahead.

One man eventually used his powers of persuasion to gain the necessary concession: Jewish entrepreneur Joseph Navon (1858–1934). His plan proposing French funding got Ottoman approval in 1888, giving him control for 71 years. Unable to attract the

Although the railway extended on to Jaffa's beach by 1885, there was no harbour by which incoming ships could dock

necessary investment, Navon sold on his interest to a company that built the railway using a wealth of international expertise.

The winners were Christian tourists, whose journey to a city that was so religiously significant for them would be cut from two days to about four hours. There was also a trade incentive for the Ottoman authorities.

After construction work began the following year, progress was relatively swift on the 86 km (53 mile) route, despite the gradient from Jaffa being almost at sea level and Jerusalem nearly 2,500 feet higher.

The line, built on a metre gauge with seven stops, finally opened officially in 1892 and, according to Muslim rites, three sheep were slaughtered on the tracks before the train set off and the station was smothered in palm leaves. As the following report, published in *Scribner's Magazine* in 1893 and written by the American consul in Jerusalem Selah Merrill, makes clear, the train caused quite a stir.

'Tens of thousands of people, for the first time in their lives, have seen a railroad and a train of cars. They have had a revelation, and in the great city as well as in the dirtiest village of the land, wonder is at its height.

'The excitement can hardly be realized by the inhabitants of other countries, to whom railroads perfected by the highest engineering skill and with lavish expense are objects as familiar and common as a daily newspaper.

'We forget that, not so very long ago, in our own country we had only bridle-paths and scarcely a yearly post, while railways and steamboats had not even been dreamed of. Let all the world rejoice if this mediaeval country is experiencing a sensation which it can hardly comprehend.'

> **'They have had a revelation, and in the great city as well as in the dirtiest village of the land, wonder is at its height.'**
> Selah Merrill

## Light railway across the divide

Since August 2011, a light railway has been serving the streets of Jerusalem. For most cities, that wouldn't be noteworthy but there, where communities are divided on the grounds of race, its inauguration made headlines around the world. When they are passengers, Jews and Palestinians share the sleek, shiny carriages. It's one of the few public places where they will ever rub shoulders.

Construction began in 2002 but it was hampered by delays, not least because potentially valuable archaeological sites may have been at risk. There were arguments about the route it should take and whether it would be a target for terrorism.

However, the single line crosses from significant Jewish sites, like Israel's Holocaust memorial, into the city's business sector, by city hall and the Damascus Gate, which leads into the Old City, into two Palestinian neighbourhoods in East Jerusalem and on to a Jewish settlement.

To have drawn up a route that bypassed Palestinians would have been politically clumsy, yet there was some appetite for this in the city. One of the railway's main aims is to operate on behalf of tourists in the Holy City.

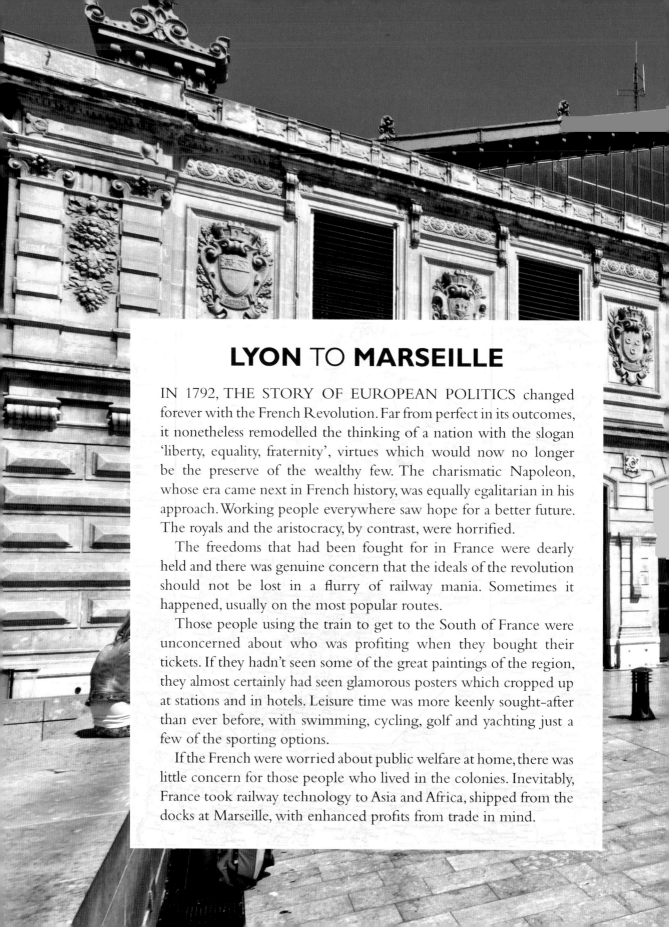

# LYON TO MARSEILLE

IN 1792, THE STORY OF EUROPEAN POLITICS changed forever with the French Revolution. Far from perfect in its outcomes, it nonetheless remodelled the thinking of a nation with the slogan 'liberty, equality, fraternity', virtues which would now no longer be the preserve of the wealthy few. The charismatic Napoleon, whose era came next in French history, was equally egalitarian in his approach. Working people everywhere saw hope for a better future. The royals and the aristocracy, by contrast, were horrified.

The freedoms that had been fought for in France were dearly held and there was genuine concern that the ideals of the revolution should not be lost in a flurry of railway mania. Sometimes it happened, usually on the most popular routes.

Those people using the train to get to the South of France were unconcerned about who was profiting when they bought their tickets. If they hadn't seen some of the great paintings of the region, they almost certainly had seen glamorous posters which cropped up at stations and in hotels. Leisure time was more keenly sought-after than ever before, with swimming, cycling, golf and yachting just a few of the sporting options.

If the French were worried about public welfare at home, there was little concern for those people who lived in the colonies. Inevitably, France took railway technology to Asia and Africa, shipped from the docks at Marseille, with enhanced profits from trade in mind.

# THE BATTLE FOR FRENCH RAILWAYS

FOR EVERY EUROPEAN NATION there was one awkward issue to resolve – who would cash in on the railway age, the government or private companies? In France, the Third Republic, which governed from 1870, had high-minded concerns about the general benefits generated by the railways, but was considered officious and long-winded in its dealings with industry. Yet private companies were thought greedy and excessively powerful by some ministers, as well as by employees.

That was certainly an accusation levelled at the Compagnie des chemins de fer de Paris à Lyon et à la Méditerranée, otherwise known as PLM. Formed in the middle of the 19th century, it held sway over the successful south-eastern routes that led to the Côte d'Azur favoured by the burgeoning middle classes of England and France. There was disquiet among many who felt the profits should have been more equally distributed.

One politician sought to find a compromise that would please the state and the six big railway companies that existed in France. Charles Louis de Saulces de Freycinet (1828–1923) drew up a blueprint for public works that would accelerate expansion for rail companies while bringing a new raft of benefits to the French population. With uncharacteristic flamboyance, he announced a three billion franc budget for building new railways in 1878 alongside a fund of one billion francs to improve canals and 500 million francs to help ports. Almost immediately, he revised the target for 24,000 km (14,900 miles) of new track for the railways to 64,000 km (39,800 miles). The aim was to couple these enhancements in infrastructure with universal education.

Freycinet wanted big French railway companies to help poor and remote communities. But his costly plans to knit private companies and state aims together soon failed

Typically, Gustave Noblemaire, the director of PLM, complained about 'the absolute domination of the state'. For his part, Freycinet was determined the tendency for the PLM and others to act as 'a state within a state' would be ended. The ongoing fracas between government and enterprise lasted for four years. In 1882, after a wobble on the Lyon stock market, France experienced an economic depression so severe that public spending, such as that announced under the Freycinet Plan, was scrapped.

Freycinet served in a dozen different governments during his long political career, four times as premier. In 1887 he lost the presidential election to Sadi Carnot (1837–1894), who became the fifth president of France's Third Republic. By trade, Carnot was an engineer before joining the government as the Minister of Public Works and Finance. Carnot's agenda was to unite France, which still had a number of unhappy monarchists among its conservative right wing and, in common with most European nations at the time, a good number of disgruntled left-wingers as well.

To bring the country together in the middle ground he toured 73 towns in France before arriving at Lyon on 24 June 1894. The city was hosting a world fair, containing all the latest technology. Spirits were high among the crowds who thronged to see him as he left the Palais de la Bourse following a banquet.

To their horror, an Italian anarchist, Sante Geronimo Caserio, leapt into Carnot's carriage and fatally stabbed him. It didn't matter to Caserio that Carnot had a different nationality to his own. (He travelled from his home village by train to carry out the crime.) In the killer's eyes, he was part of the bourgeois class that lived off the backs of the poor. Before his death by guillotine, Caserio showed no remorse.

But any hopes he had that the random act of violence would spark a revolution came to nothing. The killing caused outrage and grief in France. Fearing that the Third Republic could topple, people did finally pull together as Carnot had hoped they would. They adopted the richly patriotic 'La Marseillaise' as an anthem and selected 14 July, when the Bastille was stormed at the start of the French Revolution in 1789, as a day of national celebration.

There was one unlikely outcome: medical student Alexis Carrel (1873–1944) remained haunted by the idea that, with better knowledge of joining severed veins, he could have saved the president. In 1912, he won the Nobel Prize for work in this field, which ultimately led to organ transplants.

## Trumpeting for trippers

After the service from Saint-Étienne to Lyon opened in 1842, passengers in every carriage were supervised by a conductor bearing a trumpet. According to an account by writer Jules Janin (1804–1874), the trippers took their seats, filling each carriage in turn. 'When everyone is seated and all the carriages are linked to each other the first conductor blows his trumpet and all the others answer him,' he wrote.

'Then, by means of a handle, each conductor turns a screw which connects with the wheels; the first sets off the first carriage and this starts to move, pulling the others after it ... It is quite marvellous to travel so fast, to see nothing in front pulling you along, to feel none of the bumps and shudders associated with an ordinary carriage. To go at such a speed, go through so many mountains and cross so many precipices and all due to two iron lines running parallel.'

# POSTER ART AND THE RIVIERA BY RAIL

BY 1907 THE PLM OPERATED MORE THAN 9,800 KM (6,000 miles) of line with a network that extended into the French colony of Algeria. With flat terrain on the first leg of a journey between Paris and Marseille, its trains became famous for achieving high speeds during the trip, although the onward journey to Menton from the port was slower.

Trains using the line included the Train Bleu, also known as the Calais–Méditerranée Express, which began service in 1886, and the Côte d'Azur Rapide, introduced in 1904.

Hotels advertising in *Bradshaw's* were never short of superlatives to induce visitors to take the trip. Menton was said to have a 'pre-eminently healthy and invigorating climate' with a death rate over six summer months in 1911 numbering nine per annum for every 1,000 of the population. Meanwhile, the Grand Hotel de Cimiez, 15 minutes from Nice, was 'entirely protected from wind and dust', had 'an electric tram at the gates' and was 'first class in every respect'.

Some British railway companies urged would-be travellers to 'sleep your way from the City's fogs to the Riviera sunshine'. But the most seductive advertising came in the form of posters and it was here that PLM stole a march on some of its rivals.

After realising the value of bright and wildly alluring posters, the company sponsored artist Roger Broders (1883–

A PLM Art Deco poster designed to lure tennis lovers to Monte Carlo

1953) in the South of France, from where he produced a series of Art Deco works that long outlived PLM itself. He specialised in bold blocks of colour that filled panoramic sweeps of sun-kissed countryside. Apart from scenic views cut through by sleek locomotives, he drew fashionably dressed women enjoying apparently endless leisure time.

His style recalled some of the Cubists at work in the early 20th century. He devoted himself to posters for a decade after 1922, but during his career he also worked for car makers Renault and Peugeot and visited resorts in Italy and India. The number of visitors he enticed to the region through his insightful brushwork is unknown.

## Van Gogh and a passing train

Roger Broders wasn't the only artist to find inspiration in the region. In 1888, Vincent van Gogh (1853–1890) arrived, hoping to establish a 'studio of the south' for himself and others.

In September that year, he painted The Yellow House, where he lodged in Arles and which was next door to the restaurant where he would have his daily meal. He was delighted with the location where he felt he could 'live and breathe, meditate and paint'.

The painting is full of the vibrant colours that excited Van Gogh. In the background of the now-famous painting there's a steam locomotive – a local connection to nearby Lunel. The other line through Arles at the time was operated by PLM. A letter written afterwards by Van Gogh about a different picture featuring a train implied the locomotive was symbolic of the 'desperately swift passing of things in modern life'. For others the train puffing along in the distance behind the yellow house represents the routine of his life at the time.

Paul Gauguin (1848–1903) joined Van Gogh in Arles but their relationship quickly soured. In July 1890, the tortured Van Gogh committed suicide. The yellow house survived until the Second World War, when it succumbed to Allied bombing.

Artists who have fetched up in Provence down the years are thought to have been attracted by the clear light that bathes beautiful countryside. One theory says that the mistral, a strong wind that regularly sweeps the region for one, three, six or nine days at a time, blows through any motes in the air.

# A FRANTIC TIMETABLE BRINGS FAME TO LE TOUR

Gino Bartali winning the Tour de France in 1938. He was later a hero of the Italian Resistance who helped to hide Jews during the Second World War

AGAINST EXPECTATION, THE TRAIN PLAYED ITS PART in the success of the world's greatest bike race, the Tour de France. The man behind the race, Henri Desgrange (1865–1940), had been a humble legal clerk until a client complained about seeing his bare calves while he was cycling. As a consequence, Desgrange was compelled to give up his day job. Focusing entirely on his love of cycling, he then established a velodrome, wrote training manuals and became editor of a new sports magazine.

At an emergency meeting held in the wake of declining sales, reporter Géo Lefèvre (1887–1961) blurted out his idea of a round-France race lasting days rather than hours. Later, he admitted that he dreamt up the idea on the spur of the moment because he could think of nothing else to say. Desgrange was initially cautious, but once he found sufficient funds he announced in the magazine a five-week race with an entry fee of 20 francs. When the prize money and perks went up, a field of 60 mostly French riders finally registered.

Perhaps fearful the race would be a disaster, Desgrange stayed in Paris and dispatched Lefèvre on behalf of the magazine. And that's where the train came in – Lefèvre, dashing between the start and finish of each leg, relied on railways. Thanks to the efficient network by then in place in France, he could travel between Lyon, Marseille, Toulouse, Bordeaux, Nantes and, finally, Paris to fulfil his deadlines for the magazine.

The first winner was Maurice Garin, in 1903. He finished an extraordinary two hours and 49 minutes ahead of his nearest rival, having achieved speeds of more than 25 km (15½ miles) an hour despite the clunky bicycle he rode. The rider who finished last in that race came in almost 65 hours later.

## Bikes to locos

Somewhere at the nucleus of the locomotive story comes the history of bicycles. The creation of the bicycle was a landmark because for the first time people had propelled themselves along. Until then, all wheeled vehicles relied on horses for forward motion. There are claims and counter-claims about how bicycles came into being. Certainly, there was a German design in 1818 which involved the rider of a two-wheeled vehicle pushing himself along using one foot then the other.

Although a Scots engineer invented a treadle-powered model in 1839, the pedal as we know it wasn't added until the 1860s. Even then, bicycles had a rigid frame with iron-lined wheels, earning them the title of 'boneshakers'. After high bikes, also known as penny farthings, came the safety cycle in the 1880s, when finally bicycles had evolved into an accepted and widely used form of transport.

Circulation of the magazine, *L'Auto*, leapt by 40,000, beyond anything Desgrange or Lefèvre had anticipated.

The train played a part in the second Tour de France too, which was marred by numerous instances of cheating, including by Garin, and some physical violence by onlookers. Fans of a rider who had been disqualified in the second stage even showered the road with nails and broken glass, causing chaos among passing cyclists.

Although his first instinct was to cancel the event, Desgrange eventually agreed to competitors taking the train to the end of the stage so they could regroup before another day's cycling. Afterwards, an inquest into the event by cycling's sporting body outraged him. 'The Tour is finished,' wrote Desgrange, 'killed by its own success, driven out of control by blind passion, by violence and filthy suspicions worthy only of ignorant and dishonourable men.'

Fortunately, that wasn't the case. To reduce the temptation to cheat, a points system was introduced, later followed by exciting mountain stages. In 1919, the yellow jersey was brought in, reflecting the colour of the pages in *L'Auto*. Throughout it was Desgrange, who stamped his personality on the race.

# MARSEILLE AND LA LIGNE IMPÉRIALE

WHEN PASSENGERS FROM PARIS spilled out of the station at Marseille, they were quickly aware why the city was called 'the gateway to the Orient'. The port was buzzing with trade: imports from French colonial interests in Asia and Africa and exports to those territories and others. Its cathedral, finally finished in 1896, was built in Romanesque, Byzantine and Gothic styles, to reflect its proximity to different civilisations.

Even the railway tracks from the French capital to Marseille were dubbed 'La Ligne Impériale', to highlight the seven million square miles of empire France possessed. And for France, there was no better way to exert influence and authority in its overseas possessions than to build railways. As Britain put

French president Paul Doumer greets the king of Siam (now Thailand) in 1898. Doumer was an ardent supporter of railway projects in Indochina, both to exert French influence and gain personal fame

railways in India, so France established a network in what's now Vietnam that even extended into neighbouring China.

When he was governor-general of Indochina, as it was known, Paul Doumer (1857–1932) instituted ambitious and 'indispensable' railway projects. He knew that photos of engineering triumphs played well with the press at home in France and could even impress local people, at least for a while. But there's little doubt that much was built to immortalise his own name.

Before Doumer arrived, railway construction had already begun, with a tramway between Saigon and Cholon from 1881 and a line between Saigon and Mỹ Tho, completed in 1885. Now lines would link Hanoi and Saigon, Vietnam and Yunnan, in addition to a north–south project, thanks to loans from the compliant French government.

Initially, the theory seemed sound. There were numerous graduates of prestigious engineering schools in France keen to tackle new railway challenges when the network at home was all but complete. Such projects could provide ample work for the local population. In practice, there were a host of problems.

## False start to African ventures

It wasn't only in Asia that the French laid down tracks. African colonies like Senegal and Niger were visited by engineers employed by colonial bosses. The aim here was to connect the important ports on the African west coast with railways, so that minerals mined inland could be more easily sold and shipped. The bridge across the Senegal river, Pont Faidherbe, opened in 1897, was deemed a particular landmark, described as 'the magnificent monument of [French] national industry'. But French railway planners were unacquainted with the ferocity of Africa's rainy seasons and many parts of the new railways were soon wrecked. Surveys for a trans-Saharan railway to link French colonies in the west and north began as early as 1880. It still wasn't completed by the end of the Second World War.

Conditions for the locally recruited navvies were appalling, with 12,000 men dying from illness or accidents during the construction of the Yunnan railway. Taxes were exacted from an increasingly resentful Vietnamese population to help finance such schemes. Meanwhile, the French fashioned a monopoly in sales of salt, opium and alcohol. Indeed, from 1902 communities were compelled to buy a quantity of alcohol from the French each week, whether they wanted it or not.

Plans to develop a sphere of influence in China were almost immediately frustrated by a civil war there. Indochina was occupied by Japan during the Second World War and proclaimed its independence in 1945. So whether the investment by France paid off, on lines with typically modest traffic, is doubtful.

The French liked to portray their presence overseas as a 'civilising mission'. In fact, reprehensible French treatment of the Vietnamese steered many there to Communism, sowing the seeds for a turbulent future. Doumer was assassinated after being made the French president.

# 4

**VIENNA** TO **TRIESTE**
**BARCELONA** TO **MALLORCA**
**PISA** TO **LAKE GARDA**
**SOFIA** TO **ISTANBUL**
**FREIBURG** TO **HANNOVER**
**ATHENS** TO **THESSALONIKI**

AFTER SCRUTINY, THE CAUSES OF THE FIRST WORLD WAR and the spread of the railways in a pressure-cooker region appear closely linked. An assassin's bullet fired in Sarajevo in 1914 may have been the trigger, but there had been niggling nationalism, conspiracies, feuds and fighting alternately flaring up or simmering below the surface for decades.

The key area was the rump of Europe that lay closest to Asia, in the domain of the Ottoman empire – and the building of a railway network there coincided with soaring tensions. A belief that the Orient Express, symbolic of success and fin de siècle glamour, would distract from those escalating difficulties had no substance.

In 1913, Serbia was assertive, the Greeks ambitious, Russia watchful, the Austro-Hungarian empire defensive, the Germans seeking more influence and the Bulgarians wanting independence. Each tried to express its own agenda at least partly in the construction or administration of railway lines.

The British and French, major investors in the region's tracks and rolling stock, observed from the sidelines.

Italy would eventually be drawn into the fray, although its overriding priority was to compete on parity in industry and commerce.

Spain had tensions of its own, with the so-called 'tragic week' unfolding in Catalonia after protesting socialists, anarchists and republicans clashed with the army in July 1909, leaving scores of people dead. Soon afterwards, the abandoned first tunnel of the metro in Barcelona seemed like an open wound.

Meanwhile, Germany was fostering a toxic mix of chauvinism and victimisation among its people, set against a booming economy. As society shifted uneasily in Europe under the old order, the 1913 landscape described in detail by *Bradshaw's* was – for all these reasons and more – about to shatter irretrievably.

# VIENNA TO TRIESTE

EMPEROR FRANZ JOSEF I HELPED TO SHORE UP his empire with railways, reaching to the furthest outposts to furnish his fashionable capital, Vienna, with necessities and luxury items. The harsh reality was that labourers, drawn from the poorest rungs of society, would die in order for this to happen.

Taking the railway through the Semmering Mountains was a bold scheme, on the part of both engineer Carl von (born Carlo) Ghega and the men who worked there. Nor would one mountain crossing be enough, with traffic between central Austria and its territories increasing exponentially during the 19th century. This was the gritty nature of expanding the railway network. To underline its achievement, the Südbahn is now in three countries, Austria, Italy and Slovenia.

Yet there were some unexpected spin-offs, which were not only economic but scientific. In 1842, Austrian physicist Christian Doppler (1803–1853) described how sounds were higher pitched when the listener and the source of the sound were approaching one another. As the source moved away, the pitch was lower. To verify this, he put a musician on a train and asked him to play a single note while approaching a listener on a platform. Three years later, the experiment was replicated with a band of trumpeters and a group of listeners.

All experienced the same and the Doppler effect – then applied to sound but later to all forms of waves – was established.

The increased network should have put the Austrian empire on the front foot when it came to the First World War. But no amount of preparation could nullify the effects of internal treachery contrived by one of the most notorious spies history has known. This time it was conscripts who would die in their droves, the result of one man's pursuit of good living.

# LEARNING CURVES

AFTER COMING TO POWER IN 1848, newly installed emperor Franz Josef was mindful of the importance of railways. He would now oversee the building of the first mountain railway through the Alps at Semmering, even before prestigious architectural changes were made in Vienna and while railway building in the empire was still in its infancy.

Some of the groundwork had been laid under the auspices of his predecessor and a stretch of track in the north between Vienna and Gloggnitz had been open since 1841. That meant tourists and artists – usually found haunting the coffee shops of Vienna – could make their way to this stunning Alpine location to enjoy its flora and the panoramic views. As a consequence, they built fine new chalet homes on the slopes, signalling just how an influx of visitors could change the profile of an area; in this case, from poor to wealthy.

The section that linked Graz and Mürzzuschlag, both south of the Semmering range, was finished in 1844. That left the difficult mountain range in the middle to traverse in order to unite both short sections.

Starting in 1848, 20,000 workers set to, building 16 viaducts – several with two-storey arches – 14 tunnels, more than 100 stone bridges and 11 iron bridges to span the 42 km (26 mile) distance. All that in addition to a number of one-in-four gradients and perpetual tight curves as the railway hugged the mountainside throughout the Semmering Pass.

It all occurred at a time when railway-building technology was relatively underdeveloped; for example, there was no powerful explosive available to help with the tunnelling. But without the 'Südbahn', as it was known, Vienna would have been hemmed in on one side by an impenetrable physical barrier with no access to the port at Trieste, the 'Austrian Riviera', denting its prestige and prosperity.

The most demanding were the upper regions of the line, from Gloggnitz to the Semmering summit tunnel at a height of 1,431 metres (4,695 ft). At the time, no railway had been built as high.

In July 1854, the entire route was completed, with an extension to Trieste, on the Adriatic coast, added three years later. Curiously, the total length of all the tunnels was 1,477 metres (4,846 ft), exactly the same distance as the 16 major viaducts, which was a combined total of one-fifth of the line length. As trains chugged across sweeping vistas, dipping this way and that with the lie of the land, the journey must have been an exhilarating one for passengers unused to railways on such a grand scale.

The route was marked at regular intervals by some 57 two-storey houses, built for those whose job it was to inspect tracks made more fragile by the number of bends and the steepness of the slopes.

## But is it art?

Austrian society was ready to embrace changes in the nation's transport system. But when it came to the arts it was a different story. On 31 March 1913 at the Great Hall in Vienna, a concert of modern music ended in a brawl, with the audience taking exception to the dissonant notes being played. Conductor Arnold Schoenberg (1874–1951) was leading the orchestra in music written by himself and others when the mêlée broke out. Understandably distressed by the hostility, the composer later commented: 'If it is art, it is not for all, and if it is for all, it is not art.' Famous for the punches thrown, the centenary of the Skandalkonzert was marked by musicians playing the same programme – with some listeners still finding it too atonal for their tastes.

# PEAK OF ACHIEVEMENT

THE GENIUS BEHIND THE PROJECT was Venetian-born Carlo Ghega (1802–1860), whose breathtaking vision resulted in the railway between Gloggnitz and Mürzzuschlag being added to the UNESCO World Heritage List in 1998 as ' one of the greatest feats of civil engineering during the pioneering phase of railway building'.

According to UNESCO: 'The continued operation of the line is a sound testimony to the engineering genius of Carl von Ghega, the project engineer. The property also derives its appearance from the villas and hotels constructed in its immediate vicinity in the late 19th and early 20th centuries, showing the impact of the railway line on the surrounding landscape.' This

**Without these two-storey arches the viaduct could not reach the height necessary to bridge the plunging valley**

was 'an outstanding technological solution to a major physical problem'. One of its outstanding features remains the double-decker viaduct crossing the Kalte Rinne, meaning 'cold furrow', built in natural stone to complement the environment in the elegant style of the ancient Romans.

So demanding was the route that an innovative type of locomotive was commissioned, to better cope with the relentless mountain contours. A competition was held to bring forward a new design to tackle the challenge. None of the four entries was deemed entirely suitable, so a fifth option was commissioned, incorporating the best qualities of them all. When the design was agreed, 26 new-style locomotives were ordered. After 1959, Ghega's tracks carried electric trains although some heritage trips still occur.

## A heavy toll

The death toll during the construction of the Semmering railway was more than 700. Some estimates say as many as 1,000 people perished, mostly from the effects of typhus or cholera. However, in 1850 the human cost was amplified by the deaths of 14 men who were killed by a rock fall at a particularly precarious point. Soon, those in charge were persuaded that the preferred route on the outside of the mountain was simply too dangerous. Ghega decided to burrow through limestone and make a tunnel instead. The mountain slope still bears the scar of the work that had been carried out, and abandoned following the deaths.

He certainly did his homework prior to starting the monumental task. Ghega first visited America to see how mountain railways were built there. And there were some challenges on site before a pick axe had been wielded. Although there had once been a well-trodden crossing in the area, it had fallen into disuse and there were no reliable maps. Consequently, Ghega set out to survey the landscape himself. To do so, he developed the necessary surveying tools, some of which went on to be widely used in other railway engineering projects.

Although his assiduously plotted plans were completed in 1847, there was still a question mark over the scheme, with many politicians and the press believing it was unfeasible. One hope, that it would provide considerable employment, was realised. The line was divided into 14 sections, each being assigned to a different construction firm. From the start, a total of more than 1,000 men and 400 women were taken on. That figure eventually increased to more than 20,000.

When it was finished, those who supported the building of the railway buoyantly declared there was now nowhere too inaccessible for tracks to be laid. The Semmering railway became an inspiration for other nations with difficult terrain to breach. Unsurprisingly, Ghega, who was of Albanian descent, was by 1853 the chief planner of the railway network in Austria. He died of tuberculosis in Vienna before being able to complete another bold railway line in Transylvania.

Café Central, in Vienna's Freyung district, is one of many meeting places in the city

# COFFEE CULTURE

ONE OF THE GREATEST PLEASURES IN VIENNA for residents and visitors alike was to sit inside a coffee house, to read the newspaper, catch up with friends or to debate the latest issues. There's a theory that the custom started back in the 17th century after the Ottomans abandoned sacks of coffee beans in the vicinity following an unsuccessful siege in 1683.

However it started, the habit caught on and the coffee houses, typically elegant and urbane, were usually packed. In 1913, the customers included Stalin and Trotsky, both using different names at the time and in exile. They apparently met for the first time in Vienna and even then there was little warmth between the two, despite their shared aspirations for revolution in Russia.

One of the art students in the city was Adolf Hitler and the factory workers had among their number a young Marshal Tito, who would eventually rule Yugoslavia. Moving in more hallowed circles was Sigmund Freud, the man credited by many at the time with unlocking the secrets of the mind.

In 1867, Jews had been given equal rights by the emperor, permitting them access to education. Freud and other intellectuals drawn from this section of Viennese society now rubbed shoulders at the coffee houses with a new breed of industrialist and any number of firebrands and philosophers who arrived there by train.

What Vienna needed to underpin this was a ready supply of coffee. With easy access to the port at Trieste, supplies would in theory be more dependable and less expensive. The train became the workhorse that kept the enthralling facades of the coffee houses in business.

## A tram car's story

Today's tripper to Trieste might well use the same tram car as those visitors from Bradshaw's day. According to the city's transport group, the Austrian-built tram car bearing No. 411 is the oldest one still running in Europe today.

It first went into service when the three kilometre line between Trieste and Opicina opened in 1902, among six carriages being used. At that time it was marked as Number One. It looks different now, however, because initially the drivers' platforms were open to the elements. But in 1908 windscreens were put in to weatherproof the tram, which was lengthened too, to increase the original capacity of 44 passengers. At last, the driver could hang up the large waterproof cape that he had once used to protect himself and the controls during inclement weather.

The tram car survived changes made in 1928 when the original rack railway technology was replaced with the workings of a funicular. That's when tractors were introduced to push the cars up the track and to put a brake on their descent down the one-in-four hill.

But when a different type of car was introduced during the 1930s, this one was withdrawn from service and kept as a 'spare' to be used in case of breakdowns. A special platform was added to the roof so that it could also be used for repair work on the overhead cables.

In 1992, aged 90, the tram car was restored by staff who completed the refurbishment with the same green livery that defined the cars on the line in the 1920s. Even the newer cars on the line date from either 1935 or 1942, when wartime shortages left their interiors a little more stark than their predecessors.

The tram was designed to tackle the hill that separates the port, almost at sea level, from Opicina, standing at a lofty 329 metres (1,080 ft), the polished steel traction cable that enables the operation 950 metres (3,117 ft) long. Previously, passengers on the regular train service had a 32 km (20 mile) detour along flatter terrain.

The cars run on a single metre-gauge track with passing loops. Today's drivers control the discreetly small tractors remotely from inside the carriage.

# BRENNER PASS

FOR CENTURIES THE BRENNER PASS was well worn by populations migrating to Europe who had identified it as the lowest point at which the Alps could be crossed. As early as 15 BC, the first Roman road, the Via Claudia Augusta, was marked out in the saddle of the mountain range, for those on foot or on horseback. It's all the indication railway builders needed that this was the ideal route for a train. Experienced railway engineer Karl von Etzel (1812–1865) tackled the project that was designed to improve internal communications in the Austrian empire.

By the time it opened on 24 August 1867 the majority of the line lay in newly formed Italy. (Ironically, most of the population in the Tyrol would have been more at home in the Austrian empire. They spoke German – and still do – so railway signs in this part of Italy are always in two languages.)

There was an 800 metre (2,625 ft) climb to accomplish in 40 km (25 miles) between Innsbruck in Austria and Brenner, which would become the border between the two countries, followed by a longer descent into Italy. Von Etzel – who had gained his early experience in France and had even built railways through mountains before, designing a steep ramp to ease trains out

Karl v. Etzel, k. württembergischer Oberbaurath, Direktor der österreichischen Südbahn, gest. 2. Mai.
Originalzeichnung von E. Sues.

Karl von Etzel was a veteran of French and German rail projects before tackling the Brenner Pass

of Geislinger Steige in the Swabian Jura – ensured the stations were long enough to accommodate the several locomotives that would be needed to haul trains slowly uphill. (Even today three locomotives are sometimes needed for freight trains.) He also made use of spiral tunnels to achieve the gradients.

The size of the station assumed particular importance after electrification because Austrian locomotives ran on alternating current while the Italians had chosen direct current. Generations of travellers had to wait while the engines were changed before the journey could continue.

Von Etzel didn't see the railway line run in its entirety. He died – on a train – after suffering a stroke as he visited his newly built retirement home. Since its opening there have been numerous attempts to make it faster and leaner, trimming the curvatures and adding tracks.

His achievements were not restricted to the 1,500 km (930 miles) of railway track constructed under his guidance. He was a gifted communicator too, with several respected books to his name published after 1844. Even his building instructions were famous for being clear and concise.

## A new route

From its inception the Brenner Pass was a vital corridor, especially for freight, with as many as 242 trains a day passing through it before the end of the 20th century. Necessary repair work slowed the network catastrophically. In some places, it's too narrow to lay more tracks to relieve the problem, while a lack of road access makes delivery of repair materials difficult.

Plans for a replacement were made when it became known as much for being a bottleneck as for the stunning views it offered passengers. In 1989, the prospect of a Brenner base tunnel – below the existing railway and through the mountains – came under scrutiny. After lengthy consideration, plans for a 55 km (34 mile) two-bore tunnel were approved in 2009.

However, the costs involved – some eight billion euros – have proved a stumbling block, despite general agreement from funding partners, Austria, Italy and the European Union. The earliest it is likely to open is 2025.

# THE SPYING GAME

To all appearances Redl seemed a proud and loyal servant of the Austrian empire

HIS NAME IS VIRTUALLY UNKNOWN in the West. But Colonel Alfred Redl (1864–1913) is one of the most notorious spies ever unmasked, as his double-dealing cost the lives of thousands of soldiers in the opening months of the First World War.

Redl was the son of a railway clerk in the Austrian province of Galicia. He was the ninth of 14 children born into humble circumstances at Lemberg, now Lviv in the Ukraine. After excelling in his home town as a military cadet – showing a flair for languages – Redl joined the Imperial Army as an officer, despite a lack of aristocratic connections, and forged up the ranks.

By 1907 he was head of counterintelligence for the Austrian empire. He introduced new methods: recording conversations on a waxed cylinder, for example, and taking fingerprints. But he was also in pole position to leak state secrets to Austria's time-honoured enemies, Russia and Serbia. It's presumed he did so after being blackmailed by Russian agents who discovered that he was homosexual – at the time illegal in Austria. However, he was also well paid for his treachery and enjoyed living ostentatiously.

To the Russians and Serbians he gave the Austrian mobilisation plan prepared for the event of war, immediately neutering its effectiveness. When a traitor was suspected in Austria, he revealed the names of Russians at work in Vienna secretly given to him by his spymasters and they were consequently executed. Meanwhile, he passed on the names of Austrian agents undercover in Russia, who were also duly dispatched.

He was finally caught when a letter arrived at the main post office in Vienna during April 1913 that went uncollected. When it was opened by post office officials there were thousands of Austrian Kronen inside. To the police, who were called in, it looked suspiciously like an espionage payment. By now Redl had moved on from the counterintelligence department to work in a different army section. His successor, Major Maximilian Ronge, had the post office put under surveillance.

## Betrayal

The full implications of his treachery were not felt until after war was declared in July 1914. For Serbia and Russia, the promised attack by Emperor Franz Josef held no fears, as they were well versed in every element of the battle plan in advance. Consequently, the emperor's soldiers were felled by the thousand as the Austrian empire was defeated in battles with both countries before the end of August.

The addressee, a Mr Nikon Nizetas, didn't turn up until the end of May, by which time three cash-stuffed envelopes were waiting for him. Police officers who had kept watch on the post office for six weeks nearly missed their man, who slipped away before they had time to detain him. They saw the back of his departing cab as they dashed to the bank's front door. As luck would have it, they noted the cab number – and saw it again almost immediately as it returned to its rank. The cab driver led them to Hotel Klomser, where the concierge inadvertently revealed the man who had so recently arrived was Colonel Redl.

He was even recognised by some of the shocked policemen who worked in the department he once led. Senior army officers arrived, putting a revolver on his desk, in a bid to keep the matter a secret and save the army's reputation. Some hours later, Redl shot himself after admitting his guilt in writing.

There were more surprises to come, for when police broke into one of his homes in Prague they found women's clothing and an overwhelming scent of perfume. The implication that he and his associates were cross-dressing was a matter of utmost embarrassment and the regime sought to cover up the scandal, reporting Redl's suicide as stress-related.

However, the locksmith responsible for breaking in missed his football match to do so and had to explain himself to his team captain, journalist Egon Erwin Kisch.

In the absence of the star half-back, his team lost and wanted to know the reason he hadn't turned up for the game. As a consequence, he spilled the beans. When Kisch learned that Redl, barely cold in his grave after taking his own life, had lived in a lavishly appointed apartment full of expensive women's clothes he began an investigation.

Ultimately, Redl's activities were exposed through the pages of the German-language newspaper *Bohemia*, leaving the empire at a low ebb.

PROHIBIDO VIAJAR EN LOS ESTRIBOS

# BARCELONA TO MALLORCA

THERE WAS A SLOW START FOR THE RAILWAY BUSINESS in Spain, where there was a marked lack of energy and appetite for railways in the mid-19th century. Of course, hostility to the invention was experienced everywhere but was quickly overcome when trains arrived, bearing a host of benefits across Europe as the tentacles of the railway system were planned.

And if much of Spain was rural and reluctant, where this kind of attitude prevailed, Madrid was a more modern city with a cosmopolitan elite. Even so, the capital missed out on the honour of hosting the country's first railway when one determined Catalan went to work. Significantly, the view of Miquel Biada Bunyol had been shaped overseas rather than in his homeland.

Still that hesitancy is reflected too in the length of time that the people of Barcelona had to wait for the construction of the city's metro, even after official agreement had been given.

These delays may well have worked in Spain's favour. French investors were looking for fertile new ground after their domestic system approached capacity. Eventually, it attracted English money as the railway mania bubble burst in Britain in the 1840s, leaving speculators looking outside the UK, where the profitable aspects of the railway network were already in place, to countries like Spain. Sadly, much of the good work was undone in the Spanish Civil War in the 1930s, and it would take years to bring the system back to a high mark.

For Mallorca, the principle 'small is best' held good. The island's railway link between the capital Palma and 'market garden' Sóller was built expressly to carry fruit to new markets. Happily, when that was no longer profitable tourists filled the seats to keep the service viable. It wasn't Mallorca's only railway line but it might have been the most charming.

# SPAIN'S FIRST TRAIN

SPAIN'S FIRST DOMESTIC TRAIN between Barcelona and Mataró, some 30 km (20 miles) further up the coast, was treated as an oddity rather than an innovation after being opened on 28 October 1848. Indisputably a triumph of engineering with its 44 bridges, it would nevertheless be a further three years before the railway age proper got underway in Spain. There were a number of reasons for this.

Early investors in Spanish railways were mostly French and they were far more comfortable with the idea of trains radiating out of the capital, Madrid, just as their own national trains tended to do. More than that, Barcelona was in Catalonia – a region with its own distinct language and culture which got swept up within the boundaries when Spain united as a country. Yet this corner of Spain had more in common with parts of neighbouring France than it did with Madrid. Once the technology was proved, it was expedient for the Spanish government to focus on its central lines rather than an outpost like Barcelona.

It was a Catalonian who ensured the trail-blazing line was built in the first place. Entrepreneur Miquel Biada Bunyol (1789–1848) left Mataró when it came under attack by Napoleon's army in 1808. He spent some time in Venezuela and then in Cuba, where he witnessed its first train service get underway in 1837. Inspired, he returned to Catalonia determined to build the first railway there – and sought British money to do so. In August 1843, he was granted official permission from the Spanish government to go ahead.

*Although the line between Madrid and Aranjuez was opened with great ceremony in 1851, it wasn't Spain's first railway*

During the project he faced numerous difficulties. At every stage it was blighted by a lack of money and twice he was forced to call meetings in Barcelona's city hall, where he made impassioned pleas for more finance to keep the railway in business.

Opponents of it resorted to vandalism carried out under cover of darkness, in a bid to stop its progress. Bunyol would have to patrol the newly laid tracks to protect them, and it is probably in doing so that he contracted the

## Maestro

If the guitar had a home anywhere in the 19th century it was in Spain, where there were virtuosos in both flamenco and classical styles. Among the most famous was Francisco Tárrega (1852–1909), who lived in Barcelona and composed original scores for the instrument, as well as adapting the work of famous composers including Chopin and Beethoven.

A childhood accident that left him with impaired eyesight helped steer him towards a career in music. He was already an accomplished performer by the time he enrolled in the Madrid Conservatory in 1874. As a performer he toured Europe, finally settling with his wife Maria in Barcelona in 1885. Afflicted by paralysis in his right side three years before his death, he fought against the odds to continue playing in private and composing until his death.

pneumonia that eventually cost him his life. Bunyol died just months before the train service went into operation, having spent his personal fortune in pursuit of the project. But if his dream was to have Catalonia beat Spain and gain the prestigious accolade of having the first train on the peninsula then it was fulfilled.

Barcelona then became the regional hub of railways, with links to Molins de Rei, Zaragoza, Girona and Sarria opening in 1854, 1861, 1862 and 1863 respectively. Thus a network was created.

It was only a matter of time before Catalonia had its own international line, with a company formed in 1875 to extend further eastwards. France and Catalonia were finally linked by rail in 1878.

The concept of Barcelona's metro was rooted in the highly successful French model but appeared a quarter of a century later

# TRAIN DELAYS

LIKE OTHER CITIES, BARCELONA experienced a surge in population at the end of the 19th century which resulted in, among other things, chaos among the horse-drawn carriages on the road. And in common with many of Europe's metropolises, the city opted for an underground system to ease the pressure.

But it is the length of time it took for services to be up and running that set Barcelona apart from the rest. As early as 1907, the Spanish King Alfonso gave the go-ahead for the metro to be built, with Parisian chic in mind. It was originally planned to be a single line measuring little more than 7 km (4½ miles), running between the city centre and the port. However, the city council were unhappy with some aspects of the plan and no building work was carried out.

In 1911, construction did get underway, to coincide with an enlargement of the city's shops and housing. But five years later, with the site causing considerable disruption, no one was willing to continue the scheme and it was left partially completed. Another five years passed before action was finally taken on the issue, with a new company being formed. Perhaps oddly, the decision was to use the original plans turned down in 1907 – with a few modifications – and the previously built tunnel standing idle since 1916.

In 1924, 17 years after he signed the concession that permitted the building of the metro, King Alfonso officially opened it.

A second line built at the broad gauge to concur with mainline services in the city opened two years later. There were some extensions during the 1930s but then little happened for two decades before a major building programme was instituted in the late 20th century.

## Towering achievement

One man who left his universally recognised signature on Barcelona's skyline is the architect Antoni Gaudí (1852–1926). His landmark creation is the unfinished Sagrada Família, a temple begun in 1882. When its first architect resigned, the project fell to Gaudí and he soon abandoned the neo-Gothic design for something more richly innovative which has since captivated millions of visitors.

It wasn't his only work, however, and another six of his buildings have been recognised by UNESCO for being outstanding. According to the organisation: 'His work is rooted in the particular character of the period, drawing on the one hand from traditional Catalan patriotic sources and on the other from the technical and scientific progress of modern industry.

'Gaudí's work is a remarkable reflection of all these different facets of society and has a unique and singular character. In fact, his works are particularly associated with *Modernisme*, and in this sense, Gaudí can be regarded as the most representative and outstanding of the *Modernista* architects.'

From 1914 Gaudí, who was unmarried and a devout Catholic, dedicated himself entirely to the project, living and working on the site, where he continued to produce designs and three-dimensional models of how he envisaged the building. Progress was slow, however, and he saw only one tower completed before he was knocked down by a tram.

Not everyone is as thrilled with the outcome, however. George Orwell branded it 'one of the most hideous buildings in the world' and hoped it would be destroyed in the Spanish Civil War. Later, a Madrid newspaper columnist called it 'the dream of a genius driven crazy by mystic reveries'.

It remains a major tourist destination and it is visitors' money that continues to pay for the lofty temple, due to be completed in 2026.

Mallorca's 'orange express' crossing the Cinc-Ponts viaduct, with the town of Sóller in the background

# A SURVIVOR'S STORY

IN THE ANNALS OF RAILWAY HISTORY ONE Mallorca train service has proved an unlikely success story. Usually, railways thrive in urban areas, where there's a large number of potential passengers and plenty of trade, especially those built early in the boom years. This line wasn't opened until just before the First World War, primarily to ship low-cost citrus fruits from the remote orchards on one side of the island to the other, between towns with a combined population of fewer than 80,000 people.

Yet the Tren de Sóller is arguably one of the most enduring of all railways, for just as it was inaugurated the role of vitamin C in preventing scurvy was finally being understood by scientists, increasing the demand for oranges. And when the oranges and lemons were later crated and taken by lorry on newly built roads, tourists stepped in and began filling the train's mahogany-lined carriages.

Before the railway, Sóller's growers faced a ten-hour journey in horse-drawn wagons across the Tramuntana mountains before they could sell their goods in Mallorca's capital, Palma. The alternative of a coastal voyage was equally time-consuming.

As early as 1893 plans for a train route were being drawn up, but several blueprints were thrown out, including one that would have taken in Valldemossa, where George Sand and her lover Frederick Chopin once lived. The more direct 28 km (17 mile) route that was finally favoured needed 13 tunnels – one of which was three kilometres long – several bridges and a five-arch viaduct to link the ports of Palma and Sóller.

When a society was formed for the construction project, virtually everyone in Sóller chipped in some money, reflecting the promise the railway held for them and their futures. It took five years to build the line, run on a metre gauge so it could if necessary link to the other railway lines on Mallorca, amounting to about 190 km (120 miles) at the time. A locomotive built in 1891 in Loughborough was the workhorse during construction, making it the first to use the line.

On 16 April 1912, with the steam locomotive festooned in flowers, the train got up a head of steam to cover the full length of the completed line for the first time, the news overshadowed by headlines announcing the sinking of the *Titanic*. The line boasted probably the oldest station in the world in Sóller. Dated 1606, it was built not for railways, of course, but was appropriated at the time for this use.

Inexplicably dubbed 'red lightning' or 'the orange express', the unhurried engine also transported fish around the island.

### Late addition

At the end of the line in Sóller there's a tram that continues the 5 km (3 mile) journey to the sea. No one knows why the railway line simply wasn't extended in the first place. But the year that railway construction ended, tram building began – using the same metre gauge – to cover the final leg of the journey.

It was powered by a 600 volt motor-driven dynamo and a power plant was installed in Sóller's station. At the time, passengers and freight were carried on it, meaning a cumbersome carriage switch for goods sent in from Palma.

In 1929, overhead cables for electrification were installed to eliminate the sparks and smoke that bothered passengers in the tunnels. Jerónimo Estades, the 'local hero' who steered the railway project to fruition, was also behind its electrification.

Even today it is slow paced, with the journey taking about an hour, a matter of some delight for today's tourists who can take in the scenery at their leisure.

# Arrivi Arrivals

| treno<br>train | | provenienza<br>origin | orari<br>time |
|---|---|---|---|
| FRECCIAROSSA AV | 9529 | MILANO C.LE | 13: |
| TRENITALIA RV | 3154 | LIVORNO C.LE | 14: |
| TRENITALIA R | 6814 | FAENZA | 14: |
| italo AV | 9926 | ROMA OSTIEN. | 14: |
| FRECCIARGENTO AV | 9426 | ROMA TERMINI | 14 |
| italo AV | 9931 | MILANO P.GAR | 14 |
| FRECCIARGENTO AV | 9427 | VENEZIA S.L. | 14 |
| TRENITALIA RV | 3122 | PIOMBINO M. | 14 |
| TRENITALIA R | 23508 | AREZZO | 14 |
| italo AV | 9986 | ROMA OSTIEN. | 14 |

solari udine

# PISA TO LAKE GARDA

IT COULD BE COINCIDENCE BUT MOST ITALIANS seem to be born with a need for speed. Like the rest of Europe they were tied to slow-going locomotives – especially heading uphill – when the age of trains first dawned. Yet as soon as technology would allow, they put increased speeds at the top of the agenda, improving journey times for passengers and freight.

It was the same in the development of cars, with some of the most famous racing marques being born in Italy. And one Italian was determined to speed up communication with the development of wireless, albeit in work that had to be carried out away from his homeland.

Here was a young country rushing towards monumental achievements to help bind all its people together in the common cause of unity.

Italy embraced the modern age without losing any of its natural charms, though. Despite an overhaul in its infrastructure and services, visitors from Britain still found its society exuding charm. By comparison, Britain seemed stuffy, hypocritical and hidebound by convention.

Of course, those people who chose Italy as a bolt hole were generally those with money. While they proclaimed the charms of the country, many Italians were themselves emigrating to America. For while visitors found life blessedly simple, the poor found simplicity tedious and grinding.

# MOVING TO A MODERN AGE

THE ITALIAN STATES WERE ONCE either small administrations or the outposts of an empire with an infrastructure made to a distant regime's specifications. When it united, Italy inherited a railway system that was ill-suited to its needs. It wasn't just that the Austrians had a different agenda regarding destinations. The first tracks and trains that served Austria and then Italy were quickly outdated, especially as far as capacity was concerned.

The line that linked Florence to Bologna was one such line. Known as the Porretta line, it was opened in 1864 across the Apennines to link the Tuscan railways with the trunk route connecting Bologna and Milan which had been completed three years earlier.

The Porretta line was popular but had some drawbacks. It was single track, like many at the time. But it also had steep gradients, which meant that passenger trains, and especially loaded freight trains, proceeded slowly, causing traffic jams behind and ahead – the single track meant that nothing could pass in the opposite direction.

*Before modernisation, the slow-moving Porretta line consisted of a single track, as this 1863 picture reveals*

In the tunnel, the locomotives, still battling to get uphill, produced prodigious amounts of smoke, to the discomfort of travellers and railway employees. It was almost intolerable even when ventilation shafts and fans were fitted to the tunnel. Alternatives were sought and several mountain lines were built in the 1890s, but these were also single track and, without the benefit of a tunnel for shelter, were prone to closure as a result of heavy snow.

As early as 1882 the designer of the original line, Jean Louis Protche (1818–1886), began looking into a new fast link including a tunnel. Although he died four years later, many of his ideas remained integral to the project.

The upgrade also typified the bold approach taken by Italian railway 'king' Riccardo Bianchi, as he transformed the existing system so it was fit for purpose and commercially competitive in the 20th century.

However, it wasn't until 1908 that the government finally earmarked 150 million lire for its construction. Even then, debate about the exact route of the line took a further three years to agree. The result was plans for a double-track line powered by electricity with 31 tunnels and a number of bridges. The aim was to have fewer stations and minimal disruptions from roads and level crossings. In 1913, the year *Bradshaw's* was published, work commenced and Bologna and Pianoro were swiftly connected.

## Tuscany triumph

In 1934, the Florence to Bologna Direttissima opened – as its name implies, a far more direct route, spanning just 97 km (60 miles) rather than the original 131 km (81 miles). The gradients were roughly halved and trains on the safer, straighter line could achieve more than double the speed they did previously. When the first line opened in 1864 passengers had a five-hour journey ahead of them, a time reduced by new locomotives and electrification. However, express trains on the new 'direttissima' covered the distance in just 75 minutes. Today's trains have lopped a further ten minutes off that.

But the onset of the First World War, when Italy fought alongside Britain and France mainly on its Austrian border, delayed further development. After the war there was the characteristic political instability that affected all the belligerents, which made a project like the railway even more overdue.

Work on the longest tunnel through the Apennines was delayed until 1920, and when it started it was far from straightforward. Not only did the sand and clay make digging difficult for the engineers, but workers were also dogged by methane gas seepage, usually dispersed by a controlled explosion. Once, a fire caused by a blast burned for more than ten weeks, causing serious damage. For these reasons, most of the 97 men who died during the railway construction perished in this 18 km (11 mile) underground stretch.

However, one important principle was established. Inside was a double-track passing station, for express trains to overtake slower local ones, endorsing the notion of a high-speed service.

# THE WONDER OF WIRELESS

WHEN NEWSPAPERS UNITED WITH NEW and faster train services, communications in Europe seemed to be thrillingly swift. But an immediacy previously unknown in sending and receiving messages was about to make the world seem smaller still in the 20th century, and it was a graduate of Bologna's historic university who pioneered the necessary wireless technology.

Guglielmo Marconi (1874–1937) didn't start from scratch but built his work on previous discoveries by men like German physicist Heinrich Hertz in 1883, who himself used groundwork laid down by James Clerk Maxwell a decade earlier.

Marconi knew that wireless technology could revolutionise international communications but was unable to interest the Italian government in its merits

Marconi began extending the range of the wireless at his family home in Italy to 2.5 km (1½ miles). However, the Italian government was apparently unmoved by the possibilities so Marconi moved to England – the centre of the maritime world, where the advantages of wireless communication were immediately obvious.

Initially, he put his wireless machinery through its paces by sending a signal across the English Channel. But he was determined messages could travel much further, despite the response of numerous naysayers who thought the curvature of the earth would interfere.

After forming a company and gaining some patents, he established a base in a small wooden hut on the Lizard in Cornwall, just yards from a house that used to signal ships using flags. And it was in these humble and somewhat bleak surroundings that he conclusively proved his theory, first on 23 January 1901 by receiving an S signal in Morse code from another of his company's bases on the Isle of Wight. The distance between the wireless stations was 300 km (186 miles). Then, later the same year, he sent a wireless message that was received in Newfoundland, Canada, 3,500 km (2,200 miles) away.

Soon ships would be able to transmit SOS messages and receive help from the nearest available vessels with the same equipment. He was even credited with saving lives after the *Titanic* disaster in 1912, even though help had not reached the doomed ship as quickly as it might.

## A family affair

Italian railway worker Rodolfo Maserati saw key changes in transport unfold in his working life. By the 20th century the locomotives that he worked alongside were achieving higher speeds than ever before. But it was through six sons that he glimpsed the future. His eldest son Carlo was one of the first test drivers for Fiat in Turin. While he worked there, Carlo designed a single-cylinder engine that he installed into a wooden chassis.

In 1903, Carlo moved to car makers Isotta Fraschini and worked with brother Alfieri. Ultimately, a family firm was created involving Alfieri and brothers Bindo, Ernesto and Ettore, making spark plugs as well as cars. Another brother, Mario, designed the Maserati logo featuring the colours from Bologna's flag and the trident featured in one of the city's fountains. The first car produced by the brothers appeared in 1926, the Tipo 26.

Both Carlo and Alfieri died young and the other brothers eventually sold the company, although the Maserati brand survived. As a champion of steam, Rodolfo had nonetheless gifted the world one of the most exciting sports cars through his talented sons.

Then radio began, although Marconi's company was by now no longer at the cutting edge of the industry. He went on to experiment with microwaves but didn't find the same commercial success as previously.

As a Nobel Prize winner, Marconi returned to Italy firstly for war service and finally to live, embracing Mussolini's Fascism before he died. Upon his death wireless stations across the world fell silent, a tribute that underscored the difference he had made to international communications.

**Paddle steamers on the Italian lakes were a source of delight to British tourists, as a way of soaking up the spectacular scenery**

# LITERATURE ON THE LINE

ALTHOUGH HE LOATHED INDUSTRIAL MODERNITY, writer D. H. Lawrence (1885–1930) could not avoid using trains. Like many writers of his generation, he used them to travel all over Europe – and railways featured in his stories as a device, to energise the plot and illuminate his characters.

Whatever grievance he had with railways was primarily reserved for those used in industry. In *Sons and Lovers* he hints the new and presumably narrow gauge railways serving bigger-than-ever mines are like the chains of slavery for workers. '[F]rom Minton across the farmlands of the valleyside to Bunker's Hill, branching off there, and running north to Beggarlee and Selby, that looks over at Crich and the hills of Derbyshire: six mines like black studs on the countryside, linked by a loop of fine chain, the railway.'

Lawrence was born in Eastwood, Nottinghamshire, also the birthplace of the Midland Railway. But when he began an affair with a married woman, Frieda Weekley, they fled abroad by rail to escape the ensuing scandal. Frieda was German, the first cousin of 'Red Baron' pilot Manfred von Richthofen, and their first stop was Germany – where Lawrence was accused of being a spy. Together they set off over the Alps, walking and using mountain railways when their budget would allow. When they got to the tranquil setting of Lake Garda they found accommodation in Gargnano, and Lawrence embarked on a purple patch, as far as writing was concerned, including the final version of *Sons and Lovers*.

As the loving couple gazed out on the lake, they would have seen the same paddle steamer services listed in the 1913 *Bradshaw's Continental Guide*, timed to depart after the arrival of the trains on the branch line at Riva or Peschiera. Indeed, today's tourists might still glimpse the same vessels on those waters.

The Swiss-built *Zanardelli* went into service in 1903, originally permitted to carry a mighty 800 passengers – reflecting the number of tourists who flocked to the area. During the First World War, she was used to ferry troops and supplies when the lake acted as a border between Italy and its enemy, Austria.

In the Second World War, after sustaining damage in an air raid, the *Zanardelli* was under American control for a while and bedecked with artwork that reflected US scenes. Withdrawn in 1959 for a decade, the steamer was finally refurbished and in 1983 was fitted with a diesel engine.

Slightly longer than her sister ship, the *Italia* embarked on her maiden voyage in 1909. Although she was sunk in an air attack in 1945 the hull was raised and renovated in time for a return to service in 1952. She was fitted with diesel hydraulics in 1980.

## Italy: classy without class

Lawrence wasn't the first writer to find Italy a soothing balm for the creative temperament. Edward Morgan Forster (1879–1970) wrote two successful books inspired by a trip to Italy with his beloved widowed mother Alice. For Forster, Italian society compared favourably with that in Britain, where he considered it too bound by pointless convention. The novels, *Where Angels Fear to Tread* (1905) and *A Room with a View* (1908), feature characters who are stiff with Edwardian propriety but whose lively inner lives defy the social norms of the day. The targets of his writing are the class system, repression and British imperialism, among other things. Mostly, those attitudes are personified in British tourists using *Baedeker's* guides with zeal. Later, Forster was a witness for the defence in the 1960 obscenity trial involving the publishers Penguin and Lawrence's novel *Lady Chatterley's Lover* – which had been published privately in Italy as early as 1928. It proved grist to Forster's mill, as the trial became infamous when prosecution counsel Mervyn Griffith-Jones asked the jury: 'Is it a book you would wish your wife or your servants to read?'

# SOFIA TO ISTANBUL

DURING THE 19TH CENTURY the Ottoman empire fought a catalogue of wars, with only limited success. So expensive were the relentless campaigns that, when it came to providing trains and industry for the vast region it ruled, there was nothing in the coffers. It was just one of a number of complicating factors that finally led to the dismemberment of the empire at the end of the First World War. On the one hand, the arrival of the Orient Express in Constantinople – later called Istanbul – seemed a prestigious event. Yet the very tracks that the luxury trains travelled on were inspiring a fatal discontent in sections of its broad society.

Forced to seek investment from other countries to provide a domestic rail service, the Ottoman regime got sucked into some costly contracts by hard-nosed and highly experienced European railway entrepreneurs. As its finances worsened, so nationalism within its boundaries erupted. Meanwhile, Germany used its influence with the Ottomans to start marginalising its perceived enemies, Britain and France.

And there were continuing power struggles between Islam, Roman Catholicism and the Orthodox religions to consider.

More worrying still for Sultan Abdul Hamid II were the rebellious mutterings in his army and among intellectuals. A group known as the Young Turks, officially the Committee of Union and Progress or CUP, finally forced the sultan to introduce constitutional reforms in 1908.

Here was an entirely new concept of having the most able and interested at the empire's helm rather than the high-born, notably radical in that part of the world. While they brought in plenty of popular changes, the Young Turks estimated that Germany would be on the winning side during the First World War and, disastrously, joined the campaign.

As far as the Ottoman empire was concerned, the installation of a railway service wasn't empowering as it had been for other nations; rather something that left it mortally wounded.

# THE ORIENT EXPRESS

UNTIL THE 1880S, OPULENCE AND RAIL TRAVEL were not words that generally sat together. One man changed that when he pursued the dream of a luxury train that would take passengers from western Europe to Asia's gateway in considerable style. Belgian Georges Nagelmackers (1845–1905) had been inspired when he travelled to America and saw Pullman coaches providing travellers with comfortable overnight accommodation during lengthy railway journeys.

In Europe, where railway cars were notoriously Spartan, he believed there would be an appetite for ornate decor and quality service among the wealthy, who were by now accustomed to international travel. He planned a train that would be worthy of its title of 'the king of trains and the train of kings'.

*Even the best engines had to stop for water, like this one. Those scheduled stops left passengers fearing attacks in the east*

The son of a banker and a friend of royalty, Nagelmackers was well placed to make his vision a reality with his high-ranking contacts. In 1874, he started the Compagnie Internationale des Wagons-Lits, or CIWL, which translates as International Sleeping-Car Company. Then he networked furiously among the European railway companies that would haul his coaches.

He soon learned that garnering investment and co-operation was not as easy as he'd hoped in a Europe divided by previous wars and laying the ground for those in the future. Nonetheless, on 4 October 1883, the first Express d'Orient was ready to leave the Gare de l'Est with a select group of passengers – most of them armed, for fear of meeting bandits on the eastern leg of the trip.

In *The Times*, journalist and passenger Adolphe Opper de Blowitz reported that Nagelmackers was 'bent' on revolutionising Continental travel 'by introducing a comfort and facility hitherto unknown and has had to struggle for ten years not only against internal difficulties and the conflicting interests of railway companies but against the indifference of the very portion of the public which is destined to profit from the result'.

### King and crewman

One illustrious passenger eschewed all CIWL comforts and insisted on travelling in the cab. Wearing overalls, King Boris III of Bulgaria (1894–1943) observed and sometimes drove the locomotive – too fast for the crew's liking, who respectfully tried to part him from the controls.

In 1934, his know-how saved a train between Sofia and Varna, after an onboard bomb knocked the driver unconscious. Having heard the explosion the king clambered outside the racing train from his saloon to the cab, brought the locomotive to a halt, then tended the driver. King Boris was probably poisoned after resisting Hitler's demands to deport Bulgaria's Jews and for refusing to declare war on Russia.

Nagelmackers was indeed catering solely for the elite. The crowd that gathered on the platform to watch the train's departure glimpsed through the window how railway travel on slam-door trains had been elevated to a new level. There was a smoking room, a ladies' boudoir and a library, with Turkish carpets on the floors, plush red armchairs and inlaid tables ready to bear crystal glasses. Bedrooms had silk-covered walls, in one of which was a pull-down bed thick with smooth sheets and soft blankets.

Those on the outside didn't see the dining room with its embossed leather ceiling and velvet drapes, where a freshly cooked five-course meal would soon be served. Nor did they know about onboard toilets with hot and cold running water.

Servants' dormitories were tucked away at the end of the carriage, along with an ice box that was filled with exotic foods. Beneath the carriage were American-style pairs of four-wheel bogies, making for a much more even ride.

As the inaugural train pulled into Strasbourg, Vienna and Budapest, it was greeted by brass bands and local dignitaries. A gypsy orchestra came onboard in Tsigany in Hungary to serenade the passengers as they made sedate progress at just 64 kph (40 mph).

Although passengers had to take a ferry over the Danube and a sea voyage from the port of Varna to reach Constantinople in the absence of suitable track, the new railway – for now still mortgaged to the hilt – was deemed a success.

# MIND THE GAPS

BY THE SUMMER OF 1889 NEW RAILWAY TRACKS had filled in the gaps and passengers from Paris could reach Constantinople 68 hours later without leaving their lap of luxury. The train crossed seven international frontiers and operated in more than eight different railway systems.

In 1891, it became officially branded the Orient Express, named not for the Far East but for the former Byzantine empire. Here was an exotic destination rarely visited by Europeans before the train service got underway. CIWL even built a hotel in Constantinople, the Pera Palace, to receive passengers in a comparable style.

However, the train did alter its course, either to suit new routes as they became available or to surmount political hurdles that arose with increasing regularity. The most prominent scuffles were two disputes in swift succession which deprived the Ottoman empire of its last remaining European possessions. In the First Balkan War – over in eight weeks – the Ottoman empire was defeated by Serbia, Bulgaria, Greece and Montenegro.

Just six months later Bulgaria was attacked by its former allies, Serbia and Greece, who were now joined by Romania and the Ottoman empire. Within two months Bulgaria was on the losing side and had to surrender territory. The short, sharp conflicts that escalated international tensions across Europe helped to set the stage for the First World War.

Unwittingly, some of the groundwork for both had been laid when railways that carried the Orient Express were built in the region, illuminating how the conflict came about.

Years before the tracks were put down – and convinced that railways were necessary for its survival – the Ottoman empire looked for foreign investment and engineers to fulfil its needs. A first concession to build a railway from Constantinople to Vienna was granted in 1868 and changed hands several times for lack of funds until the following year, when it was seized by Baron Maurice de Hirsch (1831–1896), a financier with an appetite for railway schemes.

The chosen route to the Austrian border, via Adrianople and Sofia, bypassed self-governing Serbia in favour of Bosnia and was called 'the south road'. Behind this was an Austrian desire to isolate Serbia, a country the old empire viewed with suspicion. With generous terms already agreed, Hirsch eventually established the Société Générale pour l'Exploitation des Chemins de Fer Orientaux, thankfully abbreviated to CO.

But nothing went smoothly for the company or the countries involved. There were various uprisings in the Balkan states between 1874 and 1878, making co-operation and construction almost impossible. Meanwhile, the Ottoman empire defaulted on a debt to Russia and they resumed hostilities for two years.

## Fair's fare

In Bradshaw's, the Orient Express was advertised starting from London and going via Paris, Stuttgart, Vienna, Bucharest and Constanţa on the Romanian coast, in a trip costing £19. There was an alternative too, via Brussels, Cologne and then Vienna onwards for £17.13s.3d. There were no second-class options – and both trains were known as the Orient Express.

Passengers boarding at Charing Cross on the 10 a.m. service would spend four nights aboard the train, possibly more if there were substantial delays or detours. The service between London and Vienna ran each day while the onward trip to Constantinople was only available three times a week.

By 1913 the journey entailed a ferry trip from Constanţa, as by now the most direct route through Adrianople (now Edirne) was suspended following the Balkan Wars.

Nor was the CO bringing in any revenue for the Turks. In 1881, when the company had 105 locomotives, the majority were supplied by Germany and the rest by Austria, Belgium, Britain and France. Most of the wagons came from Germany too, as did the track, the material for the station buildings and 90 per cent of the iron in the new bridges. It was an example of how Germany was cementing its influence.

The Congress of Berlin in 1878 restored peace by making Serbia, Romania and Bulgaria independent and placing Bosnia under Austrian control. It also directed that the future of the Constantinople to Vienna railway should be in the control of Austria, Turkey, Bulgaria and Serbia. The subtext was a desire by Germany to ease out French and British influences.

# PLANS DERAILED

NATURALLY, NEWLY INDEPENDENT COUNTRIES wanted railway networks of their own. Without the necessary finance to build them, it seemed to them reasonable to assume ownership of tracks already running through their territories.

Passengers travelling in luxury on the Orient Express were unaware of the political rumblings in the region

Although Bulgaria had played no part in its construction, it seized the CO line within its borders in 1888 – and even then it remained disgruntled. In 1890, Otto von Kühlmann, once president of the company, wrote to the head of the Deutsche Bank, Georg von Siemens, about the Bulgarian attitude: 'They have 300 km of railways in their country for which they have not paid anything and then they complain because they believe railway tariffs are too high.'

For their part, the Serbs and Bulgarians believed the CO put its financial interests – and those of Austria and Germany – above those of the countries in which they operated. Nor did they provide any regional benefits, outside the train service itself, while the company was run from Vienna.

They had a point. The CO was paid by the track kilometre by the Ottoman empire and, as the *Economist* put it, 'it could afford to disregard sordid considerations of profit and loss'.

In 1896, the Bulgarians began to construct a rival railway section, parallel to the one operated by the CO. The company lodged an international protest and secured the support of the German and Austrian governments, as well as the banks. For lack of funds, the new line was abandoned.

Ultimately, the Ottoman empire received two major payouts after initiating the line. The first was from Baron Hirsch, who was found to owe the Turks some 60 million francs. Arbitration revealed that Hirsch had agreed to build railways for an average price. In the event, he completed construction of the (cheaper) tracks across the plains, but the more challenging routes through the mountains were unfinished. (Hirsch, one of Europe's richest people at that time, and his wife Clara are thought to have given away £18 million to philanthropic causes, chiefly in Jewish education.) The next payout was 42 million francs from the Bulgarians after the railway was seized, money supplied by the Russians. Half was given to the CO by the Turkish government.

In 1908, CO workers took strike action, to the fury of the Bulgarians, who confiscated the company's supplies of coal and petroleum and expelled some of its employees. It's thought this backlash happened because a Bulgarian diplomat had been snubbed at an event in Istanbul. Many of the workers' demands were about safety and ultimately met by the CO management.

Wealthy passengers aboard the Orient Express were blissfully unaware of the friction created by the construction of eastward lines out of Europe and of the simmering tensions that continued in the region, fuelling the small-scale strife that suspended some services.

## Great train robbery

On 31 May 1891, audacious train robbers derailed the Orient Express, to rob passengers and take hostages. Seeing the track had been torn up, the driver braked but was unable to bring the train to a halt in time. After the engine and the first few carriages had toppled down an embankment, the armed thieves arrived on horseback, led by a bearded man who identified himself as Anasthatos.

The gang took jewellery and cash, although Anasthatos returned wedding rings and lockets to women passengers before he left. Then they forced the train driver, a British embassy official, several German businessman and some of the wealthier passengers to their hideout.

A rescue mission from Constantinople was held up by bureaucracy and then by soldiers on board who insisted on travelling at a snail's pace in case it was a trap. When an outraged Kaiser Wilhelm II threatened to invade, the Ottoman government came up with the ransom demanded for the hostages, who were duly released. Anasthatos, his men and the thousands of pounds' worth of ill-gotten gains that he secured that day were never seen again.

When the First World War finally erupted, the Orient Express service was stopped for its duration. Germany and Austria took charge of any CIWL carriages left within its borders, using them to form a rival called Mitropa. It was in competition with the Orient Express after the war, along with the Simplon Orient Express, another luxury service which took a more southerly route across Europe. It was on this train that Agatha Christie set her *Murder on the Orient Express*. From 1932, there was also the Arlberg Orient Express.

But the era for this kind of train travel was coming to an end. Over the decades the services were withdrawn, shortened, switched, shared, economised or, in one case, made even more exclusive than previously.

Smyrne.          Mouvement du Port.

## COLONIAL COMPETITION

The harbour at Izmir with lines run by the British-sponsored ORC embedded into the quay

WHILE THEY WERE NOT ENMESHED in that convoluted drama being played out on the European flank of the Ottoman empire, the British still registered some interests in railways on Turkish soil. There was British money behind the Oriental Railway Company – not to be confused with the CO – which built railways in the Izmir region.

The concession was given as early as 1856 for the line between Izmir and Aydin, the same year the first railway in the Ottoman empire between Alexandria and Cairo had opened.

For the Oriental Railway Company, British investors who had stumped up £1.2 million would reap the rewards for 50 years after the predicted date of the railway opening, which was 1860. In fact, costs got the better of the schedule. Although the first section was opened in 1858, it would be a further eight years before it was completed.

The aim was to transport minerals and fruit and vegetables from fertile valleys around the Menderes river, known in classical times as the Meander. Cave paintings reveal it has been inhabited for some 8,000 years and bears evidence of ancient Greek kings, Alexander the Great, the Byzantine emperors, the Crusaders and various Turkish sultans. But despite this illustrious heritage, the value of the goods the railway was transporting was not high and the profits were therefore limited.

Politics did play a part in the expansion of the Oriental Railway Company. While it did extend the line as far as Eğirdir by 1912, there was reluctance in Britain to provide money that might further empower the Ottoman empire in a strategically sensitive area. In one direction lay the Middle East, where Britain was cultivating petroleum interests and watched hawk-like over the Suez Canal. In the other was India, the colony that provided both kudos and material trade for Britain.

Meanwhile, the Ottoman empire kept a wary eye on the Oriental Railway Company, as building a railway to a port betrayed its self-interest.

The Ottomans might have reasonably suspected the British of sizing up the region for possible colonial expansion, given the political landscape. Perhaps for this reason, the ORC failed to win any further concessions that might have enhanced its profits in the region. But with an inability to build railways for itself, this inward-looking response by the Ottomans left the region poorly served with railway connections.

As far as railway building was concerned, the Ottomans ended up focusing not on the land in present-day Turkey but in all its dominions, particularly the Middle East. However, future ruler Kemal Atatürk (1881–1938) came to rue the lack of domestic lines. He believed that had a planned route through the Taurus Mountains to Adana at the eastern end of the Mediterranean Sea been built, the Turks might have exerted better control of the Arab lands.

## Armenian genocide

In an eerie precursor to the Holocaust which would later be organised by their German allies, the Turks used trains during a systematic genocide of Armenian Christians begun in 1915. After years of persecution, the Armenians were thought likely to side with the Russians during the First World War. According to *Bradshaw's*, there were about 40 Armenian churches in Istanbul in 1913, giving an indication of the size of the population.

A letter dated 22 November 1915 from an American rail traveller made public by the American Committee for Armenian and Syrian Relief revealed how old people and children were crammed into wagons for a train journey that ended in death or exile.

'We began to pass one train after another, crowded, jammed with these poor people being carried away to some spot where no food could be obtained. At every station where we stopped we came side by side with one of these trains. It was made up of cattle trucks and the faces of little children were looking out.'

Those on the train had paid for their passage. About a million Armenians died before the war ended, many on forced marches out of Ottoman territory. Thousands more were deported.

# THE FLORENCE NIGHTINGALE EFFECT

FOR THOSE DISMOUNTING THE ORIENT EXPRESS, Constantinople must have come as something of a shock. *Bradshaw's* is very direct in its warnings. Customs examinations are, it says, 'extremely vexatious and unreasonable', with books liable to be seized and destroyed.

Nor was the weather to British tastes:

'Travellers careful of their health should recollect that the climate in summer changes from one extreme to another and that the same day, even the same hour, may be intensely hot and cold …

In summer they should not adopt the fez which exposes novices to a sun stroke but they should wear white hats or caps.'

> **'In summer [travellers] should not adopt the fez which exposes novices to a sun stroke …'**
> *Bradshaw's*

Furthermore, Turkish time changed daily with the sun.

So what would bring the British to Constantinople before the First World War? Many came to visit the graves of soldiers killed in the Crimean War (1853–1856). Eight thousand war dead are buried in the cemetery at Haydarpaşa, close to the Selimiye barracks, also known as the Scutari barracks, where Florence Nightingale (1820–1910) and her team of 38 nurses worked hard both to save the wounded and to improve basic standards of care. Most of the victims died from typhoid and cholera.

An obelisk was put there to commemorate the soldiers, unveiled by Queen Victoria in 1857. Since then the number of British graves has risen: some civilians have been buried there, but significantly there are about 400 graves dating from the First World War of men who died as Turkish prisoners of war or during the British occupation of Istanbul between 1918 and 1923.

At the Scutari barracks during the Crimean War, Florence Nightingale fought her own battle, to raise hygiene standards and save lives

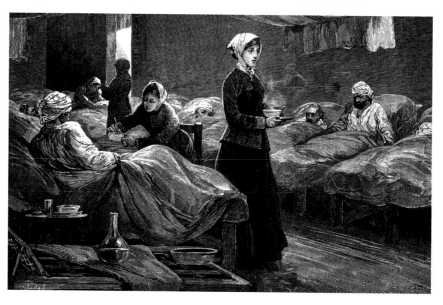

The nearby Haydarpaşa station had been rebuilt by 1909, its telltale conical towers betraying the work of German architects. Although it might look more at home on the Rhine than on the Bosphorus, it was intended to mark a new chapter in Ottoman railways after Haydarpaşa was picked as the northern end of the Baghdad and Hejaz railways – neither of which would appear for years. It was a gift from Kaiser Wilhelm II to his opposite number, Abdul Hamid II.

Construction on land reclaimed from the sea meant that 1,100 wooden piles, each measuring 21 metres (65 ft), were driven into the sodden ground by steam hammer before the six-storey station could be erected. The sandstone facades and slated pitched roof soon became a landmark.

On the Asian side of Istanbul, anyone arriving on the Orient Express would have had to catch a ferry if their onward journey started from here.

## Haydarpaşa doomed

In 1891, Sultan Abdul Hamid II had ambitions to better connect his capital city with a railway tunnel beneath the Bosphorus. French engineers drew up plans but nothing came of them, perhaps because the sultan was perceptibly losing his grip on the empire, or maybe because the ground beneath the sea was found to be particularly unstable.

But 120 years later, a tube measuring 13 km (8 miles) was set into the seabed some 60 metres (197 ft) below the water to effectively link Europe and Asia. A glassy subway, the Marmaray will initially carry commuters and the line is robust enough for high-speed trains and freight. Much of the investment in the $2.8 billion project came from Japan. Turkish prime minister Tayyip Erdoğan said his country had realised 'the dream of our ancestors'.

At its opening, Japanese prime minister Shinzo Abe said: 'Japan and Turkey are the two wings of Asia. Let us dream together of a high-speed train departing from Tokyo, passing through Istanbul and arriving in London.'

With the Marmaray refocusing rail traffic in Istanbul, there's doubt that Haydarpaşa station – which was closed for a long-term overhaul – will ever welcome a train again.

# FREIBURG TO HANNOVER

MOSTLY, COLONIAL COMPETITIVENESS and an undue expansion in the German navy are the immediate causes given for the First World War. As important as the physical manifestations of militarism is the mindset of the Germans at the time. A sense of German pride washed over the region when its people were living under numerous regimes. That wasn't appeased after German unification in 1871 and they remained united in the aim of achieving a better future under a single umbrella.

As one nation, Germany was known for its academic rigour, high culture, and for nurturing creative souls. A strong national leader might well have melded those fine qualities with the deep well of patriotism and national pride to make the country great. But Kaiser Wilhelm II did not possess the compelling character or the integrity needed for this role and he was prey to vacillation, especially after the input of advisers. For this reason, he parted company with the adequately qualified Otto von Bismarck, the statesman who had done so much to deliver the vision of a united Germany.

Folklore, extremist student groups and, unwittingly, a large conservative middle ground all fed into a belief that Germany was being short-changed on the international stage. A toxic side effect of national empowerment, it served to place Germany on the road to war.

Prosperity in cities like Hannover no doubt gave an illusion that Germany was unbeatable. No one posed the question 'what if?'…

It wasn't only the German navy that was expanding. (In 1911 Germany had 38 battleships, 43 cruisers, 129 destroyers and 16 submarines.) With railways under state control, the length of tracks increased from 6,300 km (3,900 miles) in 1879 to 31,000 km (19,300 miles) by 1902. We know from *Bradshaw's* that its army on a war footing would be some three million strong.

# BROTHERS GRIMM

FEW CHILDREN EMERGE INTO ADULTHOOD without encountering the fanciful, feel-good fairy tales drawn together by the Brothers Grimm. Yet the truth about this pair of German brothers and the stories recounted in their name has been lost in the telling.

The title page of *Nursery and Household Tales*, published in various editions in the 19th century, hints at its sinister content

Jacob Grimm (1785–1863) and his younger brother Wilhelm (1786–1859) were not so much storytellers as collectors of folklore. They witnessed how life was changing rapidly, with railways carving up the countryside and factories sprouting around the cities. Until then, stories were handed down through generations, by a father taking a long journey on foot or by horseback, or a mother passing the time while doing housework. One fear was that these tales would be lost if they were not corralled together, as the pace of life quickened.

Today, those stories associated with the brothers have a high moral plain inhabited by goodly heroes who may not win every battle over black-hearted villains but who inevitably win the war. Yet that's not how they first appeared. In their original form, the tales were vividly violent, often involving incest and savagery – and entirely unsuitable for children. After all, they had been created in the Middle Ages, at a time when Germans endured a series of brutal wars and children were often considered more of a burden than a blessing.

For example, among many differences between the Cinderella story made famous in pantomime and the one recounted by the brothers was that theirs had one of the 'ugly sisters' sever her own toe in order to fit into the shoe brought to her door by a handsome prince. The other sliced off the back of her own heel.

When they were first published in 1812, it wasn't as fairy tales for children but in a book called *Nursery and Household Tales*, aimed squarely at adults. Even today in Germany they are termed 'wonder tales' rather than children's stories.

The two men were eminent scholars with a passion for language and a yearning to see the many different German states unified as one. Apart from the fairy tales now attributed to them, they wrote about medieval literature and German legal traditions, mythology and linguistics, and were in the process of creating a German dictionary before their deaths.

Their own lives had few fairy-tale qualities. Born into comfortable surroundings, they were catapulted into adult responsibility by the untimely death of their father, leaving 12-year-old Jacob to look after his mother Dorothea and five siblings. Happily, both Jacob and Wilhelm were sponsored in their education, but they were initially disqualified from attending university in Marburg for being too poor. They won an appeal against the decision and excelled in their studies. By 1837 they were professors at the University of Göttingen, but ran into difficulties there over a point of principle.

Hannover – which had shared a king with Britain since 1714 when George I at 52nd in line to the throne was judged the closest Protestant candidate – had enjoyed the benefits of a hard-won constitution since 1833. But the death of William IV in England in 1837 ended the union between the two countries. When William's brother Ernest Augustus came to the throne in Hannover, he rejected the constitution. Seven university professors, including the Grimms, who opposed his high-handedness, were forced to quit. After leaving Hannover, they joined the university in Berlin, where they spent the rest of their lives.

By the time Wilhelm died, *Nursery and Household Tales* was in its seventh edition and contained 211 stories, including those we know today as 'Sleeping Beauty', 'Snow White', 'Rapunzel', 'Little Red Riding Hood' and 'Rumpelstiltskin'.

## The Eulenberg affair

Born with a withered arm, Kaiser Wilhelm II (1859–1941) set great store by the physical prowess associated with the military. Yet he surrounded himself with an 'inner circle' of advisers, who were either effeminate or gay. One journalist, Max Harden, became convinced the Kaiser was being badly advised by his coterie and tried to 'out' those he thought were gay. It was a long-running duel in the Edwardian era, enlivened by salacious divorce hearings and near-the-knuckle editorials, which ultimately tarnished the public perception of the Kaiser in Germany, especially among those who believed homosexuals had no place in government. However, as the advisers retreated from the spotlight, the victims of public shaming or blackmail, the door was opened for hard-line militarists to gain unprecedented and unchallenged access to the Kaiser in the years leading up to the First World War.

# HIGH-MINDED HIKERS

The imposing ruins of Heidelberg castle helped to feed the imaginations of visiting writers and philosophers

WITH ITS LOFTY RUINED CASTLE and winding river, Heidelberg has a picture-book quality that's appealed to thousands of inventive minds. Hence it became the beating heart of Germany's Romantic period in the 18th century. The reason lies with the city's university, founded in 1386 and the oldest in modern Germany.

From here, academics seeking inspiration would set forth on what became known as the 'Philosopher's Way', a scenic elevated route through woods where stunning views of the town could be glimpsed in a climate that's been compared to Tuscany. Correspondingly, they found inspiration in nature, more exotic than the norm, the same key ingredient that would fuel the work of Romantics in literature, philosophy, art and music.

The most famous figure known to have trodden that thought-provoking path is Johann Wolfgang von Goethe (1749–1832), considered the greatest German literary figure of the modern era. A poet, playwright, novelist, scientist and statesman, Goethe found more satisfaction in the unspoiled vistas of Heidelberg than he did in run-down Rome. But he was in good company. Joseph von Eichendorff (1788–1857) studied law at Heidelberg in 1808, before beginning to author his famously lyrical poems. And Friedrich Hölderlin (1770–1843), a tortured spirit whose poetry is deemed to have bridged classicism and Romanticism, is known to have wandered up that leafy route – although he did not find sufficient succour to prevent the madness with which he was later afflicted.

After the railway reached Heidelberg there was an opportunity for still more feted literary figures to visit. Mark Twain (1835–1910) was among them, trying to shake off a spell of writer's block, which he successfully did. Soon, Heidelberg was dubbed Germany's intellectual capital.

Fittingly, the first station building made from red Neckar sandstone was constructed in neoclassical style with Romantic ornament. When it first opened in 1840 – with six sets of points and 15 turntables – it only served passengers going to or from Mannheim. But soon Heidelberg had trains in its station which served Karlsruhe and Frankfurt, and later Baden, after the broad gauge chosen by Baden State Railway was replaced with standard gauge. The infrastructure was changed in the early 20th century to accommodate still more lines.

The focal point for both rail travellers and those destined for great insights on the Philosopher's Way was the castle or schloss, described by *Bradshaw's* as 'a most magnificent ruin'. Built in stages from the 12th century, it was razed by the French in 1689. The ruins were further damaged by a lightning strike in 1764, which only added to its mysterious qualities.

Despite a succession of spats in the region caused by acquisitive neighbours or contrariness between Catholics and Protestants, Heidelberg remains remarkably unscarred by conflict – being largely overlooked by bombers in the Second World War.

## Fervour for the fatherland

Another strand that fed into the story of the First World War was that of patriotic student groups, which began to appear across the German region in the 19th century. The first *Burschenschaft*, founded in 1815 at Jena, had a motto of 'honour, freedom, fatherland', and these were stirring sentiments for a people who, in their own eyes, were deprived of a nation. It soon spread, with the most enthusiastic members taking part in the 1848 revolution and some of the wars that led to the unification of Germany.

Although the goals of the *Burschenschaften* then appeared to have been accomplished, there was a post-unification revival, which saw a quest for liberalism replaced by aggressive nationalism that nurtured dreams of a pan-German Europe. Here the seeds sown for the First World War found fertile ground.

# LOSING AND WINNING

A statue dedicated to Ernest Augustus in 1910 outside Hannover's station said he was 'the father of the nation'. He was much less popular in Britain

ALTHOUGH HANNOVER SHARED A MONARCH with Britain, it benefited little from the arrangement, becoming a neglected outpost for the royals. Victoria became Britain's queen in 1837, presiding over one of the most dynamic periods of growth experienced by any modern power and gathering the world's largest empire.

But with female succession outlawed in Hannover, it had the inward-looking Ernest Augustus (1771–1851) on the throne instead, whose first act was to dissolve parliament. Hannover had been raised to a kingdom after the

Holy Roman empire, which had governed it, was dissolved in 1806. As a king, he is remembered for resisting calls by neighbouring Prussia and the Duchy of Brunswick for an east to west rail route to enter his kingdom. Only after he had participated in a trial run on the Brunswick line in 1841 did he finally agree to a railway being built to his capital. (His first train ride came a year before that of his niece, Queen Victoria – and he was soon a fully fledged convert to rail travel, not least when he later visited Britain and rode in a plushly appointed royal carriage. He immediately ordered one for himself.)

## Tram city

With a shortage of city centre trains, Hannover introduced a 'horse-drawn' railway in 1872, initially open-sided. From 1893, the electric tram was the transport of choice in Hannover – and that remains the same today.

In 2015, two new-generation trams went into service on Hannover's routes to replace 30-year-old models. Twenty-five metres (82 ft) long and fully air-conditioned, they are both in two sections and are part of an order for 50 light rail vehicles which will cost around 126 million euros. Some of the redundant trams have found a new lease of life on the streets of Budapest.

Perhaps fittingly, Hannover is the site of Germany's largest tram museum, built on the site of a former potash mine.

Despite this unpromising start he was tolerated in Hannover, less so in Britain where he had previously lived. When he died, *The Times* said: 'The good that can be said of the Royal dead is little or none.' But the outlook did not immediately improve for the little kingdom. Having defeated the neighbouring Prussians at the Battle of Langensalza in 1866, Hannover was nonetheless unwillingly annexed as part of a campaign to unite the German states.

Against expectation, it proved far more profitable than any royal association had. Mutterings of discontent against the Prussians were quelled when free trade was introduced after royal regulations that protected parochial trade guilds were swept away by the new regime. Between 1871 and 1912 the population almost quadrupled.

Its success was reflected in the mushrooming of trains serving Hannover in the second half of the 19th century. The first railway to reach the outskirts in 1843 was run by the Royal Hanoverian State Railways. But the king remained reluctant for his capital to be scarred by railways, so progress, although it did take place, was slowed until his death.

Subsumed by the Prussian state railways after 1866, by 1879 Hannover had a fine new station with seven platforms and two tunnels earmarked for freight. Out of the jaws of an apparent defeat came economic victory, compounded by a refashioning of the city by Heinrich Tramm (1854–1932), who further expanded the rail network as well as introducing a system of surburban trains. His legacy included the grand town hall, finished in 1913, the covered market and a hospital, plus the sewage system and water works.

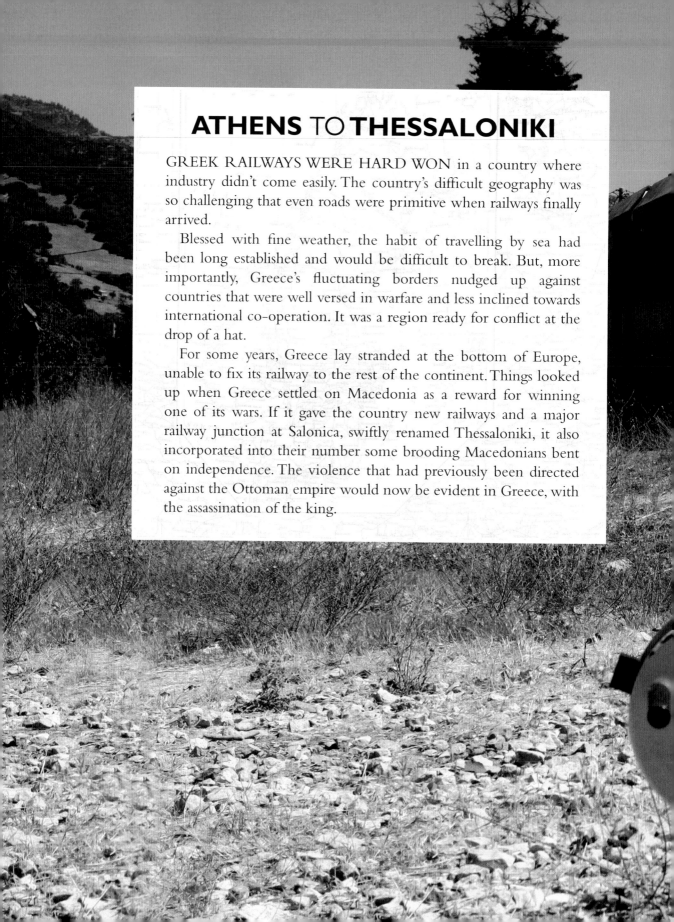

# ATHENS TO THESSALONIKI

GREEK RAILWAYS WERE HARD WON in a country where industry didn't come easily. The country's difficult geography was so challenging that even roads were primitive when railways finally arrived.

Blessed with fine weather, the habit of travelling by sea had been long established and would be difficult to break. But, more importantly, Greece's fluctuating borders nudged up against countries that were well versed in warfare and less inclined towards international co-operation. It was a region ready for conflict at the drop of a hat.

For some years, Greece lay stranded at the bottom of Europe, unable to fix its railway to the rest of the continent. Things looked up when Greece settled on Macedonia as a reward for winning one of its wars. If it gave the country new railways and a major railway junction at Salonica, swiftly renamed Thessaloniki, it also incorporated into their number some brooding Macedonians bent on independence. The violence that had previously been directed against the Ottoman empire would now be evident in Greece, with the assassination of the king.

# POLITICS AND PROCRASTINATION

BY A HAPPY QUIRK OF TIMING, Greece became an independent state in 1832, chiming nicely with the onset of the golden age of railways in Europe. Unfortunately, however, it was not best placed to take advantage of railway expansion, with a population that was thinly spread and largely poor.

*Bradshaw's* sums up the country's dilemma:

'Less than a fifth of the surface of the country is cultivated, nearly a tenth is covered by forests, almost two thirds of the land lies uncultivated and useless yet agriculture is mainly the occupation of the people, the existing manufactures not being important.'

> **'Less than a fifth of the surface of the country is cultivated ...'**
> *Bradshaw's*

It wasn't until 27 February 1869 that its first stretch of railway was completed, extending for just 10 km (6 miles) between Athens and the port of Piraeus. A steam train pulling six carriages with passengers including the country's Queen Olga and other dignitaries established the urban line, which was electrified in 1904. It took passengers and freight, including coal for the newly built gas works in Athens.

Despite the success of the link, it was another decade before the Greek parliament opened serious discussions about how the railway network would proceed. First, there was the gauge to consider. The standard gauge was preferable as far as linking up with the European network was concerned. But given budget limitations and the rugged terrain, narrow gauge railways were a viable option.

After it opened in 1869 the link between Athens and Piraeus became a vital artery for the capital city

In 1881, Prime Minister Alexandros Koumoundouros (1817–1883) signed three contracts for railway lines with standard gauges, including an international connection. But after he lost power the contract was revoked, with new prime minister Charilaos Trikoupis (1832–1896) imposing his vision of narrow gauge railways to stimulate regional economies, believing he could institute more kilometres for the same money. He had already seen the transforming effect of railways in Britain, where there were no international lines to consider.

Now in opposition, Koumoundouros declared that without compatible gauges international traffic would be limited or deterred. The debate galvanised Greece, with all sides at least agreeing upon a standard gauge line to its northern border which might one day link up to the rest of Europe.

Finally, in 1889, a contract was signed between the Greek government and a group of British capitalists to build a line from Piraeus to the Greek border, some 390 km (240 miles). Four years later work came to a halt, apparently because the construction company ran into financial difficulties. The Greek government was also short of money, having built the country's first serviceable network of roads.

Following a short war between Greece and the Ottoman empire in 1897 another company took on the task and finally reached the border in 1909.

## A long wait for the train

Greece wanted both domestic and international lines for the purposes of an improved economy and enhanced prestige. However, it would be a long time before Greece lost its historic dependency on ships. Few countries hit as many political as well as financial stumbling blocks in pursuit of establishing a railway network.

Greece needed foreign investment to bring in imported tracks and locomotives, and took out loans it could ill afford while still investing in other public programmes. The country was also boxed in by neighbouring and not necessarily friendly powers. Negotiations to plot a path into mainland Europe that was acceptable to all sides took years.

In the end, a project that should have lasted several years turned into one that endured for a quarter of a century, its architect Charilaos Trikoupis already long dead.

However, Trikoupis was rewarded by seeing a cog railway up and running in the southerly Peloponnese peninsula serving the remote communities there.

# MOVING TARGET

POISED TO END THEIR COUNTRY'S Continental isolation by joining the European network, Greek delegates opened negotiations with the Ottoman empire. Greece put forward its favoured route – the shortest – while the Ottoman government sought something different. Negotiations lasted years yet remained at an impasse.

This was hardly surprising given the heightened tensions at the border, where it wasn't just a case of the long-running antipathy between Greece and Turkey. Another factor was Macedonia, then ruled by the Ottomans.

> **'Frequent attempts were made to blow up our railway lines, fortunately mostly with only slight success.'**

But many Macedonians had long dreamed of independence and orchestrated a campaign against the railways to achieve it.

A 1903 report by the CO, the company running railways through the Ottomans' European provinces, noted an upsurge in violence by the Macedonians and their increased and 'ruthless' use of explosives:

'Frequent attempts were made to blow up our railway lines, fortunately mostly with only slight success. Several atrocities were perpetrated with [the use of] infernal machine guns against moving trains and a number of passengers were killed or injured.'

In 1911, Ottoman soldiers were still apprehensive at the Salonica–Constantinople railway junction. Thinking he saw movement in a tunnel, one soldier fired and the sound of his weapon brought trigger-happy colleagues to his aid. It sounded like a firefight had broken out between soldiers and terrorists – but the gunshots were all going one way. The movement had been in the fervid imagination of the first soldier to fire. The incident held up the train from Istanbul for eight hours.

Diplomacy over the proposed railway came to nothing as another war ensued and Greece, on the winning side, gained an unhappy Macedonia and its three railways. With renewed vigour, the Greek government set about getting its route into Europe settled and building other railways that would consolidate its territorial gains. The government bought existing railway companies, laid down more tracks and by 1916 Greece's international connections were finally made, crossing into war-affected Ottoman territory in doing so.

So there was plenty to occupy the minds of Greek politicians. And, in common with other nations, establishing a railway network was by no means the sole issue on their agenda. It is Trikoupis who is best remembered for imposing a better infrastructure on Greece. Not only did he draw up a plan for railways, but he also pushed forward plans for the Corinth Canal. Indeed, he would have begun building a bridge over the Gulf of Corinth if technology had allowed it. That wasn't achieved for another century, when it was named for him. However, there was a flip side to the ambitions that Trikoupis had during his total of seven stints as prime minister.

## Assassin at large

Although famous for his 'common touch', the Greek King George I was assassinated in Thessaloniki on 18 March 1913, a few weeks before celebrating 50 years on the throne.

He was from the Danish royal family, a candidate agreed by both the Greek parliament and Britain and France after his unpopular predecessor was ousted. King George was brother-in-law to Britain's King Edward VII. King George V and Tsar Nicholas II were his nephews and he was the grandfather of Britain's Prince Philip.

Taking a customary stroll without a bodyguard, he was shot by anarchist Alexandros Schinas, who died six weeks later in a fall from a police station window. The king's son Constantine succeeded him, a popular military leader and married to a sister of Kaiser

Wilhelm II. For the time being, Greece would be far more inclined to support the German cause than hitherto.

They eventually cost the country more money than it had in the bank. Humiliatingly, during his sixth term, Trikoupis was compelled to stand before parliament and announce: 'Regretfully, we are bankrupt.' Having failed to satisfy his country's creditors or population, he died in the first week of the 1896 Athens Olympics, an event he had opposed on the grounds of cost.

Yet despite hold-ups and setbacks, political instability and a shortage of funds, there was still a thirst to extend the railway network, but first parliament wanted to get railway administration sorted. In 1920, Hellenic State Railways was formed, to govern all lines of standard gauge in Greece. For the first two years, the French mission in Athens undertook its management, as three French lines had been absorbed. Afterwards the Greek state took charge. Much later, the narrow gauge railway built by Trikoupis in the southerly Peloponnese was also included.

As a country always pursuing greater territory, the outer limits of Greece were not finally decided until it was defeated by Turkey in 1922. By the mid-1930s Greece had more than 2,500 km (1,550 miles) of track. But although its locomotives were typically large, Greek railway lines remained relatively spare in number.

# Timeline

| | |
|---|---|
| **1830** | **The Liverpool to Manchester railway line opens in Britain, the first recognisable rail service in the world.** |
| **1835** | **Belgium runs the first steam train on the Continent, between Brussels and Malines.** |
| **1835** | **King Ludwig I of Bavaria opens the Nuremberg to Fürth line.** |
| **1837** | **Austria's Kaiser Ferdinand-Nordbahn opens, heading north out of Vienna, powered by Robert Stephenson's locomotives.** |
| **1837** | **St Petersburg and the royal retreat at Tsarskoe are linked by train.** |
| **1839** | **Germany's first long-distance line, between Leipzig and Dresden, is opened.** |
| **1839** | **Naples and Portici are linked by rail.** |
| **1839** | **The first Dutch railway is launched between Amsterdam and Haarlem.** |
| **1842** | **Lagging behind, the French government passes a law to increase rail building in France.** |
| **1846** | **Hungary's first train starts to run.** |
| **1847** | **Denmark launches its railways system with a train running between Copenhagen and Roskilde.** |
| **1847** | **Switzerland's first train, between Baden and Zürich, is dubbed 'the Spanish bun train'.** |
| **1847** | **The first *Bradshaw's Continental Guide* is printed.** |
| **1848** | **Spain's first train steams into service, serving Barcelona and Mataró.** |
| **1848** | **Vienna and Warsaw are linked by rail.** |
| **1851** | **St Petersburg to Moscow line opens.** |
| **1851** | **Spain's first long-distance railway between Madrid and Aranjuez opens.** |

| | |
|---|---|
| **1853** | George Bradshaw dies from cholera in Norway. |
| **1854** | Italy's first inter-city service linking Turin and Genoa is launched. |
| **1854** | The Semmering line links Vienna and Trieste. |
| **1856** | Portugal joins the railway age with a service between Lisbon and Carregado. |
| **1862** | Finland celebrates its first railway, built on the Russian broad gauge. |
| **1869** | Greece's first railway, between Athens and Piraeus, gets underway. |
| **1871** | Mont Cenis tunnel completed. |
| **1881** | Werner von Siemens unveils his 'electric train', which is developed into a tram. |
| **1882** | Gotthard tunnel opens. |
| **1883** | The first Orient Express runs, although passengers use train and ship to reach Constantinople. |
| **1892** | Jaffa to Jerusalem link opens for pilgrims. |
| **1900** | Paris Métro opens. |
| **1900** | Diesel unveils his new engine. |
| **1901** | Wuppertal monorail opens. |
| **1903** | The Malmbanan, built north of the Arctic Circle by the Swedes to carry freight, is finished. |
| **1903** | Thomas Cook's electric railway begins running on Mount Vesuvius. |
| **1905** | Trans-Siberia Express line completed. |
| **1908** | Hejaz Railway between Damascus and Medina opens. |
| **1913** | *Bradshaw's Continental Guide* featured in the TV series is published. |
| **1914** | The First World War begins. |

# BRADSHAW'S LEGACY

AS THE HEFTY BOOK IS SHELVED after the last European rail journey has been completed, there's a moment to reflect on what *Bradshaw's Continental Guide* has bequeathed to us.

Like no other book, it offers a glimpse of what life was like before the First World War – and reveals what might have been had the war not taken place. With the benefit of scholarly investigation, we know today that Europe was locked on a course that led to the cataclysmic conflict after numerous threads knotted together, which could not be unravelled. Its momentous events cast a long shadow over what life was like before war broke out. With *Bradshaw's*, a detailed picture emerges of this neglected time in history.

Although it was published in 1913, there's little on its pages to imply the inevitability of hostilities. Certainly, for the observant reader there are hints inside about some of the stresses already apparent. One entry warns that the rail service to Istanbul via Belgrade has been suspended due to the Balkan Wars, among the myriad conflicts bound tightly together with the start of the Europe-wide conflict.

The rash of assassinations that marked the Edwardian era come to light in the pen portrait of each country's ruling regime, with the Portuguese, Serbian and Greek kings among the dead. A raft of politicians met a similar fate.

There are several references, none of them flattering, to the poverty of Jewish quarters in foreign cities, more pertinent to a war that occurred later in the 20th century.

But politics is not the primary purpose of the guide. It's written mostly to convey the thrill of travelling to foreign lands for those unaccustomed to doing so. That wealthy Britons enjoyed 'the Grand Tour' from the 18th century is well known. But in the early 20th century the middle classes were on the rise and all those who sighed longingly over Lord Byron's eloquent words about Rome could finally hop on a train and see that city's classical splendour for themselves, should they have £9.10s.5d. to spare for the return fare. Sharing that same sense of liberation experienced by a generation long gone, today's readers, by delving through the guide's densely packed pages, are transported back into a past their ancestors would recognise.

If knowledge is power, then the traveller who went bearing a *Bradshaw's* had nothing to fear. It had within its covers the daily railway timetables for countries across Europe, revealing that in 1913 it was possible to join a train at Lyon at 9.56 a.m. and arrive in Marseille at midnight, or that a Brindisi train that departed at 7.11 a.m. would pull into Naples station at 18.30.

Every one of its idiosyncratically numbered pages contained a vast array of information, not just about times and prices but also about orientation. In the era before colour brochures, it was up to the guide's writer to accurately describe the layout of a city for a stranger, with the railway station as a starting point.

Its descriptions are reserved rather than rude, meticulous, humourless, enlightening, occasionally fulsome but never repetitive, which is remarkable given its scope.

Containing consulate advice, it was a safety net. Thanks to cab details, it helped the lost. Bearing a description of major churches, it provided guidance for the religiously devout.

History has never been more captivating thanks to its minutiae – and it still has the same power to inspire, helping readers then and now to pick the most appealing destinations.

Above all, this house brick of a book is the most apposite way that travellers can celebrate the train, the advent of which brought *Bradshaw's* and this new generation of British tourist into existence.

# INDEX

*(page numbers in italic type refer to illustrations)*

## A

AB Svenska Kullagerfabriken, 100
Abdul Hamid II, 38, 168–9, 217, 227
    deposed, 169
Abe, Shinzo, 227
advertisements, *62*, *124*, *186*
Albula railway, 46
Alexander II of Russia, 127, 132
Alexander III of Russia, 132
Alexander the Great, 225
Alexandra, Queen, 94
Alexandria–Cairo line, 224
Alfonso XII of Spain, 66
Alfonso XIII of Spain, 65, 204
    plot to assassinate, 69, *69*
Algeciras, Conference of, 71
Algeciras (Gibraltar) Railway Company, 70
*Aligeri*, 141
Allenby, Lord, 173
American Committee for Armenian and Syrian Relief, 225 (*see also* Armenian Christians)
Amsterdam–Northern France journey, 51–61
Anasthatos, 223
*Anna Karenina* (Tolstoy), 134–5
Ansaldo, Giovanni, 81
anti-Semitism, 112–13, 154
Aparicio, Juan Pedro, 122
Apennine mountains, 210, 211
Aranjuez line, 161, *161*
Arcachon, 115
arches, two-storey, *192*, 193
Armenian Christians, genocide of, 225
Art Deco, 19
Asquith, Herbert, 119
Association of German Engineers, 111
Astapovo station, 134, 135
Atatürk, Kemal, 225
Athens–Thessaloniki journey, 237–41

Atocha station, 67, *67*
Auschwitz, *154*, 155
'Austrian bridge', 81, *81*
Austrian empire, 148, 149, 189, 196, 199
Austrian State Railways, 31
Austro-Hungarian empire, 7, 13, 25, 26–7, 29
    map of, *26*
*Auto*, 183

## B

Baden State Railway, 233
Baedeker, Karl, 34, 215
Baghdad Railway, 227
Bake, William Archibald, 53–4
Balfour, Arthur, 171
Balkan War, First, 220
ball bearings, 100–1, *100*
Barcelona–Mallorca journey, 201–7
Barcelona–Mataró line, Spain's first domestic train on, 202
Barcelona metro, 204, *204*
Barcelona, as regional railway hub, 203
barges, 52–3, *52*
Barraclough, John, 77
Bartali, Gino, *182*
Basel–Jungfraujoch journey, 41–9
Battle of Langensalza, 235
Battle of the Somme, 61
Bavarian Ludwig Railway, 108–9, *108*
*Bayard*, 140
BBC, 7, 113
Beer, Hanna, 113
Belgian chocolate, 57
Belgian Resistance, 155
belle époque, 13, 20
Belpaire, Alfred, 57
Bergen line, conversion of, 97
Berlin, Congress of, 221
Berlin–Rhine journey, 33–40
Berlin, trams in, 35, *35*
Berlin Wall, 35
Betjeman, Sir John, 17
Bianchi, Riccardo, 143, 211
bicycles, 183
Bilbao station, *158*
Bing, Stefan, 91
Bismarck, Otto von, 229
Black Forest, *34*

Blériot, Louis, 17
Blowitz, Adolphe Opper de, 219
Bon Marché, 20
Bonaparte, Napoleon, 33, 85
Booth, Alfred, 160
Bordeaux–Bilbao journey, 115–23
Bordeaux station, *116*
Bordeaux wines, 116–17
Boris III of Bulgaria, 219
Bradshaw, George, 94, 101, 243
    cholera suffered by, 101
    grave, *101*
    railway shares bought by, 101
*Bradshaw's Continental Guide* (1913), 7, 10 (*see also Bradshaw's* guidebooks)
    journeys (Destinations 1):
        Amsterdam to Northern France, 51–61
        Basel to Jungfraujoch, 41–9
        Berlin to the Rhine, 33–40
        Hungary to Austria, 25–31
        London to Monte Carlo, 15–23
    journeys (Destinations 2):
        Bordeaux to Bilbao, 115–23
        Copenhagen to Oslo, 94–103
        Dresden to Kiel, 85–93
        Madrid to Gibraltar, 65–73
        Prague to Munich, 105–13
        Turin to Venice, 75–83
    journeys (Destinations 3):
        Haifa to Negev Desert, 167–75
        La Coruña to Lisbon, 156–65
        Lyon to Marseille, 176–85
        Rome to Taormina, 137–45
        Tula to St Petersburg, 127–35

Warsaw to Kraków,
147–55
journeys (Destinations 4):
Athens to
Thessaloniki,
237–41
Barcelona to
Mallorca, 201–7
Freiburg to Hannover,
229–35
Pisa to Lake Garda,
209–15
Sofia to Istanbul,
217–27
Vienna to Trieste,
189–99
legacy of, 244–5
published, 21, 101
*Bradshaw's* guidebooks, 7,
8, 34 (*see also Bradshaw's
Continental Guide* (1913))
Belgium praised by, 57
on Circumvesuviana, 145
Dresden praised by, 87
Dutch praised by, 54
on Greece, 238
on Heidelberg Castle,
233
on Jerusalem, 167
on Leipzig, 90
on Pyrenees, 115
on Santiago Cathedral,
160
warnings in, 66, 226
Brandt, Alfred, 45
Braque, Georges, 7
bread train, 43
Breda, Ernesto, 83
locomotive built by, *82*
Brenner Pass, 196–7, *197*
British empire, 7, 234
broad gauge tracks, 97, 115,
120–1 (*see also* narrow
gauge tracks)
Broders, Roger, 180
Brooke, Rupert, 7
Brothers Grimm, 230–1, *230*
Brown, Charles, 45
Brunel, Isambard Kingdom,
54, 120
Budapest:
Chain Bridge, 27, *27*
Europe's first
underground system
in, 25
Budweis line, 107, *107*

Bunyol, Miquel Biada, 201,
202–3
*Burschenschaften*, 233
Busse, Otto, locomotive
designed by, *82*
Byron, Lord, 244
Byzantine empire, 220, 225

**C**
Café Central, Vienna, 194,
*194*
Camillo Benso, Count of
Cavour, 78–9, *78*, 81, 83
Canadian Pacific Company,
30–1
Cannes, 15
Carlos I of Portugal, 164,
*164*, 165
Carnegie, Andrew, 55
Carnot, Sadi, 179
Carpathian Mountains, 150
Carrel, Alexis, 179
Carriage 2419, 61, *61*
Caserio, Sante Geronimo,
179
Central Station, Amsterdam,
53, *53*
Chain Bridge, Budapest,
27, *27*
Channel Tunnel, 17, *17*
Charing Cross station, 17
Charles Albert of Piedmont,
142
Cherepanov, Miron, 129
Cherepanov, Yefim, 129
chocolate manufacture, 57
Chopin, Frederick, 207
Christie, Agatha, 223
Chrzanów factory, 153
'Cinderella', 230
Cinématographe, 22
Circumvesuviana, 144–5,
*144*
CIWL (Compagnie
Internationale des Wagons-
Lits), 218
Clark, Adam, 27
Clark, William Tierney, 27
clocks and time, 47, *47*, *116*
CO (Société Générale pour
l'Exploitation des Chemins
de Fer Orientaux), 220–3
Colaço, Jorge, 165
Committee of Union and
Progress ('Young Turks'),
217

Compagnie des chemins de
fer de Paris à Lyon et à la
Méditerranée (PLM), 178,
180
Compagnie Internationale
des Wagons-Lits (CIWL),
218
Compañía Vapores del Sur de
España, 71
Conan Doyle, Sir Arthur, 48
concentration camps, 154–5,
*154* (*see also* anti-Semitism;
Nazi Germany)
Conference of Algeciras, 71
Congress of Berlin, 221
Cook, Thomas, 30
Copenhagen–Oslo journey,
94–103
Corinth Canal, 240
corkscrew tracks, 46, *46*
Credit Mobilier, 67
Credit Suisse, 42
Cresta Run, 49, *49*
Crimean War, 226
Cuypers, Petrus J. H., 53

**D**
Demidov factory, 129
Denis, Paul von, 109
Der Blaue Reiter movement,
7
Derbyshire, Worcester and
Staffordshire Railway, 158
*Description of a Railway on a
New Principle* (Robinson),
37
Desgrange, Henri, 182–3
destinations and journeys, *see
under Bradshaw's Continental
Guide*
Deutsche Bank, 38, 222
Deutsche Reichsbahn, 154
Deutsches Museum, 111, *111*
Dickens, Charles, 105
diesel power, 17, 19, 73, 103,
110–11, *110*
Diesel, Rudolf, 17, 110–11
*Doctor Zhivago* (Pasternak),
127
Doppler, Christian, 189
double-decker viaduct, *192*,
193
Doumer, Paul, 184–5, *184*
Douro line, 162–3, *162*
Dover, Port of, 17
Dresden–Kiel journey, 85–93

Dresden–Leipzig line, 88–9, *88*
Dresden station, 89
dynamite, 43, 44

**E**
eau de Cologne, *38*
*Economist*, 222
Edward VII of Britain, 63, 65, 115, 118–19, *118*, *119*, 164, 241
  death of, 119
Edward Dean Adams Power Plant, 35
Eichendorff, Joseph von, 233
Eiffel, Gustave, 116, 117, *117*
  station canopy built by, *122*
Eiffel Tower, 19, 117
Einstein, Albert, 39, *39*
*El Hullero*, 122–3
*El Topo*, 122
electric trains, 35, 45, 102–3
Elizabeth II of Britain, 17
English Channel, 17
Erdoğan, Tayyip, 227
Ernest Augustus of Hannover, 231, 234–5
  statue dedicated to, *234*
Escher, Alfred, 42, 45
Essen, Krupp works in, 36–7, *36*
Etzel, Karl von, 196–7, *196*
Eulenberg affair, 231
Europe's first railway service, 56, *56*
Eurostar, 16
events, timeline of, 242–3
Exposition Universelle, 19, *19*, 21
*Express d'Orient, see* Orient Express
extermination camps, 155
  (*see also* anti-Semitism; Nazi Germany)

**F**
Faisal, Prince, 171
Farina, Johann Maria, 38
Faringdon, Lord, *see* Henderson, Alexander
Favre, Louis, 42–3, 44, 45
Ferdinand I of Austria, 106
Ferdinand II of Italy, 140
Ferdinand, Kaiser, 29
*Figaro*, 17

'Final Solution', 154
Finn, Alexander, 70
First Balkan War, 220
First World War, 7, 8, 13, 33, 41, 51, 55, 93, 119, 137, 141, 167, 211, 215, 220
  and Arab states, 171
  and Armenian Christians, 225
  Armistice, signed in railway carriage, 61, *61*
  mobilisation for, 58–9, *58*
  Orient Express halted by, 223
  railways in everyday life during, 60–1, *60*
  Russian public apathy towards, 98
  and spread of railways, 187
Flamme, Jean-Baptiste, 57
Florence–Bologna Direttissima, 211
*Flying Hamburger*, *110*, 111
Folkestone, Port of, 17
folklore, 230–1, *230*
Forster, E. M., 79, 215
Franco, Gen. Francisco, 73
Franco-Prussian War, 20, 37
Franz Ferdinand, Archduke, 93
Franz Josef I, 25, 26–7, 28, 30, 189, 190
Frederick IX of Denmark, 103
Frederick the Great, 148
Freiburg–Hannover journey, 229–35
French colonial empire, 184
French Revolution, 85, 176
  and Bastille storming, 179
Freud, Sigmund, 194
Freycinet, Charles Louis de Saulces de, 178–9, *178*
funicular railways, 87, *87*, 145, *145*
'Funiculi Funicula', 145

**G**
Galician Carl Ludwig Railway, 147, 150, 153
Gare d'Austerlitz, 19
Gare de l'Est, 19, 219
Gare de Lyon, 18, 19
Gare du Nord, 19
Gare Montparnasse, 19

Gare Saint-Lazare, 19
Garibaldi, Giuseppe, 79, 141
Garin, Maurice, 183
Garland, Maj. Herbert, 172
Gaudí, Antoni, 205
Gauguin, Paul, 181
George I of Britain, 231
George I of Greece, assassination of, 241, *241*
George V of Britain, 58, 65, 241
German folklore, 230–1, *230*
Gerstner, Franz Anton von, 107, 128–9
Gerstner, Franz Josef, 107
Ghega, Carlo, 189, 192–3
Gibraltar, 70–3, *72*
  tunnel through, 72–3
Gloggnitz–Mürzzuschlag line, 192–3, *192*
Goethe, Johann Wolfgang von, 233
gondolas, 92, 93, *123*
Gothenburg–Stockholm line, electrification of, 103
Gotthard Railway Company, 43
Gotthard tunnel, 42–3, *42*, 45, 46
Goudriaan, Bernard, 54
*Great British Railway Journeys*, 7
Great War, *see* First World War
Great Western Railway, 54
Gregory XVI, Pope, 78
Griffith-Jones, Mervyn, 215
Grimm, Dorothea, 231
Grimm, Jacob, 230–1
Grimm, Wilhelm, 230–1
Gronowski, Chana, 155
Gronowski, Ita, 155
Gronowski, Leon, 155
Gronowski, Simon, 155
Grunewald station, 155
Guggenheim Museum, 123

**H**
Habsburgs, 26, 27
Haifa, 8
Haifa–Negev Desert journey, 167–75
hajj, 169
Handyside, Andrew, 53
Hannover, Britain shares monarch with, 231, 234

Hannover station, *234*
Harden, Max, 231
Haswell, John, 29
Haussmann, Baron, 19
Hawkshaw, John, 89
Haydarpaşa station, 227
Heidelberg Castle, 232–3, *232*
Heidrich, Erich, 123
Heine, Heinrich, 20, 90
Heine, Dr Karl, 85
Hejaz Railway, 167, 168–9, *168*, 170, 172, 227
    book about, 169
Hellenic State Railways, 241
Henderson, Alexander, 70
Hertz, Heinrich, 212
highest station, 8
Hilfiker, Hans, 47
Hirsch, Baron Maurice de, 220, 222–3
Hitler, Adolf, 49, 73, 194, 219
Hoffmann Machine Company, 100
Hölderlin, Friedrich, 233
Holocaust, 113, 154, 225 (*see also* Jews in Europe)
    Israel's memorial to, 175
Holsboer, Willem Jan, 46
Holy Land, 8, 160
Holy Roman empire, 235
horse-drawn wagons, 105, 107, *107*, 109, 235
Hugo, Victor, 56–7
Hungary, 25
Hungary–Austria journey, 25–31
hydro power, 102, *102*

**I**
*Impavido*, 141
Imperial Express, 25
Imperial and Royal State Railways, 153
individual destinations and journeys, *see under Bradshaw's Continental Guide*
International Sleeping-Car Company, *see* Compagnie Internationale des Wagons-Lits
Isabella II of Spain, 66, 161
Isotta Fraschini, 213
*Italia*, 215
Italian lakes, *214*

Italy's fist train, 140, *140*
Izmir–Aydin line, 224
Izmir, harbour at, *224*

**J**
Jaffa, 8
Janin, Jules, 179
Jerez, 68–9
Jerusalem, 8
    Jaffa linked with, 174–5, *174*
    light railway in streets of, 175, *175*
Jews in Europe, and Winton train, *112*, 113–14
John XXIII, Pope, 139
John Paul II, Pope, 139
journeys and destinations, *see under Bradshaw's Continental Guide*
J. P. Morgan, 55
Jungfraujoch, 8

**K**
Kafka, Franz, 112
Kaiser Ferdinand-Nordbahn, 29
Kaiserin Elizabeth-Bahn, 29
Keats, John, 138
Keppel, Alice, 115
Kiel Canal, 92–3, *92*
King's Cross station, 16, 17
Kisch, Egon Erwin, 199
Klein, Ludwig, 107
Klein, Nina, 113
Klimt, Gustav, 7
Koumoundouros, Alexandros, 238
Kraków station, 150, *150*
Krupp, Alfred, 36–7
Krupp, Friedrich, 37
Krupp works, Essen, 36–7, *36*
Krupskaya, Nadezhda, 98
Kühlmann, Otto von, 222

**L**
La Caruña–Lisbon journey, 156–65
La Ciotat, 22
*Lady Chatterley's Lover* (Lawrence), 215
Lahmann, Dr Heinrich, *87*
Lake Garda, 215
Lamiable, Charles, 70
Langensalza, Battle of, 235

Lapland railway, Arctic Circle, 97
Lateran Treaty, 138
Lawrence of Arabia, 8
Lawrence, D. H., 214–15
    and *Chatterley* trial, 215
Lawrence, T. E. ('of Arabia'), 167, 171, 172–3, *172*, *173*
Lefèvre, Géo, 182–3
Legrand, Alexis, 19
Leipzig–Dresden Railway Company, 89
Leipzig line, 87
Leipziger Baumwollspinnerei, 90, *90*
Lenin, Vladimir, 8, 98–9, *98*, 135
Leopold I of Belgium, 56
'Ligne Impériale', 184–5
*L'illustré*, 20
List, Friederich, 85, 86
'Little Red Riding Hood', 231
Livesey, Fernando, 159
Livesey, James, 159
locomotives:
    Busse-designed, *82*
    diesel, brought into service, 17
    first electric, 45
    numbers in service, 23, 59
    Pacific 231, 21
    RA 3701 ('Queen of Locomotives'), 83
    repairs, *36*
    on screen, *22*, 23
    seen as gift from British, 156
    speeds achieved by, *see* speeds of trains
    on turntable, *152*
    at Vatican, *138*
    and war effort, Britain's contribution to, 61
Łódź, Industrial Revolution's transformation of, 153
Lombard, Capt. Louis, 70
London–Monte Carlo journey, 15–23
Ludwig I of Bavaria, 108
Luís Filipe of Portugal, 164
Lumière, Auguste, 22
Lumière, Louis, 22, 23
Lunn, Arnold, 49
Lunn, Sir Henry, 48
Lunn, Peter, 49

Lunn Poly, 48
Lyon–Marseille journey, 176–85

**M**

Madrid–Aranjuez line, 161, *202*
Madrid, first station in, 67, *67*
Madrid–Gibraltar journey, 65–73
Madrid–Zaragoza–Alicante Railway (MZA), 66
Magdeburg disasters, 93
mail trains, 16, 77
Maillot, Porte de, 21
Malmbanan line, 97, 103
Manuel II of Portugal, 164
Marconi, Guglielmo, 212, *212*, 213
Marconi Transatlantic Wireless Telegraph, 30
Märklin, Theodor, 91
Marmaray, 227
Marne, River, 23
Marseille Cathedral, 220
Maserati, Alfieri, 213
Maserati, Bindo, 213
Maserati, Carlo, 213
Maserati, Ernesto, 213
Maserati, Ettore, 213
Maserati, Mario, 213
Maserati, Rodolfo, 213, *213*
Maunsell, Lt Col. F., 169
Maxwell, James Clerk, 212
Mecca, 8
*Mechanics' Magazine*, 109
Medina, 8
Meissner, Heinrich, 169
Melkikov, Pavel, 131
Merrill, Selah, 174–5
Métro (Paris), 20, 21, *21*
Midland Grand hotel, 17
Mikhail, Grand Duke, 133
Miller, Oskar von, 105, 111
Mr Henderson's Railway, 70
Mitropa, 223
model railways, 91, *91*
Moltke, Helmuth von, 34–5
Mont Cenis, 43
   tunnel through, 76, *76*
Monte Carlo, 15
Montefiore, Moses, 174
Montparnasse derailment, 23
Moore, Sir John, 161
Moreno, Jesús, 121

Morral, Mateu, 69
Morrison, John, 70, 71
Morse code, 212
Morton, Frederic, 29
Moscow metro, 131, *131*
Mould, George, 158, 159
Mould, John, 159
movie-making, 22, *22*, 153
*Murder on the Orient Express* (Christie), 223
Murray, John, 34
Mussolini, Benito, 213
MZA (Madrid–Zaragoza–Alicante Railway), 66

**N**

Nagelmackers, Georges, 218–19
Napoleonic Wars, 18
narrow gauge tracks, 46, 59, 97, 115, 122, 149, 161, 163, 230, 238 (*see also* broad gauge tracks)
National Railway Museum, Pietrarsa, 141
nationalisation:
   in France, 155
   in Italy, 83, *142*, 143
   in Poland, 153
   in Portugal, 164
   in Russia, 127
   in Switzerland, 41
   in UK, 17
Navon, Joseph, 174
Nazi Germany:
   and anti-Semitism, 112–13, 154
   and Auschwitz, *154*, 155
   and Czechoslovakia annexation, 112 (*see also* Winton train)
Neuhaus, Jean, 57
Neuhaus, Louise, 57
*New York Times*, 30
Newhaven, Port of, 17
Nicholas I of Russia, 128, 130–1
Nicholas II of Russia, 8, 25, 58, 119, 132, 133, *133*, 241
Nicholson, James, 169
Nightingale, Florence, 226, *226*
Nizetas, Nikon, 199
Nobel, Alfred, 43
Noblemaire, Gustave, 178
Norte, 67

North Sea, 20
*Nursery and Household Tales* (Grimm), *230*, 231

**O**

Oblieght, Ernesto, 145
Olga of Greece, 238
Olympic Games:
   1896 (Greece), 241
   1900 (Paris), 21
   1936 (Germany), 49
Olympic Games (1900), 21
'orange express', Mallorca, *206*, 207
Öresund Bridge, *103*
Orient Express, 61, 187, 217, 218–23, *222*, 226, 227 (*see also* Simplon Orient Express)
   fares charged on, 221
   First World War halts, 223
   official branding of, 220
   robbers derail, and take hostages from, 223
Oriental Railway Company (ORC), 224–5, *224*
Ottoman empire, 7, 13, 168, 170–2, 187, 217, 220–1, 222, 224, 225
   and First Balkan War, 220
   Greece's war with, 239
   Greek negotiations with, 240
   and Orient Express ransoms, 223
   and Oriental Railway Company, 225

**P**

paddle steamers, *214*
Palestine Exploration Fund, 171
Palmer, Henry Robinson 37
Panhard et Levassor, 21
Paris:
   Eiffel Tower, 19
   Exposition Universelle, 19
   population, 20
   stations, *18*
Paris–Orléans Railway, 67
Pasternak, Boris, 127
Peace Palace, Hague, 55, *55*
Penguin, 215
Peninsular War, 161
'people steeples', 8

Péreire, Émile, 67, 115
Péreire, Isaac, 67
Petöfi, Sándor, 26
Peugeot, Armand, 20
Philip, Prince, 241
Philosopher's Way, 232–3
Picasso, Pablo, 7
Pihl, Carl, 97
Pilsen beer, 106
Pisa–Lake Garda journey, 209–15
Pius XI, Pope, 138–9
Place de Rennes, 23
PLM (Compagnie des chemins de fer de Paris à Lyon et à la Méditerranée), 178, 180
Polish emigration to US, 150, 151, *151*
Pompeii, *139*, 144
Pont Faidherbe, 185
Porretta line, 210–11, *210*
Porta Nuova, Turin, 79–80, *79*, *80*
Portuguese empire, 164
poster art, 180, *180*
Prague–Munich journey, 105–13
Princip, Gavrilo, 25
privatisation, in Italy, 142
Protche, Jean Louis, 211
Prussian empire, 148, 149
Public Schools Alpine Sports Club, 48
Pullman coaches, 218

**Q**
'Queen of Locomotives', 83

**R**
Radek, Karl, 99
rail accidents, 23
railway clocks, 47, *47*
'Rapunzel', 231
Red Army, 135
'Red Baron' (Manfred von Richthofen), 215
Redl, Col. Alfred, 189, 198–9, *198*
Reichenbach Falls, 48
Reina Cristina hotel, 71
Rendsburg Bridge, *92*, 93
Rhaetian Railway, 46
Rhône, River, 23
Richthofen, Manfred von ('Red Baron'), 215

Ringstrasse, Vienna, 28, *28*
rivers and waterways, 23, 52–3, *52*
*Robert Stephenson*, 89
Robson, John, 87
*Rocket*, 18
Rocky Mountains, 31
Roman empire, 139
Roman roads, 139, *139*, 196
Rome–Taormina journey, 137–45
Ronge, Maj. Maximilian, 199
*A Room with a View* (Forster), 215
Rothschild, James de, 66
Royal Hanoverian State Railways, 235
Royal Mail Steamer, 160
Royal Privileged Ludwig Railway Company, 108–9, *108*
'Rumpelstiltskin', 231
Ruskin, John, 81
Russian (1917) Revolution, 135
Russian empire, 7, 13, 97, 128
Rziha, Franz, 44

**S**
Sagrada Família, 205, *205*
St Pancras station, 16, *16*, 17, *120*
Salonica–Constantinople junction, 240
Salzburg–Tyrol pass, *30*
San Sebastián station, *122*
Sand, George, 207
Santander–Madrid line, 158–9, *158*
Santiago, pilgrims flock to, 160, *160*
São Bento station, 165, *165*
Sapieha, Leon, 151
Schafbergbahn, 8, 31, *31*
Schick, Conrad, 174
Schlieffen Plan, 60
Schoenberg, Arnold, 191
*Scribner's Magazine*, 174–5
Second World War, 33, 61, 97, 112, 185, 215
  tunnels excavated during, 73
Seine, River, 21, 23
Semmering Mountains, 189, 190–1, *190*

Semmering Pass, 8
*Seven Pillars of Wisdom* (Lawrence), 173
Sewell, Don, 159
Shelley, Percy, 138
sherry production, 68–9
Siam, king of, *184*
Sicily, boat train to, 141, *141*
siderodromophobia, 23
Siemens, Carl von, 35
Siemens, Georg von, 222
Siemens, Werner von, 35
Silesia, rich in coal and minerals, 148
Simplon Orient Express, 45, *221*, 223 (*see also* Orient Express)
Simplon tunnel, *44*, 45
*Skandalkonzert* (Schoenberg et al.), 191
SKF, 100
skiing, 48, *48*
Škoda, 106, *106*
Škoda, Emile, 106
'Sleeping Beauty', 231
Smiles, Samuel, 121
Smith, Adam, 87
smoking policy, *98*, 99
'Snow White', 231
Société Générale pour l'Exploitation des Chemins de Fer Orientaux (CO), 220–3
Sofia–Istanbul journey, 217–27
Somme, Battle of, 61
Sommeiller, Germain, 43, 77
*Sons and Lovers* (Lawrence), 214
Soult, Marshal, 161
Spain, first domestic train in, 202
Spanish Civil War, 201, 205
speeds of trains, 17, 23, 83
  Orient Express, 219
Sprinzels, Peter, 113
Sprowston postmill, 100
Stalin, Joseph, 194
steel wheels, 36–7
Steiner, Ernst, 113
Stephenson, George, 18, 54, 67, 80, 108–9, 121, 129, *139*
Stephenson, Robert, 29, 80, 97
Stuart, Herbert Akroyd, 111

Suez Canal, 45, 170–1, *170*, 225
Swedish State Power Board, 35
Switzerland, 13
Szechényi, István, 27

**T**

Tárrega, Francisco, 203, *203*
Tárrega, Maria, 203
Taurus Mountains, 38, 225
Taylor, A. J. P., 58
Taylor and Prandi, 81
Thatcher, Margaret, 17
*That's Life*, 113
Third empire, 20
Thomas Cook travel agency, 30, 34, 48
    and Vesuvius funicular, 145
*Thunder at Twilight* (Morton), 29
time, standardising, 47, *47*, 101
time and clocks, 47, *47*, *116*
timeline of events, 242–3
*Times*, 219, 235
*Titanic*, 161, 207, 212
Tito, Marshal Josip, 194
Tivoli Gardens, Copenhagen, 99
Tolstoy, Leo, 8, 127, 134
    mourning for, *134*
Tolstoy, Sophia, 135
Topham, Jones and Railton, *72*
Tour de France, 182–3, *182*
towed wagons, 105, 107, *107*, 109, 129, 235
Train Bleu, 180
Tramm, Heinrich, 235
trams, 35, *35*, 195, *195*, 207, *207*, 235
    Hannover museum dedicated to, 235
Tramuntana mountains, 206
Trans-Siberian Railway, 132–3, *132*
Tren de Sóller, 206–7, *206*
Trikoupis, Charilaos, 238, 239, 240–1
Trotsky, Leon, 135, *135*, 194
Troyat, Henri, 134
Trulock, John, 159
Tsarkoe Selo line, 131

Tula–St Petersburg journey, 127–35
Turin–Venice journey, 75–83
turntables, *152*, 233
Twain, Mark, 233
two-storey arches, *192*, 193

**U**

UNESCO, 47, 192, 205
Upper Silesia Railway Society, 149

**V**

van Gogh, Vincent, 181, *181*
Vatican City, 137, 138–9, *138*
*Vesuvio*, 140
Vesuvius, 139, 144, 145, *145*
Via Claudia Augusta, 196
Victor Emmanuel II of Italy, 78, 138
Victoria Eugenie, Princess, 65
    plot to assassinate, 69, *69*
Victoria, Queen, 65, 118, 226
    accession of, 234
    first train ride of, 235
Victoria station, 17, *221*
Vienna:
    remodelling programme for, 28–9
    suicides in, 29
Vienna–Trieste journey, 189–99
Vincennes, Porte de, 21
Vingtrie, Armand Bayard de la, 140
Vizcaya Bridge, 123, *123*
Volvo, 100

**W**

W. G. Bagnall Ltd, *72*
Walker, James, 89
Walschaerts, Egide, 57
Warren, Capt. Charles, 171
Warsaw–Kraków journey, 147–55
waterways and rivers, 23, 52–3, *52*
Weekley, Frieda, 215
Weisser Hirsch sanatorium, 87
*Where Angels Fear to Tread* (Forster), 215
Whistler, George, 130
White Army, 135
Wierzbicki, Ludwik, 153

Wilhelm I, Kaiser, 93
Wilhelm II of Germany, 33, 51, 58, 119, 223, 227, 229, 241
    physical prowess valued by, 231
William I of the Netherlands, 53
William IV of Britain, 231
Wilson, Edmund, 99
Wilson, William, 108–9
Wingqvist, Sven, 100
winter weather, *96*
Winton, Grete, 113
Winton, Nicholas, 113
Winton train, *112*
wireless, advent of, 212–13
Wolsztyn:
    as major Polish junction, 152
    turntable at, *152*
World War One, *see* First World War
World War Two, *see* Second World War
World's Fair, *19*
Worsdell, Thomas, 89
Wuppertal, 37, *37*

**Y**

Yasenki station, 134
*The Yellow House* (van Goch), 181, *181*
Young Turks (Committee of Union and Progress), 217
Yunnan railway, 185

**Z**

*Zanardelli*, 215
Zimpel, Charles, 174

# PICTURE CREDITS

## PICTURE CREDITS

Pictures of Michael Portillo courtesy of Fremantle Media Ltd.

Endpapers and contents page: *Bradshaw's* Railway Map of Europe; 2: © Pawel Libera Images/Alamy; 14–15: © Mike Booth/Alamy; 16: © David Williams/Corbis; 17: © qaphotos.com/Alamy; 18: Julian Elliott/Getty Images; 18: © Photo Art Collection/Alamy; 20: Leernage/Getty Images; 21: © viennaslide/Alamy; 22: Association Frères Lumière /Getty Images; 24–25: Francesco Iacobelli/AWL Images/Getty; 26 © Kohl-Illustration/Alamy; 27: Mary Evans/Sueddeutsche Zeitung Photo; 28: Mary Evans/IMAGNO/OsterreichischesVolkshochschularchiv; 30: © Walter Geiersperger/Corbis; 31: © Topham Picturepoint (TopFoto); 34: © Swim Ink 2, LLC/Corbis; 35: © imageBROKER/Alamy; 36: © Bettmann/Corbis; 37: Orlando/Three Lions/Getty Images; 38: © Lordprice Collection/Alamy; 39: © Pictorial Press Ltd/Alamy; 40–41: JTB Photo/Universal Images Group/Getty; 42: © INTERFOTO/Alamy; 44: Press Association; 46: © Olaf Protze/Alamy; 47: Keith Levit/Design Pics/Getty Images; 48: Fine Art Images/Heritage Images/Getty Images; 49: ullstein bild/Getty Images; 50–51: © kavalenkava volha /Alamy; 52: TopFoto.co.uk; 53: TopFoto/HIP; 55: © Sjoerd van der Hucht/Alamy; 56: Universal History Archive/UIG/Getty Images; 58: © Chronicle/Alamy; 60: © Berliner Verlag/Archiv Germany/dpa/Corbis; 61: © The Keasbury-Gordon Photograph Archive/Alamy; 64–65: © Sebastian Wasek/ Alamy; 67: Mary Evans/Grenville Collins Postcard Collection; 69: © Illustrated London News Ltd/Mary Evans; 71: Guy Vanderelst/Getty Images; 72: © Sorin Colac/Alamy; 73: Keystone-France/Getty Images; 76: Universal History Archive/Getty Images; 78: Mary Evans Picture Library; 79: TopFoto; 80: Alinari Archives/Getty Images; 81: © Oldtime / Alamy; 82: © Niels Quist/Alamy; 84–85: © Kuttig - Travel - 2/Alamy; 87: © epa european pressphoto agency b.v./Alamy; 88: Culture Club/Getty Images; 90: © Agencja Fotograficzna Caro/Alamy; 91: ullstein bild/Getty Images; 92: © Helle: Jochen/Arcaid/Corbis; 96: © Premium Stock Photography GmbH/Alamy; 98: De Agostini Picture Library/Getty Images; 100: © J. Marshall/Tribaleye Images/Alamy; 102: © Roine Magnusson/Johnér Images/Corbis; 103: © Cultura RM/Alamy; 104–105: PNC/Getty Images; 106: Mary Evans/SZ Photo/Scherl; 107: ullstein bild/Getty Images; 108: Science & Society Picture Library/Getty Images; 110: ullstein bild/Getty Images; 111: Michael Fellner/Getty Images; 112: Michal Cizek/Getty Images; 114–115: © George Munday/Alamy; 116: © jmeyersforeman/Alamy; 117: © Archive Farms Inc./Alamy; 118: Roger Viollet Collection/Getty Images; 119: Print Collector/Getty Images; 120: © Hemis/Alamy; 122: © Karol Kozlowski/Alamy; 123: © Charles Stirling (Travel)/Alamy; 128: Bruno Morandi/Robert Harding/Getty Images; 129: Heritage Images/Getty Images; 130: Heritage Images/Getty Images;131: © Alex Segre/Alamy; 132: Cultura Travel/Philip Lee Harvey/Getty Images; 133: © World History Archive/Alamy; 134: © Photos 12/Alamy; 135: © Heritage Image Partnership Ltd/Alamy; 136–137: Mondadori/Getty; 138: ullstein bild/Getty Images; 139: Mary Evans/Epic/Tallandier; 140: DEA /A. DAGLI ORTI/Getty Images; 141: © LOOK Die Bildagentur der Fotografen GmbH/Alamy; 142: © MARKA/Getty Images; 144: © MARKA/Alamy; 145: ullstein bild/Getty Images; 146–147: Janek Skarzynski/Getty Image; 148: © Glyn Fletcher/Alamy; 150: © Paul Gapper/Alamy; 151: Underwood Archives/Getty Images; 152: © Andrzej Gorzkowski Photography/Alamy; 154: Christopher Furlong/Getty Images; 158: © Robert Harding Picture Library Ltd/Alamy; 160: © villorejo/Alamy; 161: © PRISMA ARCHIVO/Alamy; 162: © Colin Garratt/Milepost 92 1/2/Corbis; 164: © Chris Hellier/Alamy; 165: © Chris Sattlberger/Corbis; 166–167: © Keith J. Smith /Alamy; 168: Mary Evans Picture Library; 170: Universal History Archive/Getty Images; 171: Universal History Archive/Getty Images; 172: ullstein bild/Getty Images; 173: Culture Club/Getty Images; 174: © Hulton-Deutsch Collection/CORBIS; 175: Independent Picture Service/Getty Images; 178: Getty Images; 180: © Lordprice Collection/Alamy; 181: © PAINTING/Alamy; 182: Mary Evans Picture Library; 184: Photo 12/Getty Images; 188–189: Imagno/Getty Images; 190: © Walter Geiersperger/Corbis; 191: Imagno/Getty Images; 192: Imagno/Getty Images; 194: © Hemis/Alamy; 195: Alinari Archives/Getty Images; 196: © INTERFOTO/Alamy; 197: © epa european pressphoto agency b.v./Alamy; 198: Hulton Archive/Getty Images; 200–201: © Jeremy Lynton/Alamy; 202: Universal History Archive/Getty Images; 203: © Pictorial Press Ltd/Alamy; 204: © travelstock44/Alamy; 205: © Prisma Bildagentur AG/Alamy; 206: © Matthias Scholz/Alamy; 207: © Robert Harding World Imagery/Alamy; 210: Alinari Archives/Getty Images; 212: Hulton Archive/Getty Images; 213: Eric VANDEVILLE/Gama-Rapho/Getty Images; 214: © Latitude Stock/Alamy; 218: © John Bradshaw/Alamy; 221: © Shawshots/Alamy; 222: Universal Images Group/Getty Images; 224: © Chronicle/Alamy; 226: Universal Images Group/Getty Images; 227: © Santi Rodriguez/Alamy; 228–229: © LOOK Die Bildagentur der Fotografen GmbH/Alamy; 230: De Agostini Picture Library/Getty Images; 232: © Albert Knapp/Alamy; 234: Paul Popper/Popperfoto/Getty Images; 236–237: © ZUMA Press, Inc./Alamy; 238: © Universal Images Group/Alamy; 239: © Greek photonews/Alamy; 241: © The Art Archive/Alamy

# TO TRAVELLERS

## AND ALL LEAVING HOME FOR A CHANGE,

*Take a supply of* **ENO'S** *with you.*

ENO'S 'FRUIT SALT' prevents any over-acid state of the blood, and should be kept in every bedroom in readiness for any emergency. It is Pleasant, Cooling, Health-giving, Refreshing, and Invigorating. You cannot overstate its great value in keeping the blood PURE AND FREE FROM DISEASE.

It is, in fact, Nature's Remedy, and Unsurpassed.

**CAUTION.**—*Examine the Capsule, and see that it is marked* 'ENO'S FRUIT SALT.' *Without it you have the sincerest form of flattery—IMITATION.*

Prepared only by **J. C. ENO, Limited,**
'**FRUIT SALT' WORKS, LONDON, S.E.**

1 3 5 7 9 10 8 6 4 2

Simon & Schuster UK Ltd
222 Gray's Inn Road
London
WC1X 8HB

www.simonandschuster.co.uk

Simon & Schuster Australia, Sydney

Simon & Schuster India, New Delhi

A CIP catalogue record for this book is available from the British Library

Hardback ISBN: 978-1-4711-5149-1
Ebook ISBN: 978-1-4711-5150-7

Publishing Director: Iain MacGregor
Researcher and writer: Karen Farrington
Designed by Neal Cobourne, Ourkid Design
Printed and bound in Germany by Mohn Media GmbH

The publishers would like to thank everyone at Fremantle who has supported
this book. For unlimited help and advice, with grateful thanks to John Comerford
and Alison Kreps. To Katie Wixon who helped organise the research and supply
of the official photographs from the four series. To Cat Ledger, Esther Johnson,
Judi O'Brien and Mark Chare for vital backup. And, of course, special thanks to
Michael Portillo for his invaluable contribution. To Daniel Mirzoeff,
Pam Cavanagh and Alex McLeod at the BBC for their support.